T4-AJR-077

The Big6™ Workshop Handbook

The Big6™
Workshop
Handbook

Implementation and Impact

FOURTH EDITION

MICHAEL B. EISENBERG

ROBERT E. BERKOWITZ

 LINWORTH

AN IMPRINT OF ABC-CLIO, LLC
Santa Barbara, California • Denver, Colorado • Oxford, England

Copyright 2011 by ABC-CLIO, LLC

All rights reserved. No part of this publication may be reproduced, stored in a retrieval system, or transmitted, in any form or by any means, electronic, mechanical, photocopying, recording, or otherwise, except for the inclusion of brief quotations in a review, or reproducibles, which may be copied for classroom and educational programs only, without prior permission in writing from the publisher.

Library of Congress Cataloging-in-Publication Data

Eisenberg, Michael B., 1949–
    The Big6 workshop handbook : implementation and impact / Michael B. Eisenberg,
Robert E. Berkowitz. — Fourth edition.
        p. cm. — (Big6 Information Literacy Skills)
    Summary: "The latest edition of the Big6 Workshop Handbook contains the information that is current and essential to understanding and implementing this premier information literacy model"— Provided by publisher.
    Includes bibliographical references and index.
    ISBN 978-1-58683-422-7 (pbk. : acid-free paper)
1. Information retrieval—Study and teaching.   2. Information retrieval—Study and teaching—United States.   3. Electronic information resource literacy—Study and teaching.   4. Electronic information resource literacy—Study and teaching—United States.   I. Berkowitz, Robert E., 1948–   II. Title.   III. Title: Big 6 workshop handbook.   IV. Title: Big six workshop handbook.
    ZA3075.E4   2011
    025.5'24071—dc22   2010051618

ISBN: 978-1-58683-422-7

15   14   13   12   11   1   2   3   4   5

Linworth
An Imprint of ABC-CLIO, LLC

ABC-CLIO, LLC
130 Cremona Drive, P.O. Box 1911
Santa Barbara, California 93116-1911

This book is printed on acid-free paper ∞

Manufactured in the United States of America

Contents

List of Worksheets and Figures. vii

Foreword xiii

About the Authors xvii

Part 1: Introduction to the Big6™ and Super3™ 1

Part 2: Learning the Super3™ 25

Part 3: Learning the Big6™ 45

Part 4: Themes of the Big6™ 79

Part 5: Technology and the Big6™ 93

Part 6: Standards, Tests, and the Big6™ 121

Part 7: Micro Planning: Instructional Design 179

Part 8: Assessment 229

Part 9: Macro Planning: How to Develop School and District Information
          Literacy Programs. 245

Part 10: The Parent Connection 277

Part 11: Big6™ and Super3™ Program Planning 293

Index 305

List of Worksheets and Figures

Worksheets

Worksheet 1.1: Number Connecting Exercise 7

Worksheet 1.2: Planning for Change: Opening Questions 13

Worksheet 1.3: Information Literacy: The Big6™/Super3™ Approach: Opening Activity 14

Worksheet 2.1: Understanding the Super3™ Exercise 34

Worksheet 2.2: Super3™ Matching Exercise I—Interpretive Level 35

Worksheet 2.3: Super3™ Matching Exercise II—Interpretive Level 36

Worksheet 2.4: Super3™ Process 37

Worksheet 2.5: Super3™ Plan 38

Worksheet 2.6: Super3™ Do 39

Worksheet 2.7: Super3™ Do 40

Worksheet 2.8: Super3™ Review 41

Worksheet 3.1: Developing Big6™ Understandings Literal Level—Describe The Big6 54

Worksheet 3.2: Developing Big6™ Understandings—Literal Level 55

Worksheet 3.3: Developing Big6™ Understandings—Literal Level Based on Standards 56

Worksheet 3.4: Interpretive Level: Science Homework 58

Worksheet 3.5: Interpretive Level: Social Studies Book Report 59

Worksheet 3.6: Interpretive Level: Social Studies Group Work 60

Worksheet 3.7: Interpretive Level: Literature Essay 61

Worksheet 3.8: Interpretive Level: Animals Picture Book 62

Worksheet 3.9: Interpretive Level: Science Experiments 63

Worksheet 3.10: Interpretive Level: Vocabulary Homework 64

Worksheet 3.11: Interpretive Level: Music Class 65

Worksheet 3.12: Interpretive Level (Higher Education): Health Activities 66

Worksheet 3.13: Interpretive Level (Higher Education): Geology 67

Worksheet 3.14: Interpretive Level (Higher Education): English 68

Worksheet 3.15: Applied Level: Nutrition Posters 69

Worksheet 3.16: Applied Level: Earth Science Project 70

Worksheet 3.17: Applied Level: Art Research 71

Worksheet 3.18: Applied Level: Social Studies Group Project 72

Worksheet 3.19: Applied Level: Environmental Science. 73

Worksheet 3.20: The Curriculum Connection 74

Worksheet 4.1: Big6™ Applications 83

Worksheet 4.2: The Big6™ in Everyday Contexts 84

Worksheet 4.3: Big6™ Stages 88

Worksheet 4.4: The Curriculum Connection 90

Worksheet 5.1: Technology in Context—Opening Activity 99

Worksheet 5.2: Technology within the Big6™ Framework I 102

Worksheet 5.3: Technology within the Big6™ Framework II. 103

Worksheet 5.4: Technologies and the Big6™ 105

Worksheet 5.5: The Big6™ and Technologies. 106

Worksheet 6.1: Standards to Big6 Connection 131

Worksheet 6.2: Big6 to Standards Connection 132

Worksheet 6.3: Standards Examples I—ELA 135

Worksheet 6.4: Standards Examples II—Math 136

Worksheet 6.5: Standards Examples III—Various. 137

Worksheet 6.6: Standards to Big6™ 144

Worksheet 6.7: Big6™ to Standards 145

Worksheet 7.1: Developing Big6™ Understandings (Integrated Curriculum Situation) 184

Worksheet 7.2: Unit & Lesson Implementation (Integrated Big6™-Unit Planning Guide A) . . .185

Worksheet 7.3: Unit Planning Guide (Integrated Big6™-Unit Planning Guide B). 186

Worksheet 7.4: Big6™ Unit Planning 188

Worksheet 7.5: Lesson Plan Format 190

Worksheet 7.6: Generic Lesson Plan Format. 191

Worksheet 7.7: Big6™ Instructional Design Checklist. 192

Worksheet 7.8: Big6™ Instructional Strategies. 193

Worksheet 7.9: Sample Super3™—Plan. 194

Worksheet 7.10: Sample Super3™—Do 195

Worksheet 7.11: Sample Super3™—Review 196

Worksheet 7.12: My Super3™ Animal Project Cover Page 199

Worksheet 7.13: My Super3™ Animal Project—Plan 200

Worksheet 7.14: My Super3™ Animal Project—Do I 201

Worksheet 7.15: My Super3™ Animal Project—Do II. 202

Worksheet 7.16: My Super3™ Animal Project—Review I 203

Worksheet 7.17: My Super3™ Animal Project—Review II 204

Worksheet 7.18: Activate a Big6™ Tool to Improve Learning (Grades 7–12) 209

Worksheet 7.19: Know Your Information Sources (Grades 7–16)........................211

Worksheet 7.20: Diamond Thinking (Grades 6–12) 213

Worksheet 8.1: Data Collection Sheet 234

Worksheet 8.2: Postcard Assessment Exercise 235

Worksheet 8.3: Big6™ Assessment Scoring Guide..............................243

Worksheet 9.1: Curriculum Information Seeking Strategies 253

Worksheet 9.2: Data Collection 254

Worksheet 9.3: Curriculum Mapping 259

Worksheet 9.4: Integration Planning Worksheet 266

Worksheet 9.5: Unit x Big6™ Matrix 271

Worksheet 9.6: K–12 Integrated Big6™/ Curriculum Timeline 273

Worksheet 10.1: Parent Exercise: Developing an Understanding in Context 283

Worksheet 10.2: Big6™ Situations: Possible Actions............................284

Worksheet 10.3: Assignment Organizer....................................286

Worksheet 11.1: Personal Planning 297

Worksheet 11.2: School or District Planning.................................298

Worksheet 11.3: Program Assessment.....................................299

Worksheet 11.4: Benefits 300

Worksheet 11.5: Next Steps Planning 301

Worksheet 11.6: Putting it all Together 302

Figures

Figure 1.1: The Information Age: Implications for Learning and Teaching 15

Figure 1.2: The Super3™ 20

Figure 1.3: The Super3™ and Big6™ Alignment 21

Figure 1.4: The Big6™ Skills, view 1 22

Figure 1.5: The Big6™ Skills, view 2 23

Figure 1.6: Comparison of Information Skills Process Models........................24

Figure 2.1: Super3 PowerPoint Slides 32

Figure 2.2: Super3 to Big6 Match 42

Figure 2.3: Answer Key for Worksheets 43

Figure 3.1: Levels of Information Problem Solving 50

Figure 3.2: The Big6™ Skills Approach to Information Problem-Solving 51

Figure 3.3: Big6™ Skills Learning Objectives 52

Figure 3.4: Information Problem-Solving in School, Life, and Work Contexts 53

Figure 3.5: Worksheet Answer Key 76

Figure 4.1: All Subjects, Ages, Grade Levels 82

Figure 4.2 84

Figure 4.3 85

Figure 4.4 86

Figure 4.5 87

Figure 4.6 89

Figure 4.7 91

Figure 5.1 98

Figure 5.2: Technology within the Big6 Framework 104

Figure 6.1: Information Literacy and ICT Standards 130

Figure 6.2: Montana Content and Performance Standards 133

Figure 6.3: Applying Big6™ Skills, AASL Standards and ISTE NETS to Internet Research . . .134

Figure 6.4: Standards Examples I—ELA Linked to Big6™ 138

Figure 6.5: Standards Examples II—Math Linked to Big6™ 139

Figure 6.6: Standards Examples III—Various Linked to Big6™ 140

Figure 6.7: Standards Examples I—ELA in Order by Big6™ & Grade Level 141

Figure 6.8: Standards Examples II—Math in Order by Big6™ & Grade Level 142

Figure 6.9: Standards Examples III—Various in Order by Big6™ & Grade Level 143

Figure 6.10: Big6™ Skills Aligned with National Academic Content Standards
　　　　　　　 and ICT Literacy Standards 146

Figure 6.11: Big6™ Skills Aligned with Montana Content Standards .147

Figure 6.12: Janet Murray's Big6™ Skills Aligned with National Academic
　　　　　　　 Content Standards and ICT Literacy Standards 153

Figure 6.13: The Big6™ and Standard Tests 156

Figure 7.1 197

Figure 9.1 251

Figure 9.2: Curriculum Mapping Sample (K–6) 260

Figure 9.3: Curriculum Mapping Sample (7–12). 261

Figure 9.4: Curriculum Mapping Sample (K–6) 262

Figure 9.5: Curriculum Mapping Sample (7–12). 263

Figure 9.6: Curriculum Mapping Sample (K–6) 264

Figure 9.7: Curriculum Mapping Sample (7–12). 265

Figure 9.8: Unit x Big6™ Matrix—Elementary 267

Figure 9.9: Unit x Big6™ Matrix—Secondary 268

Figure 9.10: Unit x Big6™ Matrix—Ms. Hall—4th Grade Teacher 269

Figure 9.11: Unit x Big6™ Matrix—Social Studies Department 270

Figure 9.12: Sample Integrated Big6™/Curriculum Timetable. 274

Figure 10.1: Overview 281

Figure 10.2: Helping with Homework Chart 282

Figure 10.3: Sample Parent Letter 285

The BIG6™ Foreword

Welcome to the Big6™—the most widely used approach to information literacy in the world!

By using the Big6, you join tens of thousands of educators who are committed to ensuring that students, from pre-school to post-graduate levels, gain and apply essential information literacy skills to all types of endeavors.

In our view, information literacy is as fundamental to student success in school and life as reading and writing. Basic literacy—reading and writing—are at the core when one considers the "essentials" of learning. The traditional "3 R's"— reading, writing, and arithmetic—are indispensable building blocks of learning and achievement.

However literacy in the 21st century goes far beyond the 3 R's. UNESCO (United Nations Educational, Scientific and Cultural Organization), for example, offers the following definition of literacy, ". . . the ability to identify, understand, interpret, create, communicate, compute and use printed and written materials associated with varying contexts. Literacy involves a continuum of learning to enable an individual to achieve his or her goals, to develop his or her knowledge and potential, and to participate fully in the wider society" (UNESCO, 2004).

Today, we hear discussions of media literacy, technology literacy, digital literacy, financial literacy, civic literacy, social literacy, and others. We recognize the usefulness of these various literacies; however, we believe that "information literacy" is even more fundamental than these. Information literacy is now elevated to the same essential level as reading and writing. Information literacy—the ability ". . . to recognize when information is needed and have the ability to locate, evaluate, and use effectively the needed information"—is basic to all human endeavors and necessary for all human problem-solving, decision-making, and learning (ALA, 1989). Here's another definition of information literacy: the Big6 Information Problem Solving Skills.

Today, students need to learn and use information and technology in school and beyond more than ever. Again, there is widespread recognition that "basic skills" include more than reading, 'riting, and 'rithmetic. There's a 4th "r"—research! What do we mean by research? Information literacy! Yes, but what is information literacy and how do you explain and teach it to students in meaningful ways? The answer to that is clear and direct: the Big6.

We first developed the Big6 in 1987 as a simple, flexible, and broadly applicable approach to teaching and learning essential information literacy skills. We've expanded and refined the Big6 approach over the years by working with thousands of teachers and many more students. For example, although we use the phrase "Big6" to refer to our entire approach to information literacy learning, when we say, "Big6" we include:

- The Big6 process (6 stages and 2 sub-stages under each).

- The Super3 process (Plan, Do, Review).

- Technologies and technology skills within the Big6 process.

- Connections to national, association, state, and school district standards.

- Integration with subject area curriculum and assignments.

- Instructional design and assessment.

- Applications to standardized tests.

- Micro planning—lessons and activities tied to units.

- Macro planning—systematic by teacher, grade, subject area, or school.

This 4th edition of the *Workshop Handbook* is therefore tried and tested many times over. It is practical and immediately useful. Our previous handbooks were successfully used all over the world as a guide for Big6 professional development workshops and self-study to help classroom teachers, teacher-librarians, technology teachers, administrators, and parents learn the Big6 approach.

The new edition of the *Workshop Handbook* includes new and revised worksheets, answers to training exercises, a major revision to the section on the Super3, lists of resources, and explanations on how to use the various materials in Big6 training contexts. We have included a new chapter on integrating Big6 Skills with state and national curriculum standards and on information skills for success on tests. All together, this 4th Edition focuses on learning about, using, and teaching the Big6 Skills approach to information and technology skills.

The Big6™ Workshop Handbook is written to help classroom teachers, teacher-librarians, technology teachers, administrators, parents, community members, and students to do the following:

- Learn about information literacy and the Super3/Big6 processes.

- Use the Big6 process in their own activities (educational, personal, and business).

- Implement a Big6 approach to information and technology skills in classrooms, libraries, and labs; in individual schools and districts; in regions and states; and even as part of national and international initiatives.

At its most fundamental level, the Big6 is a six-stage process model for information problem-solving and decision-making. We have spent over 20 years working in public and private education, business, government, and communities to improve information problem-solving and technology skills. The Big6 is widely recognized as a conceptual but also practical approach to the design and implementation of information and technology skills instruction in schools. The Big6 and Super3 comprise the information literacy curriculum. Implementing this curriculum requires full integration with subject area curriculum and assignments.

The Big6 approach helps people learn essential information and technology skills necessary for success. The publications and services surrounding the Big6 approach include books, journal articles, posters, cards, bookmarks, videos, the Big6 listserv, directory, and the Big6 Web site for educators and parents. (For more information on all of these resources and services visit www.big6.com to contact Big6 Associates, or contact Linworth Publishing). Everyone involved with the Big6— our staff, trainers, and the hundreds of thousands of teachers and students who use the Big6—are really part of a "movement" that continues to gain momentum. This movement recognizes the importance of information literacy for success in the 21st century, and that the Big6 approach provides the goals and means to ensure that students learn and apply information literacy in all they do.

Parts 1–4 of the book help the reader identify the need for information and technology skills and develop a working understanding of the Big6, Little 12, and Super3. Part 5 concentrates on technology and how to use technology in a meaningful way through integration within the Big6 framework, and the new Part 6 links the Big6 to state and national standards. Part 7 turns to implementing the Big6 on the micro (lesson and unit) level, and Part 8 offers specific approaches to assessment using the Big6 stages. Part 9 focuses on systematic planning of Big6 programs on the school or district level by using efficient curriculum-mapping and planning documentation techniques. Part 10 provides content for parent roles in information literacy learning. The final section of the book, Part 11, helps educators to set their own agenda and plans for Big6 program success.

If you are discovering the Big6 for the first time, this *Workshop Handbook* will guide you through the basic concepts, help you to gain proficiency in the Big6 and help you develop a strategy for implementation based upon your own school or district situation. This book (and the www.big6.com Web site) are excellent sources of information about the Big6 approach and how to implement it in your educational setting.

If you already use the Big6, this fourth edition will provide additional insight and will help you to expand your efforts. We encourage you to use *The Big6™ Workshop Handbook* to support local, school-based Big6 professional development initiatives.

As we said in a previous edition of this *Workshop Handbook*, please, "Remember to THINK BIG! Education and teaching essential information and technology skills is critically important to student success in school and in later life. Information literacy skills are not optional—they are basic skills for success in the 21st century. This *Workshop Handbook* is written to help you effectively implement the Big6 approach to information and technology literacy programs in your educational setting."

We love to hear from all Big6ers. Visit our Web site: www.big6.com, or email us directly at info@big6.com.

We would like to thank Sue Wurster of Big6™ Associates and Cyndee Anderson from Linworth Publishing for their assistance in preparing this new edition. And, a special thanks to our publisher and always enthusiastic supporter, Marlene Woo-Lun, a truly unique and supportive person—we are so fortunate to work with you. And finally, to Laura Robinson—daughter, friend, and co-teacher: we couldn't have done it without you!

Mike Eisenberg & Bob Berkowitz
Seattle, Washington, and Rochester, New York

American Library Association. 1989. "Presidential Committee on Information Literacy: Final Report." Chicago: American Library Association.

UNESCO Education Sector. 2004. "The Plurality of Literacy and its implications for Policies and Programs: Position Paper." Paris: United National Educational, Scientific and Cultural Organization, 2004, p. 13, unesdoc.unesco.org/images/0013/001362/136246e.pdf.

About the Authors

MICHAEL B. EISENBERG

Mike Eisenberg is the "founding dean" of the Information School at the University of Washington, having served from 1998 to 2006. During his tenure, Mike transformed the unit from a single graduate degree into a broad-based information school with a wide range of research and academic programs, including an undergraduate degree in informatics, masters degrees in information management and library and information science (adding a distance learning program and doubling enrollment), and a doctorate degree in information science. For many years, Mike worked as professor of information studies at Syracuse University and was the founding Director of the Information Institute of Syracuse (including the ERIC Clearinghouse on Information & Technology, AskERIC, and GEM, the Gateway to Education Materials).

Mike is well-known for his work in information literacy and information, communications and technology (ICT) skills development. The apex of this work was the creation (with Bob Berkowitz) of the Big6 approach to information problem-solving, the most widely used information literacy program in the world. Mike has worked with thousands of students—pre-K through higher education—as well as people in libraries, business, education, government, and communities to improve their information and technology skills. Mike's current efforts focus on information literacy, the expanding role of libraries, virtual online environments, and information science education K-20.

Besides his numerous books (with Bob Berkowitz) on the Big6, Mike is also author (with Carrie Lowe and Kathy Spitzer) of *Information Literacy: Essential Skills for the Information Age* and dozens of scholarly articles in information science. Mike is a frequent keynote speaker at conferences, presents numerous workshops and training sessions each year, and consults with school districts, libraries, businesses, and government agencies on information resources, services, curriculum, technology, and management. He has worked as a teacher, library media specialist, program administrator, and consultant.

Mike has received widespread recognition including the 2009 Association for Library & Information Science Education Award for Professional Contribution, the 2006 Distinguished Service Award from the American Association of School Librarians and Baker & Taylor, the 2003 Presidential Award from the Washington Library Association, and the 1990 Distinguished Alumni Award, School of Information Science and Policy of the Nelson A. Rockefeller College of Public Affairs and Policy, University at Albany.

Mike Eisenberg
Professor and Dean Emeritus
The Information School of the University of Washington
Suite 370, Mary Gates Hall, Box 352840
Seattle, WA 98195–2840
Mike_eisenberg@big6.com
www.ischool.washington.edu/mbe

ROBERT E. BERKOWITZ

Co-creator of the Big6™ Approach, Bob Berkowitz is an educator first and foremost. He earned degrees from George Washington University (MA in Education), State University of New York at Albany (MLS), and North Adams (MA) State College (School Administrator's Certification).

Bob has over 30 years of teaching experience in both rural and urban settings. He began his career teaching language arts in high school. Bob enhanced his professional expertise by becoming a school library media specialist. He successfully managed and taught in school libraries at the elementary, middle school, and high school levels. His credentials are rounded out with additional experience as district coordinator for library and information programs and university instructor. His breadth of experiences uniquely qualifies him to be a consultant and trainer to educators at every level regardless of their professional degree, interests, length of service, or responsibilities.

Often requested to share his ideas at conferences, workshops, and seminars, Bob is a dynamic and passionate educator who taps his 30+ years in education to deliver powerful information to bring about educational change. He readily establishes rapport with library media specialists, teachers, and administrators regardless of their subject area specialties or grade level assignments. Bob's Big6 workshops and speeches are interactive, informative, innovative and inspiring. He is able to draw from his abundant experiences to customize his presentations to the needs of any audience.

Bob's contributions in education are far reaching. Both at home and around the world, his words and actions have inspired and empowered educators to transform their instructional practice based on the Big6 Approach, thus effectively preparing students for the rest of their lives. A central theme of his work is that we must prepare students for their future, not for our past.

In 2000, Bob was named a W. K. Kellogg Foundation Expert in Residence. He has been an Adjunct Instructor at Syracuse University's School of Information Studies, and Consultant to Mansfield State University's School Library & Information Technologies graduate program. Bob acted as Library Media Specialist Consultant to a research skills-based English curriculum project that won National Council of Teachers of English recognition as a Center of Excellence in English and the Language Arts.

Bob and Mike Eisenberg have collaborated on a number of books and projects, most notably *Teaching Information & Technology Skills: The Big6™ in Secondary Schools* (2000), *Teaching Information & Technology Skills: The Big6™ in Elementary Schools* (1999), *Helping with Homework* (1996), *Information Problem-Solving: The Big Six Approach to Library & Information Skills Instruction* (1990), *Curriculum Initiative: An Agenda and Strategy for Library Media Programs* (1988), and *Resource Companion to Curriculum Initiative* (1988).

Other works by Bob Berkowitz include: *Big6™ Research Notebook* (2007), "Moving Every Child Ahead: The Big6™ Success Strategy" (May/June, 2002), *MultiMedia Schools*; and "Acing the Exam: How Can Librarians Boost Students' Test Scores?" (October, 2002), *School Library Journal.*

Currently, Bob is a School Library Media Specialist with the Wayne Central School District, Ontario Center, NY.

Part 1:
Introduction to the Big6™ and Super3™

▶ 1.0 Introduction: Planning for Change 3

▶ 1.1 Number Connecting Exercise 4

▶ 1.2 Planning for Change: Opening Worksheets .5

▶ 1.3 The Information Age: Implications for Learning & Teaching 5

▶ 1.4 The Big6/Super3 Approach to Information Literacy 5

The Big6™ Introduction to the Big6™ and Super3™

1.0 Introduction: Planning for Change

In his workshops, Mike often starts with a Calvin and Hobbes cartoon about change. It's the cartoon that shows Calvin and Hobbes coming down a hill in a wagon. Calvin says, "I thrive on change." Hobbes says, "You? You threw a fit this morning because your mom put less jelly on your toast than yesterday." Calvin then says, "I thrive on making other people change."

Education today is all about change. There are all kinds of new demands on teachers and students—some driven by environment and mandates, but the more profound demands are created by fundamental changes in our society—the information society. We live in an increasingly complex information world. Education—schools, teachers, caregivers—must come to grips with what knowledge and skills students really need and then make sure that students gain the needed knowledge and skills.

We can no longer rely on the old ways of doing things, for example classrooms based on the teacher as "sage on the stage," carefully doling out information through textbooks and lectures, and assessing through tests. Instead, teachers are more "guides on the side," helping students to navigate through and use a wide range of electronic and print resources, coaching and assisting, and assessing through a range of means including individual and collaborative projects. The information society demands that students need to find, use, and process a wide range of information, often in a very short period of time. Students learn these skills through guidance, teamwork, and projects. And, we assess their skills and knowledge by looking at the authentic results of their efforts.

In the Foreword, we discussed how information literacy is as basic and fundamental as reading and writing. Information literacy is not optional—it is essential. Students already use a very different set of tools and technologies than their parents did for schoolwork and learning. But tools and technologies will continually change. The Big6 approach to information literacy is not about particular tools or technologies. The Big6 helps students to learn underlying skills and processes and how to use new tools and technologies as they become available. Students need to be flexible and so do their teachers, schools, and districts.

Making the requisite changes that help students to gain essential skills will not necessarily be easy, but it is vital that we do so. The materials in this chapter can help. The chapter is designed to help you understand the nature of instructional change, how to overcome resistance to it, and how to approach others to make changes with you.

1.1 Number Connecting Exercise

The first activity in the Workshop Handbook—the Number Connecting Exercise—is designed to address people's natural aversion to change. As you and other participants go through this exercise, it becomes evident that shifts of focus or process are okay—healthy and appropriate. Several elements must be in place in order to effect change. These elements include the following:

Compatibility: Compatible with current instructional practice

Complexity: Easy to understand and explain to others

Observability: Observable as change

Try-ability: Easy to try without taking a big risk.

CCOT—that's one way to remember these aspects of creating change—CCOT. Despite the complex look of this first activity, it satisfies the CCOT principles of change. Numbers, number recognition, and number sequencing are well-known skills among the vast majority of adults and children alike. Teachers often ask students to engage these kinds of skills (Compatibility). The exercise is simple to do even though there is a time constraint that adds to the challenge, and there are only two instructions (Complexity). The visual nature makes it easy for the participant to see what he or she has done, and whether the participant has changed his or her approach (Observability). All participants will feel comfortable trying this exercise; it minimizes risk factors that may inhibit a participant's willingness to engage in the task.

Potential risk factors include embarrassment, fear of failure, or lack of time. The participants do this activity on their own and are not required to share the results, thus eliminating the potential for embarrassment. There is no way for a participant to fail in the exercise because there are multiple opportunities to practice the skills, and each person will improve to some degree. Lastly, the activity takes only two and one-half to three minutes to complete, which effectively eliminates the excuse that trying the exercise will take too long (Try-ability).

Bob designed the Number Connecting Exercise to make some key points about change:

■ Change: Be careful not to get too complacent, too comfortable. Change is just around the corner.

- Repetition: We learn through repetition.
- Patterns: There are patterns that we can learn to help us be effective and efficient.
- Shared experiences: Sharing common experiences helps to bring people together.

The Number Connecting Exercise is our first introduction to change and the challenges facing students and educators.

1.2 Planning for Change: Opening Worksheets

Following the Number Connecting exercise is a second introductory exercise. The goals here are two-fold: to get us thinking about (1) our personal aspirations for the workshop and (2) our initial thoughts about information literacy and information literacy skills programs. We use the umbrella title "Planning for Change" for these worksheets as we begin learning about the Big6 approach to information literacy while continually thinking about ways to easily integrate the Big6 into classrooms, schools, and districts.

1.3 The Information Age: Implications for Learning & Teaching

The third section in Part 1 is a set of PowerPoint slides used to present a discussion about the challenges of the information society. We all know that the amount of available information is overwhelming. There are also serious questions about the quality and credibility of information—particularly information gathered via the Internet. Our experience is that most people need a system for "sorting and sifting" all of this information. They also want a successful method for becoming efficient and effective information problem solvers. That's the Big6!

The PowerPoint slides offer a context for the Big6 in terms of information literacy and information needs in our society. We recognize that you will supplement these PowerPoint slides with slides of your own. You will have numerous opportunities to personalize your Big6 presentation throughout this handbook, and we encourage you to do so. Think about the different audiences for the Big6, and how you would customize your presentation of the information. Also consider how you will evaluate whether you were successful so that you can improve for the next time.

1.4 The Big6/Super3 Approach to Information Literacy

The last section in Part 1 includes overview handouts of the Super3 and Big6. These are useful handouts to copy and share directly with students as well as other instructional staff. (Yes! Making copies of individual pages for internal use in your school or class is definitely permitted.) An additional handout shows the connection between the Super3 stages and the Big6 Skills.

The last handout shows the connection between the Big6 and the information literacy standards developed by the Association of College and Research Libraries (ACRL, 2000. Information *Literacy Competency Standards for Higher Education*, Chicago: American Library Association). Many professional organizations and educational departments have developed information literacy standards. Any and all can be directly linked to the Big6. The ACRL standards are our favorites because they are focused, concise, and reflect a process-approach to information literacy. Furthermore, although aimed at higher education, we find the ACRL standards to be relevant and applicable to the K-12 environment.

In summary, this first part introduces change and a new approach to thinking about (1) the skills and knowledge that students really need, and (2) how to help students gain those skills and knowledge.

We believe that students need to be effective and efficient information problem-solvers, and that we need to change our schools and ourselves in order to help students succeed.

Worksheet 1.1:
Number Connecting Exercise

Directions

Please do not turn the page until you are told to do so.

The next five pages are sheets of numbers. The numbers are scattered all over the page, but they are all there and it will be your job to find them. To get you started, the number one will always be found at the top left corner; it has a circle around it.

Your job will be to use a pen to connect the numbers in order beginning with number one, then two, then three, and so on. You should work as fast as you can because your goal is to connect as many numbers as possible. However, please note that:

1. You must begin with the number one and you cannot skip any numbers. Thus, you cannot connect 30 to 31 until you have already connected the previous 29 numbers.
2. Lines can cross. When you are done, there will not be a picture of anything.

There are five pages of numbers. You will be allotted 30 seconds per page. On each page, you must begin again with the number one. Work as fast as you can. You will be told when your time is up. Do not turn to the next page until told to do so.

① 53 39 15 16 54

27 51 28 40 6

13 17 5 2 26 62

3 41 14 50

29 38 30

37 49 25 18 4

42

7 23 55 46 36

43 31

35 22 12 34

19 57

11 44 24

8 32 58

47 33 45 20

21 9 59 48 60 10 56

1 53 39 15 16 54

27 51 28 40 6

13 17 5 2 26 62

3 41 14 50 30

29 38

37 49 25 18 4 42

7 23 55 46 36

35 43 31

11 19 57 22 12 34

44 24

8

47 33 45 20 32 58

21 9 59 48 60 10 56

① 53 39 15 16 54

27 51 28 40 6

5 2 26 62

13 17 3 41 14 50 30

29 38

37 49 25 18 4 42

7 23 55 46 36

35 43 31 22 12 34

11 19 57 44 24

8

47 33 45 20 32 58

21 9 59 48 60 10 56

① 53 39 15 16 54
27 51 28 40 6
13 17 5 2 26 62
3 41 14 50 30
29 38
37 49 25 18 4
42
7 23 55 46 36
35 43 31
22 12 34
19 57
11 44 24
8
47 33 45 20 32 58
21 9 59 48 60 10 56

① 33 9 25 23 45

49 41 37 59 13

19 51 35 15 21 29

3 27 7 55 47

11 31

43 57 17 53 39 5

34 12 36 20 56 22

2 46

18 54 8

50 28 58 40 14 30

42 26 44 38 6 48

4 10 52 24 60 16

32

Worksheet 1.2:
Planning for Change: Opening Questions

Answer these questions as specifically as possible. Be prepared to share your answers with others in the workshop.

1. I hope to leave this workshop with the following knowledge:

2. I hope to leave this workshop with the following skills:

3. If I could simply wave a magic wand to improve the information and technology skills instructional program in my school or district, I would want the following changes to occur:

Worksheet 1.3:
Information Literacy: The Big6™/Super3™ Approach: Opening Activity

Complete these statements as specifically as possible. Be prepared to share your answers with others in the workshop.

1. The purpose of information literacy skills instruction is:

2. An effective information literacy skills instruction program gives students the opportunity to:

3. An effective information literacy skills program helps classroom teachers to:

4. An effective information literacy skills program helps teacher-librarians, technology teachers, and other teaching specialists to:

The Information Age: Implications for Learning & Teaching

Notes:

Information Age — Problems

- Everyone – information access, overload, quality
- Students – gaining essential information knowledge & skills
- Schools – providing meaningful learning opportunities
- Society – providing opportunity for our children to succeed at the highest possible levels.

© M. Eisenberg 2009

Information Problem #1: Overload

"The amount of new information stored on paper, film, magnetic, and optical media doubled in three years.."

© M. Eisenberg 2009

Information Overload

Today, a <u>daily</u> *New York Times* has more printed information in it than a person would come across in an entire <u>lifetime</u> in the 17th Century.

www.reuters.com/rbb/research/dflfor/rame.htm

© M. Eisenberg 2009

Figure 1.1 The Information Age: Implications for Learning and Teaching

Web Example

"Should my child be immunized? Are immunizations safe?"

- **Found 145,000 sites via Google**

- **If spent 5 minutes on each, would take about 12,083 hours to review.**

- **Assuming at least 100-200 that appear to be right on target. Using these meaningfully could easily take an additional 50 - 100 hours.**

- **Total Potential time to spend: 503 days or almost 2 years!!!!!**

© M. Eisenberg 2009

Education Solution to Information Overload?

- **Speed things up?**

- **Pack in more and more content?**

- **Add more technology?**

© M. Eisenberg 2009

Information Problem #2: Quality

"More than 2/3 of teens said within the last year that they use the Internet as their major resource when doing a big project for school..."

© M. Eisenberg 2009

Figure 1.1 The Information Age: Implications for Learning and Teaching (*continued*)

Information Literacy in an Information Society

Quality

In a study of 500 sites used by Colorado high school students to do research, only 27% of the sites were judged to be reliable for academic research!

Ebersol, Samuel, "Uses and Gratifications of the Web among Students," Journal of Computer-Mediated Communication, 6(1): September 2000, www.ascusc.org/jcmc/vol6/issue1/ebersole.html

© M. Eisenberg 2009

The Solution?

- **Discourage Web Use?**

- **Pre-select resources?**

- **Filtering?**

© M. Eisenberg 2009

Alternative Solution

- **To have students use information and technology effectively and efficiently for success in school, work, and their personal lives.**

- **To focus on process as well as content.**

- **For students to be lifelong learners and independent thinkers.**

© M. Eisenberg 2009

Figure 1.1 The Information Age: Implications for Learning and Teaching (*continued*)

Information Literacy

- A new *basic* of the 21st century
- The 4th "R" – research
- The most basic of the basics!

© M. Eisenberg 2009

Information Literacy

"To be information literate, a person must be able to recognize when information is needed and have the ability to locate, evaluate, and use effectively the needed information."

American Library Association, 1989

© M. Eisenberg 2009

Talking about …

Process

© M. Eisenberg 2009

Figure 1.1 The Information Age: Implications for Learning and Teaching (*continued*)

For the Youngest
The Super3

Beginning **Plan**

Middle **Do**

End **Review**

© M. Eisenberg 2009

Information & Technology Literacy
The Big6™ Skills

1. Task Definition

   2. Info Seeking Strategies

      3. Location & Access

         4. Use of Information

           5. Synthesis

              6. Evaluation

© M. Eisenberg 2009

Valued Skills

- Problem Solving
- Information Use
- Speaking
- Independent Work
- Technology
- Group Work
- Writing
- Reading

www.washington.edu/oea/

© M. Eisenberg 2009

Summary – Solutions

- **Information literacy.**
- **Recognized as essential.**
- **The most basic of basics.**
- **Infused through education and society at all levels.**

© M. Eisenberg 2009

Notes:

_____

_____

_____

_____

_____

_____

_____

_____

_____

_____

_____

_____

_____

_____

_____

_____

_____

_____

_____

Figure 1.1 The Information Age: Implications for Learning and Teaching (*continued*)

The Big6™/Super3™ Approach to Information Literacy

Super3

Beginning   **Plan**

Middle   **Do**

End   **Review**

Figure 1.2 The Super3™

Super3-Big6 Alignment

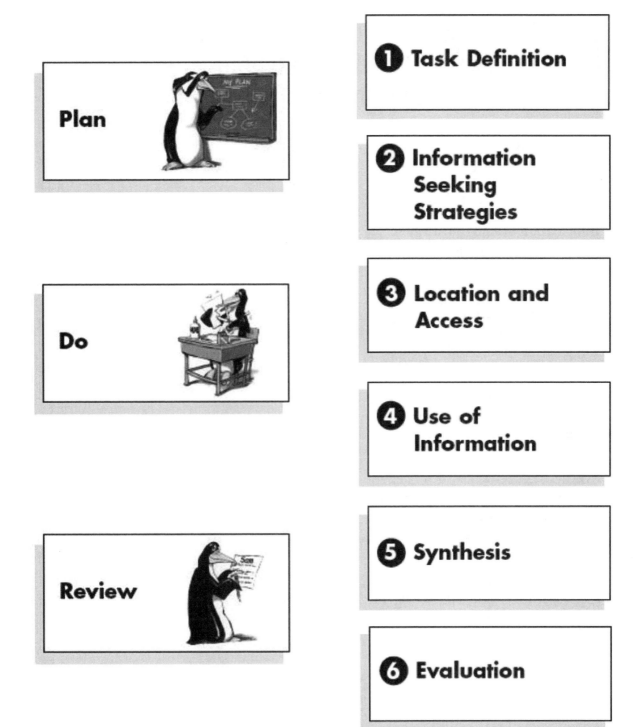

Plan

❶ **Task Definition**

❷ **Information Seeking Strategies**

Do

❸ **Location and Access**

❹ **Use of Information**

Review

❺ **Synthesis**

❻ **Evaluation**

Figure 1.3 The Super3™ and Big6™ Alignment

The Big6 Skills Model of Information Problem-Solving

1. **Task Definition:**
   1.1   Define the problem.
   1.2   Identify the information needed.

2. **Information Seeking Strategies:**
   2.1   Determine all possible sources.
   2.2   Select the best sources.

3. **Location and Access:**
   3.1   Locate sources.
   3.2   Find information within sources.

4. **Use of Information:**
   4.1   Engage (e.g., read, hear, view).
   4.2   Extract revelant information.

5. **Synthesis:**
   5.1   Organize information from multiple sources.
   5.2   Present information.

6. **Evaluation:**
   6.1   Judge the result (effectiveness).
   6.2   Judge the process (efficiency).

Figure 1.4 The Big6™ Skills, view 1

The Big6™ Skills Approach to Information Problem-Solving

The Big6™ Skills

The Big6 is a process model of how people of all ages solve an information problem.

1. **Task Definition**
   1.1 Define the information problem
   1.2 Identify information needed to complete the task (to solve the information problem)
      - What's the task?
      - What types of information do I need?

2. **Information Seeking Strategies**
   2.1 Determine the range of possible sources (brainstorm)
   2.2 Evaluate the different possible sources to determine priorities (select the best sources)
      - What are possible sources?
      - Which are the best?

3. **Location and Access**
   3.1 Locate sources (intellectually and physically)
   3.2 Find information within sources
      - Where is each source?
      - Where is the information in each source?

4. **Use of Information**
   4.1 Engage (e.g., read, hear, view, touch) the information in a source
   4.2 Extract relevant information from a source
      - How can I best use each source?
      - What information in each source is useful?

5. **Synthesis**
   5.1 Organize information from multiple sources
   5.2 Present the information
      - How can I organize all the information?
      - How can I present the result?

6. **Evaluation**
   6.1 Judge the product (effectiveness)
   6.2 Judge the information problem-solving program (efficiency)
      - Is the task completed?
      - How can I do things better?

The Big6™ is copyright © 1987 by Michael B. Eisenberg and Robert E. Berkowitz.

Figure 1.5 The Big6™ Skills, view 2

Comparison of Information Skills Process Models

Eisenberg/Berkowitz
Information Problem-Solving
(The Big6 Skills)

ACRL Information Literacy
Competency Standards

1. Task Definition
    1.1 Define the problem
    1.2 Identify info requirements

1. Determines the nature and extent of the information needed.

2. Information Seeking Strategies
    2.1 Determine range source
    2.2 Prioritize sources

3. Evaluates sources...critically

3. Location & Access
    3.1 Locate sources
    3.2 Find info

2. Accesses needed information effectively and efficiently.
5. Accesses and uses information ethically and legally.

4. Information use
    4.1 Engage (read, view, etc)
    4.2 Extract info

3. Evaluates information...critically
5. Understands many of the economic, legal and social issues surrounding the use of info.

5. Synthesis
    5.1 Organize
    5.2 Present

3. incorporates selected info into his or her knowledge base and value system.
4. Individually or as a member of a group, uses information effectively to accomplish a specific purpose.

6. Evaluation
    6.1 Judge the product
    6.2 Judge the process

Figure 1.6 Comparison of Information Skills Process Models

Part 2:
Learning the Super3™

▶ 2.0 Introducing the Super3™ 27

▶ 2.1 Think Process! 28

▶ 2.2 Plan: Beginning 29

▶ 2.3 Do: Middle 29

▶ 2.4 Review: End 30

▶ 2.5 Super3™ for Older Students
and Special Learners 30

▶ 2.6 Parents Can Help Too 30

▶ 2.7 Super3™ in Action 31

▶ Answers Key 43

The BIG6 Learning the Super3

2.0 Introducing the Super3

By Laura Eisenberg Robinson

The Big6 has been the focus of our discussion so far, but what is the "Super3?" The Super3 is our approach to information literacy for younger children as well as for those students who might be initially overwhelmed by the full Big6 framework. Like the Big6, the Super3 emphasizes a problem solving process, practical skills for students to implement and use, and meaningful and relevant learning.

The Super3 contains the same basic elements as the Big6 but uses simpler language to present the concepts. Super3 is presented in an easier manner for younger students to understand and remember. Here are the Super3 stages:

1. Plan—(Beginning)

2. Do—(Middle)

3. Review—(End)

This information problem-solving motto, Plan-Do-Review, is easy to remember and helpful to young students who are starting to learn information problem-solving skills. This chapter, Part 2, explores the Super3 in detail and helps you develop an expertise with this information problem-solving approach for the youngest learners: the Super3.

2.1 Think Process!

Designed for children in Pre-K through 3rd grade, the Super3 helps younger students become better thinkers and problem-solvers by learning and focusing on "process." Children begin to solve problems even before they enter school. These problems may include what older learners and adults consider minor, everyday things like picking out clothes, deciding what toys to play with, or figuring out how to interact with friends, siblings, or neighbors. For young children, however, these can be sophisticated decisions. As they grow older, problems and situations become more complex and intricate. The goal of the Super3 process is to help you provide students with the tools to successfully solve problems and complete their tasks. The process is designed to help students think about their task in terms of what they will do, how they will do it, and what their final result will be.

The Super3 process is a:

- Way of doing things
- Course of action
- Plan
- Approach
- Method

The Super3 is all about using a "process" with three parts that are simple to remember: Plan, Do, and Review! The Super3 provides an overall framework for students to learn **how** to get things done. It helps learners across all curriculum areas and is widely applicable to:

- Schoolwork (completing a book report or writing 3 sentences)
- Recreation (how to play checkers or how to become better at soccer)
- Decision-making in real life (deciding what field trip to go on or deciding what to buy Grandma for her birthday)

So, in summary, the Super3 process can help young students to:

- Improve their thinking and problem-solving skills
- Complete tasks and do a more thorough job with assignments and projects
- Recognize what they are doing and why
- Label and talk about the work/activity they are doing

Further, the Super3 allows educators to make the information problem-solving process:

- Simple enough for kids to "get it" and remember what they are doing
- Complex enough to adequately represent the full process
- Flexible enough to accommodate all learners, and to allow for different approaches
- Applicable across a range of problem or task situations

That's the Super3!!

2.2 Plan: Beginning

Plan (Beginning) is the important first step of the Super3 process and it is a stage that students do not always consider naturally. More often, students jump right into the middle of a project and begin to do their assignments. The key is to help students understand the importance of making a plan. For example, when kindergarten students are given a picture to color, spend a moment to discuss the step that they take when choosing colors. What are they doing when they choose a blue crayon for the sky? They are planning how they will tackle the assignment to achieve the desired effect. This is really no different than a 12th grader planning which resources she will consult first when writing her term paper about Hamlet.

Help your students begin to think about using a process to create the foundation for educational success throughout their school career. Elementary students do a great deal of planning in their daily routine. Planning activities may include examples like the following:

- Choosing teams for a kickball game
- Picking blocks to build a castle
- Selecting a picture book to check out from the library media center
- Deciding where to place his or her mat for naptime.

Planning is a natural function of human thought. It is our responsibility as educators to help students recognize the importance of the planning process.

2.3 Do: Middle

Do (Middle) is the action stage when students work on and complete various activities. Students will find the sources they may need, read and view the necessary information, and put it all together. During the Do stage, students might draw, paint, write, read, and listen. Do (Middle) may involve organizing and presenting the particular information, and then putting elements together to finish the job.

For example, students might do the following activities:

- Draw a picture of their favorite story
- Cut out pictures from a magazine to show what they ate for breakfast
- Work in small groups to solve math problems
- Interview an adult about their job

You can model the Do stage in a variety of ways. For example the teacher could model, demonstrate, and show the stages of the writing process. A student might interview an older student about his or her hobbies, interests, and favorite activities. Many teachers already instruct by modeling teaching and learning with their classes. Connecting these crucial activities to the Super3 can reinforce the role of these skills in the overall information problem-solving process. The Super3 gives students and teachers a familiar context in which to apply their understandings, skills, and techniques within a recognizable process.

2.4 Review: End

Young students often forget about the Review (End) stage. Many kids feel that once they complete a task or assignment, their job is done. However, to truly build a foundation for academic success, young students must not forget to evaluate what they have produced. Just as Big6 #6—Evaluation—asks students to evaluate both process and product, Review is a multi-faceted concept as well. For example, when asking students about their work, don't only ask them if they created a quality product; also ask them about the path they took to complete the assignment, and whether or not they would do it differently next time.

One way to get your students into the Review (End) routine is to make it a part of your everyday assignments. When planning an activity, build in evaluation time. Have students look over their work before they turn it in, and put their initials on the back of the paper if they feel the product they created meets the assignment criteria and is their best work. Be very specific and clear about your expectations when assigning work to your students because clear expectations will give them a better foundation for reviewing their work.

2.5 Super3 for Older Students and Special Learners

Although the Super3 is designed for younger students, it is also beneficial for children with special needs, English Language Learners (ELL), or older students who are not yet familiar with or ready for the Big6.

The terminology and detail of the full Big6 process can be overwhelming for some students. The Super3 is more manageable and easy to learn while still encompassing the full process of information problem-solving. Students readily grasp the three stages and teachers can add more details and complexity over time. Once students gain proficiency in the Super3, there is an easy transition to the stages and sub-stages of the full Big6 process.

2.6 Parents Can Help Too

Parents can easily become involved in helping their children learn and use the Super3. Talk to parents about the importance of information problem-solving on open house or curriculum night and encourage families to make the Super3 a regular part of home life. Explain the Super3 process and how you and the students use it in the classroom.

Send home a weekly or monthly newsletter or classroom update to share the Super3 activities that happen in the classroom. Encourage parents to ask meaningful and specific questions about the work their children complete and how they feel about their finished task or project. This activity will help avoid the "What did you learn at school today? Nothing!" syndrome at the dinner table and will help reinforce the importance of the Super3 inside and outside of the classroom.

Guiding questions for families to ask include:

- What part of the Super3 did you focus on today?
- What was your favorite part about doing this project?
- What might you do better next time?
- What is the next step for your work?

2.7 Super3 in Action

Explanations

The first set of materials in Part 2 includes handouts and PowerPoint presentation examples that explain the Super3 process in detail. The materials discuss what the Super3 is, who the Super3 is designed for, and why teachers might use the Super3.

Next you will find detailed explanations of each stage: Plan, Do, and Review along with guiding questions to help students as they progress through each stage. It is our hope that these slides and handouts will help you, the educators, to integrate the Super3 into your current classroom activities and practices.

Exercises

Worksheet 2.1—Literal Level includes specific curriculum examples of activities from Kindergarten through grade 3. This gives you practice in correlating student actions to the Super3 stages.

Worksheets 2.2 and 2.3 are classroom based examples. We encourage you to use these exercises to deepen your understanding of the Super3 and to help implement the Super3 into real curriculum situations. Completing the exercises will help you begin to think about the Super3 in the day-to-day activities of Kindergarten to 3rd grade classrooms.

Next, we include worksheet pages (Worksheets 2.4 to 2.8) of examples of the three different stages. These are ready-to-use consumables that depict just how easy, helpful, and appropriate the Super3 is for younger students.

As you know, the Super3 is a spin-off of the Big6 information problem solving skills. We end this part with slides (Figure 2.2) correlating the Super3 to the Big6. This correlation is helpful when explaining both processes to parent groups, administrators, and secondary/post educators.

Super3: it's like a story…

Plan Beginning

Do Middle

Review End

Super3: What is it?

- A process:
  - a way of doing things
  - a course of action
  - a plan
  - an approach
  - a method

- A framework for students to learn how to get things done

- A simple, familiar pattern, easy for children to remember

Super3: Who uses it?

- Young learners

- Preschool through grade 3

- Students, classroom teachers, teacher-librarians, technology teachers, reading teachers, care givers, parents, families

---

Super3: Why use it?

The Super3 helps young learners in all curriculum areas.

The Super3 process is widely applicable:
- Schoolwork
  - to complete a worksheet or make a picture
- Recreation
  - to improve at soccer or learn to play checkers
- Decision-making in personal life
  - what game to play with a friend, or what birthday present to get for mom

---

Themes of the Super3

1. The Super3 is all about helping children to think about, recognize, and talk about "process."

2. The Super3 provides a common vocabulary for talking about process.

3. The Super3 is adaptable and flexible; it can be applied to any subject area, assignment or decision.

4. Using the Super3 is not always a linear. Sometimes students jump around or loop back.

5. The Super3 is a simplified version of the information problem-solving process. It leads naturally to a more detailed explanation—the Big6.

Plan: Beginning

I think about my task and how I will complete my project.

✓ What am I supposed to do?
✓ What will a "good job" look like?
✓ What information do I need?
✓ Where will I get my information?
✓ What is my plan?

Figure 2.1 Super3 PowerPoint Slides

Plan: Teaching TIPS

- ✓ **Have students evaluate samples of previously completed work.**

- ✓ **Give LESS rather than more direction on tasks.**

  Have students generate questions about the task.

- ✓ **Have students restate the task or rewrite it in their notebooks.**

Do: Middle

I do my work.
- ✓ I get the information I need.
- ✓ I put it all together.
- ✓ I might read, draw pictures, use the computer, or write.
- ✓ I cite my sources.

Do: Teaching Tips

- ✓ **Create a word web of various "DO" tasks: reading a book, completing math problems, students coloring a world map.**

- ✓ **Ask students how many things the "DO" each day—at home and school: brushing teeth, riding bus, eating lunch, making bed, playing jump rope.**

- ✓ **Always label your actions and explain that it is all part of "DO." "I am writing about our field trip and this is the DO part of the Super3."**

Do: Teaching Tips

- ✓ Always have students cite their sources.

- ✓ It is important for students to tell where they found their information. It makes their work more trustworthy–even at the youngest ages.

- ✓ Start simple.
  - book, computer, person
  - page number, author, or website name
  - Include an area (heading, box on bottom of page) on each major assignment for the citations.
  - drawing, stickers, stamps

Review: End

I check my work to make sure it is complete.
- ✓ Is my job done?
- ✓ Did I do what I was supposed to?
- ✓ Did I cite my sources?
- ✓ Do I feel okay about my work?
- ✓ Do I need to do anything else before I turn it in?

REVIEW: Teaching Tips

- ✓ **This is ongoing, should be formal and informal, and should progress across multiple settings: whole class, small groups, pairs, and individually.**

- ✓ **Build in frequent check-in times and breaks as students work.**

- ✓ **Use checklists, questionnaires, and rubrics to help give students guidelines for checking their work.**

- ✓ **Thumbs up/down, exit slips, nod head, smiley faces.**

Figure 2.1 Super3 PowerPoint Slides (*continued*)

Worksheet 2.1: Understanding the Super3™ Exercise

Student Action	Super3 Stage
Views a video on whales.	
Looks over a worksheet to make sure it's all done.	
Chooses a topic for a project.	
Listens to a story.	
Realizes that she's not sure what she is supposed to do.	
Decides that he needs a book about butterflies.	
Goes to the library to use a computer.	
Uses the Paint program to create a title page.	

Worksheet 2.2:
Super3™ Matching
Exercise I—Interpretive Level

Curriculum Situation:	1st Grade students gather information and complete a report about a place near their home (for example: a park, museum, zoo, community center)	
Actions	**Super3**	**Explanation**
Students work in the computer lab of the library media center using pre-selected websites.		
The classroom teacher discusses how to select a place.		
Students explain what was the hardest part of the assignment		

Worksheet 2.3:
Super3™ Matching
Exercise II—Interpretive Level

Curriculum Situation:	2nd grade students set "goals for the month" for themselves in reading, writing, and math.	
Actions	**Super3**	**Explanation**
The classroom teacher and the students talk about "goals" and what they will be learning this month.		
Using a "poor" example of a completed checklist, the teacher and students discuss whether it was done correctly.		
The students fill out a Super3 planning worksheet that includes the 3 subjects and a place to write their goals.		

Worksheet 2.4:
Super3™ Process

Super3
- **Plan**
- **Do**
- **Review**

Name:_____

Process 2

PLAN

Before I start I will_____

_____

_____

_____

PLAN

In order to complete this assignment I will_____

_____

_____

_____

PLAN

I will know my job is complete when_____

_____

_____

_____

Worksheet 2.5:
Super3™ Plan

Name:_____

Plan 1

What is my job and what do I need to do?

_____

_____

_____

_____

_____

_____

Worksheet 2.6: Super3™ Do

Name:_____

Do 1

My goals for the school year are:

What happened?

Why did it happen?

When did it happen?

Who was there?

Where did it happen?

Worksheet 2.7:
Super3™ Do

Name:_____

Do 7

Story Elements

Title: _____

CHARACTERS	SETTING

PROBLEM	SOLUTION

Worksheet 2.8:
Super3™ Review

Name:_____

Review 3

☐ I read my piece to myself.

☐ My writing makes sense.

☐ My name and the date are on my writing.

☐ I have a title for my writing.

☐ I used periods, question marks, and exclamation marks.

☐ I used capital letters.

☐ My final work is neat.

☐ This is my best work.

Super3 to Big6

- As students get older, they can transition to a more sophisticated explanation of the problem-solving process:

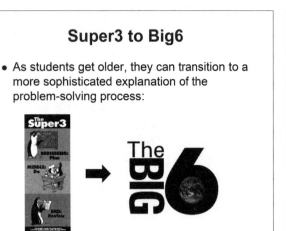

Super3 – Big6 Match

PLAN	1. Task Definition
	2. Info Seek Strategies
DO	3. Location & Access
	4. Use of Information
REVIEW	5. Synthesis
	6. Evaluation

Super3 to Big6

PLAN	Task Definition
	Information Seeking Strategies
DO	Location & Access
	Use of Information
	Synthesis
REVIEW	Evaluation

Figure 2.2 Super3 to Big6 Match

Other Super3 Ideas

- Super3 Dinosaurs (Nancy Reid, Green Bay, WI)
  PLANasaurus
  DOasaurus
  REVIEWasaurus
- Create your own Super3 mascot - make posters, bookmarks, and coloring pages with your character
- Rhymes, songs, and dances

Answer Key

Worksheet 2.1: Understanding the Super3 Exercise

1. DO
2. REVIEW
3. PLAN
4. DO
5. PLAN
6. PLAN
7. DO
8. DO

Worksheet 2.2: Super3 Matching Exercise I—Interpretive Level

A. DO
B. PLAN
C. REVIEW

Worksheet 2.3: Super3 Matching Exercise II—Interpretive Level

A. PLAN
B. REVIEW
C. DO

Figure 2.3 Answer Key for Worksheets

Part 3: Learning the Big6™

▶ **3.0 Introduction: Learning the Big6™** **47**

▶ **3.1 Information Literacy: The Big6™ Skills Process & Approach** **48**

▶ **3.2 Worksheets** **54**

▶ **Worksheet Answer Key** **76**

The BIG6 Learning the Big6™

3.0 Introduction: Learning the Big6™

In this part of the *Workshop Handbook*, we get to the heart of the Big6 approach to information and technology literacy. Here we include:

- Explanations of the Big6 at different levels and for different age groups.
- A chart to show the Big6 in different contexts: school, life, and work.
- Exercises that help develop an overall Big6 understanding.

Learning the Big6 will increase your capacity to provide effective integrated instructional activities for students. This section of the Workshop Handbook will help you to become proficient in the Big6 approach.

The goals of Part 3 are to:

- Learn the Big6 approach and corresponding vocabulary.
- Develop an understanding of "Big6 Basics"—the principles and guidelines associated with effective Big6 use and learning.
- Provide practice opportunities to learn new ideas and methods, and to develop expertise in improving Big6 instruction in your school environment.

Educators know that information problem-solving skills are basic skills. Students need to learn to create, manipulate, and make meaning out of complex and ever increasing amounts of information available through seemingly endless sources. Therefore, students need to be information literate.

The Big6 offers a conceptual and practical program for students to do just that. The Big6 is an information literacy curriculum, a problem-solving process, and a set of skills.

For teachers, the Big6 provides a systematic approach to teach information and technology skills. Students can use Big6 whenever a situation, academic or personal, requires information to solve a problem, make a decision, or complete a task.

Students who use Big6 have a context for learning various information-related skills and for using technology tools and techniques. The Big6 also offers an information problem-solving process that is easy-to-learn and practical.

3.1 Information Literacy: The Big6™ Skills Process & Approach

Explanations

The first set of materials in Part 3 (including Figures 3.1 to 3.3) will explain the stages of the Big6 as a process as well as individual skills. The main six stages are important as part of the overall Big6 process. These are the six necessary process stages for solving information problems. They represent a logical flow similar to the Super3: from Plan: Beginning (figuring out what needs to be done) to Do: Middle (gathering and using necessary information, creating a resulting product) to Review: End (evaluating success).

Review the language of the Big6 in three forms: (1) the formal statements that describe the stages in the process; (2) the detailed explanations for each Big6 Skill; and (3) the Big6 stages as questions for elementary school students.

Charts

One important strength of the Big6 is its broad applicability across many situations and settings. We firmly believe that learning needs to be relevant, meaningful, and purposeful. Students constantly question the usefulness of what they learn in school. The Big6 helps to resolve this uncertainly and allows students to see the relevance of their work. Further, the Big6 Skills that children learn at school will apply to their lives beyond school. If they learn to be effective and efficient information problem-solvers in school, they will be effective and efficient information problem-solvers beyond school.

The chart in Figure 3.4 describes the Big6 process in the context of three specific settings: school (an assignment); life (selecting a movie to attend); and work (creating a report). We also provide a blank chart so you can brainstorm school-home-work situations from an audience. Have students work through each according to the Big6—in small groups or use with the entire audience.

At first glance, the Big6 often seems like common sense. "It's simple," some say—and on one level it is simple. However, the Big6 also encompasses some complex critical thinking abilities. The Big6 worksheets in this handbook will help students to understand the Big6 and appreciate the nuances of skills at each stage.

Exercises

First, you will need to develop a working knowledge of the Big6 to become an independent user and teacher of the Big6 approach. This knowledge will enable you to communicate the standard Big6 vocabulary and to integrate the Big6 into instruction and assignments. Learn the Big6 terminology, have a clear and accurate understanding of what each term means, and integrate the approach into content instruction.

The exercises in this section of the Workshop Handbook will take you from literal to interpretive to applied levels of Big6 knowledge:

- **Literal Level:** What are the Big6 terms as defined by the authors?
- **Interpretive Level:** What does each Big6 term mean?
- **Applied Level:** How can I use Big6 in the context of content instruction?

The Interpretive level builds on a Literal understanding (the facts) of the Big6 terms, and the Applied level brings together the Literal and Applied levels to enable you to design and use the Big6 in teaching and learning activities.

(L) Literal Level: Worksheet 3.1 furthers your Big6 understandings by asking you to define the Big6 Stages in your own words. Worksheet 3.2 requires you to identify the Big6 Skill(s) students use when they engage in different activities. This is a literal level application of the information that was previously explained. The purpose of this exercise is to improve your ability to analyze and label student actions by using Big6 terms. Worksheet 3.2 uses a similar approach, but in 3.3 the selected actions come directly from various states' subject area standards.

(I) Interpretive Level: Worksheets 3.4–3.14 require an Interpretive response. To complete the worksheets, explain which Big6 Skills to teach in each situation, and then explain why that Big6 Skill is the relevant choice.

(A) Applied Level: The remaining worksheets (3.15–3.19) provide practice on the Applied level. The worksheets provide a structure in which to apply the Big6 process and skills in a wide range of academic situations.

All the worksheets in this chapter provide a structured, scaffolding approach in which to learn the Big6. The worksheets require you to recall information about the Big6 and definitions, to interpret their meaning in context, and to use Big6 in open-ended curriculum scenarios. In later chapters, you will use the Big6 to design instructional units, lessons, and activities as well as to integrate the Big6 into existing curricular elements.

Draw upon your content knowledge and the contexts in which you teach, then apply the Big6 to real school and life situations. The three-level approach (LIA) will help you construct meaning for yourself and you will soon become an independent Big6er.

We are all information consumers—in school, work, and life settings. In order to put our students in a position to be effective consumers as well, we must provide them with tools to understand the nature of information and use information throughout their lives. The Big6 provides a framework for teaching students this most important lesson. Working through this chapter will increase your confidence to understand and apply the Big6 process and will reveal the deep thought and specific skills required in each Big6 stage.

Levels of Information Problem Solving

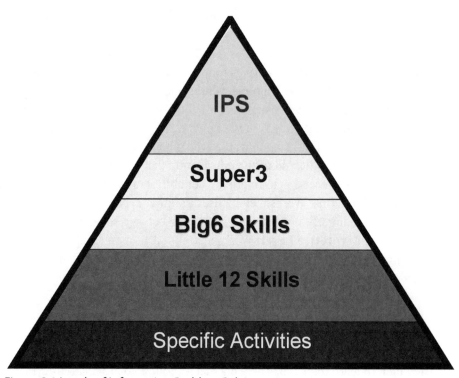

Figure 3.1 Levels of Information Problem Solving

The Big6™ Skills Approach to Information Problem-Solving

1. Task Definition

1.1   Define the problem.

1.2   Identify the information needed.

2. Information Seeking Strategies

2.1   Determine all possible sources.

2.2   Select the best source.

3. Location & Access

3.1   Locate sources.

3.2   Find information within sources.

4. Use of Information

4.1   Engage (e.g., read, hear, view).

4.2   Extract relevant information.

5. Synthesis

5.1   Organize information from multiple sources.

5.2   Present the result.

6. Evaluation

6.1   Judge the result (effectiveness).

6.2   Judge the process (efficiency).

Figure 3.2 The Big6™ Skills Approach to Information Problem-Solving

Big6™ Skills Learning Objectives

Big6™ #1
Task Definition

The student demonstrates the ability to:
- Determine the information problem to be solved
- Reformulate a complete statement of the task
- Pick out keywords embedded in a question
- Ask a good question
- Understand and follow printed and/or oral directions

Big6™ #2
Information Seeking Strategies

The student demonstrates the ability to:
- Develop alternatives and to seek a variety of materials
- Determine which information is most/least important
- Recognize that information can be gathered from many sources, including investigation, observation, and human resources
- Use appropriate criteria for selecting sources

Big6™ #3
Location and Access

The student demonstrates the ability to:
- Determine what sources are available
- Independently gather resources
- Determine if the source is usable
- Access appropriate information systems, including online databases, online public access catalog, and electronic multimedia

Big6™ #4
Use of Information

The student demonstrates the ability to:
- Distinguish facts from opinion
- Accurately and completely summarize/paraphrase the main idea from written and oral sources
- Accurately cite sources
- Read, listen, view, and touch carefully to acquire information

Big6™ #5
Synthesis

The student demonstrates the ability to:
- Organize information in clear, coherent presentations
- Present information in ways appropriate to the task
- Participate effectively in discussions and debates
- Produce personally designed products to communicate content

Big6™ #6
Evaluation

The student demonstrates the ability to:
- Demonstrate a high degree of confidence in the quality of the product produced
- Assess the product for completeness, strengths, and weaknesses
- Develop criteria to determine the effectiveness of the process used to solve the problem
- Provide recommendations to improve results
- Determine the need for further information

Figure 3.3 Big6™ Skills Learning Objectives

Information Problem-Solving in School, Life, and Work Contexts

Information Problem-Solving Process	School Context: Completing an assignment for class	Life Context: Deciding which movie to attend on Saturday night	Work Context: Reporting on five year product sales
Task Definition	Finding out that the task involves writing a two-part essay and realizing that a key to success is using documented supporting evidence.	Figuring out that it will be necessary to attend a 7:00–7:30 p.m. showing in order to get the babysitter home on time.	Producing a table and chart representing sales figures by product and salesperson over 3 years. Recognizing that reliable sales data over time is needed.
Information Seeking Strategies	Considering potential information sources and deciding that current newspaper and magazine articles would be best.	Deciding to look at the entertainment section of the newspaper to determine the showing times of movies.	Determining that there are at least 3 places where sales figures are kept: fulfillment, accounting, and marketing.
Location & Access	Using an online index to search for appropriate newspaper and magazine articles.	Locating the newspaper upstairs next to the bed. Using the "Quick Guide" on the first page to locate the entertainment section.	Requesting raw data files from each of the 3 departments.
Use of Information	Reading the articles and typing notes directly into a word processing program, noting the sources.	Reading the movie ads and focusing on times and locations.	Examining the various files and extracting the data by relevant categories and years.
Synthesis	Using a word processor, creating an outline, then drafting the essay.	Determining that there is only one movie playing at the time you both want to see a movie.	Using an electronic spreadsheet program to organize and compare data and sources. Using graphing capabilities to create a series of charts.
Evaluation	Realizing that your details are weak on one of the two parts and that you should go back and find additional information.	Realizing that the newspaper was a good source for the necessary information and that you successfully met your task.	Rechecking to ensure data accuracy. Getting feedback on charts from a co-worker.

Figure 3.4 Information Problem-Solving in School, Life, and Work Contexts

Worksheet 3.1:
Developing Big6™ Understandings
Literal Level—Describe The Big6

Describe each of the Big6 Skills in your own words.

Big6™ Skills	Description
1. Task Definition	
2. Information Seeking Strategies	
3. Location and Access	
4. Use of Information	
5. Synthesis	
6. Evaluation	

Worksheet 3.2:
Developing Big6™ Understandings—
Literal Level

In the space provided, indicate which of the Big6™ skills students are using when they perform each of the following activities:

TD	=	Task Definition
ISS	=	Information Seeking Strategies
L&A	=	Location & Access
UI	=	Use of Information
S	=	Synthesis
E	=	Evaluation

When a student

_____ 1. chooses between an encyclopedia and a magazine for information on the political situation in the Middle East.

_____ 2. creates a monthly classroom newsletter about climate changes in the world.

_____ 3. interviews a long-time community resident about local history.

_____ 4. assesses the presentations of other students.

_____ 5. uses PowerPoint to create a multimedia show about holiday celebrations in other cultures.

_____ 6. reflects on personal information skills that need to be improved.

_____ 7. uses advanced Google commands.

_____ 8. evaluates the effectiveness of different specific media (e.g. video, audio, animation, print, etc.).

_____ 9. writes a thesis statement.

_____ 10. finds word definitions in a dictionary.

_____ 11. answers questions with the use of a textbook.

_____ 12. selects a specific topic for a science fair project.

See Answer Key on pp. 76

Worksheet 3.3: Developing Big6™ Understandings— Literal Level Based on Standards

In the space provided, indicate which of the Big6™ skills students use when they perform each of the activities:

TD	=	Task Definition
ISS	=	Information Seeking Strategies
LA	=	Location & Access
U	=	Use of Information
S	=	Synthesis
E	=	Evaluation

When a student is able to:

_____ 1. Design, develop, publish products (Web pages, videotapes) using technology and information resources. (SC)

_____ 2. Identify problems and define their scope and elements. (MO)

_____ 3. Correctly use standardized citations. (FL)

_____ 4. Review and revise communications to improve accuracy and clarity. (MO)

_____ 5. Apply a creative process in the arts: Gather information from diverse sources. (WA)

_____ 6. Evaluate the processes used in recognizing and solving problems. (MO)

_____ 7. Draw conclusions using a variety of techniques. (FL)

_____ 8. Apply a performance process in the arts: Identify audience and purpose. (WA)

_____ 9. Draw mathematical ideas and conclusions from reading, listening, and viewing. (MO)

_____ 10. Determine the value and reliability of content collected on Web sites and other online resources. (MI)

_____ 11. Analyze information from a variety of sources. (NC)

_____ 12. Use technological tools to exchange information and ideas. (MO)

_____ 13. Begin using note-taking strategies to record facts and opinions from sources. (SC)

_____ 14. Organize and classify economic information by distinguishing relevant from irrelevant information, placing ideas in chronological order, and selecting appropriate labels for data. (NY)

_____ 15. Use details from text to analyze the text for accuracy of information. (MO)

_____ 16. Create and share electronic documents and multimedia materials with educators and other students. (MI)

Worksheet 3.3: *(continued)*

_____ 17. Use self-evaluation rubrics and teacher evaluation rubrics to assess final products. (SC)

_____ 18. Apply a creative process in the arts: Conceptualize the context or purpose. (WA)

_____ 19. Make hypotheses about economic issues and problems, testing, refining, and eliminating hypotheses and developing new ones when necessary. (NY)

_____ 20. Begin preparing a Works Cited list. (SC)

Note: The above statements are taken from various state standards documents. As individual standards and state documents change frequently, specific items may no longer be current. Below, we cite the main Web site for standards documents for the states included.

- Florida Department of Education (FL): http://www.floridastandards.org/Standards/FLStandardSearch.aspx
- Michigan Department of Education (MI): http://www.michigan.gov/mde/0,1607,7-140-28753—,00.html
- Missouri Department of Elementary & Secondary Education (MO): http://dese.mo.gov/standards/
- New York State Education Department (NY): http://www.emsc.nysed.gov/ciai/
- North Carolina Department of Public Instruction (NC): http://www.ncpublicschools.org/curriculum
- South Carolina Department of Education: http://ed.sc.gov/topics/curriculumstds/
- Washington Office of Superintendent of Public Instruction: http://www.k12.wa.us/CurriculumInstruct/EALR_GLE.aspx

See Answer Key on pp. 76

Worksheet 3.4:
Interpretive Level: Science Homework

Curriculum Context: For homework, Sally must answer questions at the end of a chapter in her science textbook.

	Student Activities	Big6™	Explanation
A	Sally decides that she will need to use her science book to answer the questions.		
B	Sally writes the answers to the questions, noting the page number(s) where she found the answers.		
C	Sally thinks about how she used the bold headings to locate the answers and realizes it was a helpful technique.		
D	Sally calls her friend Tanya about the assignment. Tanya reminds Sally to write the answers in complete sentences.		
E	Sally reads a section looking for the answer to question four.		
F	Sally uses the bold headings to get the section that seems to be the right one for question four.		

The Big6™ Skills © 1987 Eisenberg & Berkowitz

Big6™ Skills

1. **Task Definition**
   1.1 Define the problem.
   1.2 Identify the information needed.

2. **Information Seeking Strategies**
   2.1 Determine all possible sources.
   2.2 Select the best source.

3. **Location & Access**
   3.1 Locate sources.
   3.2 Find information within sources.

4. **Use of Information**
   4.1 Engage (e.g., read, hear, view).
   4.2 Extract relevant information.

5. **Synthesis**
   5.1 Organize information from multiple sources.
   5.2 Present the result.

6. **Evaluation**
   6.1 Judge the result (effectiveness).
   6.2 Judge the process (efficiency).

See Answer Key on page 76

Worksheet 3.5:
Interpretive Level: Social Studies Book Report

Curriculum Context: A social studies class has been assigned a book report. Students are to read a biography and write a book report.

	Activities	Big6™ Skills
A	Students complete a self-assessment sheet and attach it to the final draft of their book report.	
B	While reading, students are required to take notes using a graphic organizer.	
C	Students go to the library to select a biography to read for their assignment.	
D	Students are told that the library media specialist has reserved books that are appropriate for the assignment.	
E	Students read the assignment requirements and ask questions to clarify the classroom teacher's expectations.	
F	Students prepare their book reports using word processing tools.	

The Big6™ Skills © 1987 Eisenberg & Berkowitz

Big6™ Skills

1. **Task Definition**
   1.1 Define the problem.
   1.2 Identify the information needed.

2. **Information Seeking Strategies**
   2.1 Determine all possible sources.
   2.2 Select the best source.

3. **Location & Access**
   3.1 Locate sources.
   3.2 Find information within sources.

4. **Use of Information**
   4.1 Engage (e.g., read, hear, view).
   4.2 Extract relevant information.

5. **Synthesis**
   5.1 Organize information from multiple sources.
   5.2 Present the result.

6. **Evaluation**
   6.1 Judge the result (effectiveness).
   6.2 Judge the process (efficiency).

See Answer Key on page 76

Worksheet 3.6:
Interpretive Level: Social Studies Group Work

Curriculum Context: Middle school students are working on interdisciplinary group projects on regions of the United States, including cultural, social, geographic, and historical aspects.

	Student Activities	**Big6™**	**Explanation**
A	Group three uses the online catalog to find books while group four is searching for articles using a search engine.		
B	The groups brainstorm possible sources of information and decide to use magazines, books, their parents, and the World Wide Web.		
C	The students discuss which Web sites were useful and why.		
D	Group four prints out a magazine article.		
E	Each student group selects an area of the United States as the focus of its report.		
F	Group five delivers their report in the form of an audio podcast.		

The Big6™ Skills © 1987 Eisenberg & Berkowitz

Big6™ Skills

1. **Task Definition**
   1.1 Define the problem.
   1.2 Identify the information needed.

2. **Information Seeking Strategies**
   2.1 Determine all possible sources.
   2.2 Select the best source.

3. **Location & Access**
   3.1 Locate sources.
   3.2 Find information within sources.

4. **Use of Information**
   4.1 Engage (e.g., read, hear, view).
   4.2 Extract relevant information.

5. **Synthesis**
   5.1 Organize information from multiple sources.
   5.2 Present the result.

6. **Evaluation**
   6.1 Judge the result (effectiveness).
   6.2 Judge the process (efficiency).

See Answer Key on page 77

Worksheet 3.7:
Interpretive Level: Literature Essay

Curriculum Context: Joe, a 10th grade student, has just finished reading *The Call of the Wild*. As part of a take-home exam, he is required to write an essay comparing various aspects of his life to Buck's life.

	Student Activities	Big6™	Explanation
A	Joe marks appropriate sections in the book with post-its, then enters some relevant quotations into a word processing document.		
B	Joe realizes that he earned an A on his essay because he referred to specific examples in the book.		
C	Joe scans through the book to find the section where Buck first hears the "call of the wild."		
D	Joe realizes that the task involves writing a coherent and organized essay with specific comparisons between his life and Buck's life.		
E	Joe determines that it will be necessary to use a copy of the Call of the Wild, but a critical analysis in a book or magazine would also help.		
F	Joe prepares a chart of events in his life and in Buck's life, then uses word processing to write and print his essay.		

The Big6™ Skills © 1987 Eisenberg & Berkowitz

Big6™ Skills

1. **Task Definition**
   1.1 Define the problem.
   1.2 Identify the information needed.

2. **Information Seeking Strategies**
   2.1 Determine all possible sources.
   2.2 Select the best source.

3. **Location & Access**
   3.1 Locate sources.
   3.2 Find information within sources.

4. **Use of Information**
   4.1 Engage (e.g., read, hear, view).
   4.2 Extract relevant information.

5. **Synthesis**
   5.1 Organize information from multiple sources.
   5.2 Present the result.

6. **Evaluation**
   6.1 Judge the result (effectiveness).
   6.2 Judge the process (efficiency).

See Answer Key on page 77

Worksheet 3.8:
Interpretive Level: Animals Picture Book

Curriculum Context: A 2nd grade class is studying animals that live in a nearby area. Each student is to make a book that includes a picture of three animals and a very short story (a sentence or two) about each animal.

	Student Activities	Big6™	Explanation
A	The students and teacher brainstorm to identify some animals that live in a nearby area. Students may use one from this list but must decide on two others on their own.		
B	The teacher debriefs with the class. What was the most difficult part of the assignment?		
C	The teacher-librarian helps the students find the books and magazines about animals in the library media center.		
D	The students decide that a visit to a local nature center would be helpful.		
E	The library media specialist shows students how to take notes using PowerPoint and MS Word.		
F	Some students draw pictures of the animals with crayons or paint while other students paste pictures from old magazines.		

The Big6™ Skills © 1987 Eisenberg & Berkowitz

Big6™ Skills

1. **Task Definition**
   1.1 Define the problem.
   1.2 Identify the information needed.

2. **Information Seeking Strategies**
   2.1 Determine all possible sources.
   2.2 Select the best source.

3. **Location & Access**
   3.1 Locate sources.
   3.2 Find information within sources.

4. **Use of Information**
   4.1 Engage (e.g., read, hear, view).
   4.2 Extract relevant information.

5. **Synthesis**
   5.1 Organize information from multiple sources.
   5.2 Present the result.

6. **Evaluation**
   6.1 Judge the result (effectiveness).
   6.2 Judge the process (efficiency).

See Answer Key on page 77

Worksheet 3.9:
Interpretive Level: Science Experiments

Curriculum Context: Students are preparing science projects. Each student is required to design, run and report on a simple experiment. Students are given no other directions.

	Activities	**Big6™ Skills**
A	Students use a data table to record their findings.	
B	Ronnie decides to look for websites that have science experiments.	
C	Ronnie completes a science report worksheet to write his final lab report.	
D	Students are confused about the assignment and ask their teacher for a list of specific requirements.	
E	Ronnie uses the library OPAC to find books that have easy-to-do science experiments.	
F	Ronnie compares the time he spent on the assignment with the Time Management - Gantt Chart he prepared before he began.	

The Big6™ Skills © 1987 Eisenberg & Berkowitz

Big6™ Skills

1. **Task Definition**
   1.1 Define the problem.
   1.2 Identify the information needed.

2. **Information Seeking Strategies**
   2.1 Determine all possible sources.
   2.2 Select the best source.

3. **Location & Access**
   3.1 Locate sources.
   3.2 Find information within sources.

4. **Use of Information**
   4.1 Engage (e.g., read, hear, view).
   4.2 Extract relevant information.

5. **Synthesis**
   5.1 Organize information from multiple sources.
   5.2 Present the result.

6. **Evaluation**
   6.1 Judge the result (effectiveness).
   6.2 Judge the process (efficiency).

See Answer Key on page 77

Worksheet 3.10:
Interpretive Level: Vocabulary Homework

Curriculum Context: Students in 9th grade are given a vocabulary list of literary devices (e.g., metaphor, allusion, hyperbole, etc.) to define. The teacher requires that they rewrite the definitions in their own words and provide an example of each device.

	Student Activities	Big6™	Explanation
A	Students use the glossary in the back of the book to find a term.		
B	The teacher says that students can use a dictionary or the glossary in the textbook.		
C	Each student assesses the amount of time that the assignment took.		
D	Students determine that to be successful they must write the definitions in their own words.		
E	Students make a word processed list of terms and rewritten definitions.		
F	A student takes notes from the dictionary before writing the definition in his or her own words.		

The Big6™ Skills © 1987 Eisenberg & Berkowitz

Big6™ Skills

1. **Task Definition**
   1.1 Define the problem.
   1.2 Identify the information needed.

2. **Information Seeking Strategies**
   2.1 Determine all possible sources.
   2.2 Select the best source.

3. **Location & Access**
   3.1 Locate sources.
   3.2 Find information within sources.

4. **Use of Information**
   4.1 Engage (e.g., read, hear, view).
   4.2 Extract relevant information.

5. **Synthesis**
   5.1 Organize information from multiple sources.
   5.2 Present the result.

6. **Evaluation**
   6.1 Judge the result (effectiveness).
   6.2 Judge the process (efficiency).

See Answer Key on page 77

Worksheet 3.11:
Interpretive Level: Music Class

Curriculum Context: Students in a 4th grade music class are studying "note and rest values."

	Student Activities	**Big6™**	**Explanation**
A	One group creates a computer quiz in *PowerPoint*.		
B	The class discusses which of the tests were hard and why.		
C	The classroom teacher explains that students will work in groups and the assignment is to make a test for others.		
D	The teacher-librarian directs the students to the music books.		
E	One group decides that they want more information so they head to the library.		
F	Students photocopy pages from three books in the library media center.		

The Big6™ Skills © 1987 Eisenberg & Berkowitz

Big6™ Skills

1. **Task Definition**
   1.1 Define the problem.
   1.2 Identify the information needed.

2. **Information Seeking Strategies**
   2.1 Determine all possible sources.
   2.2 Select the best source.

3. **Location & Access**
   3.1 Locate sources.
   3.2 Find information within sources.

4. **Use of Information**
   4.1 Engage (e.g., read, hear, view).
   4.2 Extract relevant information.

5. **Synthesis**
   5.1 Organize information from multiple sources.
   5.2 Present the result.

6. **Evaluation**
   6.1 Judge the result (effectiveness).
   6.2 Judge the process (efficiency).

See Answer Key on page 77

Worksheet 3.12: Interpretive Level (Higher Education): Health Activities

Curriculum Context: Ms. Courtney asks the students in her health class to think about the preventive medicine vs. curative medicine. Their discussion results in an assignment that requires students to design a campaign to bring public attention to a health care need.

	Activities	Big6™ Skills
A	Students create digital posters and brochures.	
B	Students decide that it is important to have a clear understanding of the words "preventive" and "curative."	
C	Students use a peer assessment survey to judge their products.	
D	The students decide to start their information search with Wikipedia.	
E	Some students take notes using a word processing program so they can copy, cut and paste text onto their brochure template.	
F	The students use Wikipedia search and navigation tools.	

The Big6™ Skills © 1987 Eisenberg & Berkowitz

Big6™ Skills

1. **Task Definition**
   1.1 Define the problem.
   1.2 Identify the information needed.

2. **Information Seeking Strategies**
   2.1 Determine all possible sources.
   2.2 Select the best source.

3. **Location & Access**
   3.1 Locate sources.
   3.2 Find information within sources.

4. **Use of Information**
   4.1 Engage (e.g., read, hear, view).
   4.2 Extract relevant information.

5. **Synthesis**
   5.1 Organize information from multiple sources.
   5.2 Present the result.

6. **Evaluation**
   6.1 Judge the result (effectiveness).
   6.2 Judge the process (efficiency).

See Answer Key on page 77

Worksheet 3.13:
Interpretive Level (Higher Education):
Geology

Curriculum Context: Geology students are working on group projects to consider the influence of weathering, erosion, and deposition, as well as glaciation and tectonic activity on regional U.S. landscape types.

	Student Activities	Big6	Explanation
A	Group 3 uses OCLC WorldCat to find monographs while group 4 uses ProQuest to find articles.		
B	The groups brainstorm possible sources and list websites, magazines, books, government agencies, and local experts.		
C	The students discuss which web sites and search tools were useful and why.		
D	Group 4 uses a wiki as a common area for note taking.		
E	Each group selects an area of the U.S. to focus on.		
F	Group 5 delivers their report in the form of a YouTube video.		

The Big6™ Skills © 1987 Eisenberg & Berkowitz

Big6™ Skills

1. **Task Definition**
   1.1 Define the problem.
   1.2 Identify the information needed.

2. **Information Seeking Strategies**
   2.1 Determine all possible sources.
   2.2 Select the best source.

3. **Location & Access**
   3.1 Locate sources.
   3.2 Find information within sources.

4. **Use of Information**
   4.1 Engage (e.g., read, hear, view).
   4.2 Extract relevant information.

5. **Synthesis**
   5.1 Organize information from multiple sources.
   5.2 Present the result.

6. **Evaluation**
   6.1 Judge the result (effectiveness).
   6.2 Judge the process (efficiency).

See Answer Key on page 77

Worksheet 3.14:
Interpretive Level (Higher Education):
English

Curriculum Context: Class is held in a computer lab. English students are to write explanatory essays on the following topic: "For 3 of the world's religions, compare and contrast their beliefs on life after death, fate, and living a good life."

Student Activities	Big6	Explanation
Students use Google and other web tools to locate relevant Web sources.		
Students learn how to analyze the assignment as a 3x3 graphic chart.		
The students discuss the effectiveness of the graphic chart approach.		
Each student fill out a chart with notes from various online sources.		
For this assignment, students are encouraged to use Web resources only.		
Students write their essays from their charts.		

The Big6™ Skills © 1987 Eisenberg & Berkowitz

Big6™ Skills

1. **Task Definition**
   1.1 Define the problem.
   1.2 Identify the information needed.

2. **Information Seeking Strategies**
   2.1 Determine all possible sources.
   2.2 Select the best source.

3. **Location & Access**
   3.1 Locate sources.
   3.2 Find information within sources.

4. **Use of Information**
   4.1 Engage (e.g., read, hear, view).
   4.2 Extract relevant information.

5. **Synthesis**
   5.1 Organize information from multiple sources.
   5.2 Present the result.

6. **Evaluation**
   6.1 Judge the result (effectiveness).
   6.2 Judge the process (efficiency).

See Answer Key on page 77

Worksheet 3.15:
Applied Level: Nutrition Posters

Describe one or two activities that relate to each of the Big6™ Skills for the following curriculum content.

Curriculum Context: Students in a 1st grade class are studying nutrition and food groups. Students are required to make posters that describe what they learned. Each poster should include examples of foods that belong in each food group. Additionally, each food group must be correctly labeled.

Big6™	Student Activities

The Big6™ Skills © 1987 Eisenberg & Berkowitz

Big6™ Skills

1. **Task Definition**
   1.1 Define the problem.
   1.2 Identify the information needed.

2. **Information Seeking Strategies**
   2.1 Determine all possible sources.
   2.2 Select the best source.

3. **Location & Access**
   3.1 Locate sources.
   3.2 Find information within sources.

4. **Use of Information**
   4.1 Engage (e.g., read, hear, view).
   4.2 Extract relevant information.

5. **Synthesis**
   5.1 Organize information from multiple sources.
   5.2 Present the result.

6. **Evaluation**
   6.1 Judge the result (effectiveness).
   6.2 Judge the process (efficiency).

Worksheet 3.16:
Applied Level: Earth Science Project

Describe an activity that relates to each Big6™ Skill for the following Curriculum Context.

Curriculum Context: Students studying earth science are required to prepare a project that demonstrates how minerals impact their daily lives.

Big6™ Skills	Activities
1. Task Definition 1.1 Define the problem 1.2 Identify information needed	
2. Information Seeking Strategies 2.1 Determine possible sources 2.2 Select the best sources	
3. Location and Access 3.1 Locate sources 3.2 Find information within sources	
4. Use of Information 4.1 Engage (e.g., read, hear, view) 4.2 Extract relevant information	
5. Synthesis 5.1 Organize information from multiple sources 5.2 Present the information	
6. Evaluation 6.1 Judge the product (effectiveness) 6.2 Judge the problem-solving process (efficiency)	

Worksheet 3.17:
Applied Level: Art Research

Describe an activity that relates to each of the Big6™ Skills for the following Curriculum Context.

Curriculum Context: In an Art class, the teacher has students research how various artists were influenced by history. Students are required to create a multimedia presentation.

Big6™ Skills	Activities
1. Task Definition 1.1 Define the problem 1.2 Identify information needed	
2. Information Seeking Strategies 2.1 Determine possible sources 2.2 Select the best sources	
3. Location and Access 3.1 Locate sources 3.2 Find information within sources	
4. Use of Information 4.1 Engage (e.g., read, hear, view) 4.2 Extract relevant information	
5. Synthesis 5.1 Organize information from multiple sources 5.2 Present the information	
6. Evaluation 6.1 Judge the product (effectiveness) 6.2 Judge the problem-solving process (efficiency)	

Worksheet 3.18:
Applied Level: Social Studies Group Project

Describe one or two activities that relate to each of the Big6™ Skills for the following curriculum content.

Curriculum Context: Students in 11th grade social studies are divided into small groups to study significant U.S. Supreme Court cases. Each group is assigned a specific case on which to report. Each group is to prepare a 3-part project (oral, visual, and written) to explain the background behind the case, the decision, and the impact of the decision.

Big6™	Student Activities

The Big6™ Skills © 1987 Eisenberg & Berkowitz

Big6™ Skills

1. **Task Definition**
   1.1 Define the problem.
   1.2 Identify the information needed.

2. **Information Seeking Strategies**
   2.1 Determine all possible sources.
   2.2 Select the best source.

3. **Location & Access**
   3.1 Locate sources.
   3.2 Find information within sources.

4. **Use of Information**
   4.1 Engage (e.g., read, hear, view).
   4.2 Extract relevant information.

5. **Synthesis**
   5.1 Organize information from multiple sources.
   5.2 Present the result.

6. **Evaluation**
   6.1 Judge the result (effectiveness).
   6.2 Judge the process (efficiency).

Worksheet 3.19:
Applied Level: Environmental Science

Describe one or two activities that relate to each of the Big6™ Skills for the following curriculum content.

Curriculum Context: Undergraduates in an introductory environmental science course must write a 7-10 page essay on one of the following 3 topics: The Nature, Effects, and Costs of Acid Rain in the U.S. and Canada; The Nature, Effects, and Costs of Cutting Down the Rain Forest; or The Nature, Effects, and Costs of Noise and Sound Pollution.

Big6™	Student Activities

The Big6™ Skills © 1987 Eisenberg & Berkowitz

Big6™ Skills

1. **Task Definition**
   1.1 Define the problem.
   1.2 Identify the information needed.

2. **Information Seeking Strategies**
   2.1 Determine all possible sources.
   2.2 Select the best source.

3. **Location & Access**
   3.1 Locate sources.
   3.2 Find information within sources.

4. **Use of Information**
   4.1 Engage (e.g., read, hear, view).
   4.2 Extract relevant information.

5. **Synthesis**
   5.1 Organize information from multiple sources.
   5.2 Present the result.

6. **Evaluation**
   6.1 Judge the result (effectiveness).
   6.2 Judge the process (efficiency).

Worksheet 3.20:
The Curriculum Connection

Curriculum Unit/ Topic/Standard	Grade	Big6™ Connection	Possible Action (s) (Activity, Lesson, Assignment)

The Big6™ Skills © 1987 Eisenberg & Berkowitz

💡 Think Sheet

Answer Key

Worksheet 3.1: Literal Level

1. ISS
2. S
3. UI
4. E
5. S
6. E
7. L&A
8. E, ISS, TD
9. TD, S; also entire process
10. L&A
11. UI, S
12. TD

Worksheet 3.2: Developing Big6 Understandings Literal Level

1. ISS
2. S
3. UI
4. E
5. S
6. E
7. L&A
8. E, ISS, TD
9. TD, S; also entire process
10. L&A
11. UI, S
12. TD

Worksheet 3.3: Literal Level Based on Standards

1. TD, S
2. TD
3. S

4. E, S
5. ISS, L&A
6. E
7. S
8. TD
9. S, UI
10. ISS, UI
11. UI
12. S
13. UI
14. UI, S
15. UI
16. S
17. E
18. TD
19. TD, S, E
20. S

Worksheet 3.4: Science Homework

A. ISS
B. S
C. E
D. TD
E. UI
F. L&A

Worksheet 3.5: Social Studies Book Report

A. E
B. UI
C. LA
D. ISS
E. TD
F. S

Figure 3.5 Worksheet Answer Key

Worksheet 3.6: Social Studies

A. L&A

B. ISS

C. E

D. UI

E. TD

F. S

Worksheet 3.7: Literature Essay

A. UI

B. E

C. L&A

D. TD

E. ISS

F. S

Worksheet 3.8: Animals Picture Book

A. TD

B. E

C. L&A

D. ISS

E. UI

F. S

Worksheet 3.9: Science Experiments

A. UI

B. ISS

C. S

D. TD

E. LA

F. E

Worksheet 3.10: Vocabulary Homework

A. L&A

B. ISS

C. E

D. TD

E. S

F. UI

Worksheet 3.11: Music Class

A. S

B. E

C. TD

D. LA

E. ISS

F. UI

Worksheet 3.12: Health Activities

A. S

B. TD

C. E

D. ISS

E. UI

F. LA

Worksheet 3.13: (Higher Education): Geology

A. L&A

B. ISS

C. E

D. UI

E. TD

F. S

Worksheet 3.14: (Higher Education): English

A. L&A

B. TD

C. E

D. UI

E. ISS

F. S

Part 4:
Themes of the Big6™

▶ **4.0 Introduction:**
   Themes of the Big6™ **81**

▶ **4.1 Themes of the Big6™** **81**

▶ **4.2 Worksheets** **83**

The BIG6 Themes of the Big6™

4.0 Introduction: Themes of the Big6™

As a well-developed and widely applicable program, approach, and curriculum, there are certain conceptual understandings that help when using the Big6 and Super3 with either a broad range of people and groups or across education, work, and recreational situations.

We present these conceptual understandings in this new part of the *Workshop Handbook* as "Themes of the Big6." Note that these themes apply to the Super3 as well as the Big6.

The goals of Part 4 are to:

- Present the themes.
- Provide opportunities to develop deeper understanding of the Big6 stages and approach.
- Consider implications of the Big6 for learning and teaching.
- Develop expertise to improve Big6 instruction in your learning environment.

In Part 4, we present seven distinctive themes. Each theme is further explained with more detail, graphics, or a worksheet as appropriate.

4.1 Themes of the Big6™

(1) The Big6 process can be applied in all subjects, with students of all ages, and across all grade levels (K-20).

(2) The Big6 is adaptable and flexible; it can be applied to any information situation.

(3) Technology skills have meaning within the Big6 process.

(4) Using the Big6 is not always a linear, step-by-step process.

(5) The Big6 process is necessary and sufficient for solving problems and completing tasks.

(6) The Big6 is an ideal approach for integrating information literacy learning with all subject area curricula at all grade levels.

(7) The Big6 provides a common vocabulary for "metacognition"—that helps everyone talk about how they learn and solve problems.

Theme #1: The Big6 process can be applied in all subjects, with students of all ages, and across all grade levels (K-20).

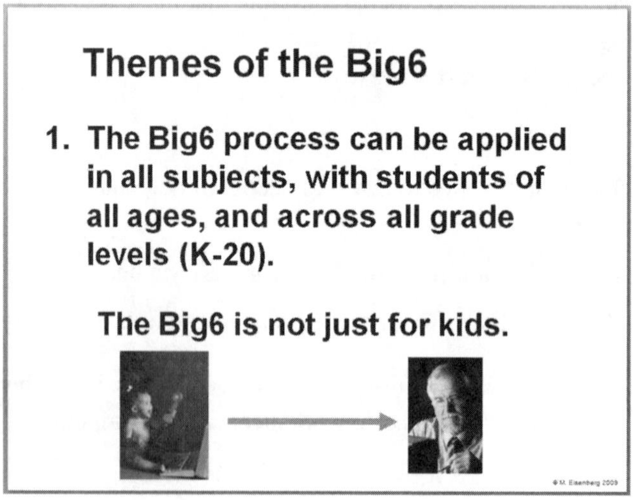

Figure 4.1 All Subjects, Ages, Grade Levels

Worksheet 4.1:
Big6™ Applications

Users	Context	Possible Big6 Applications
Middle school students	Beginning of the school year	
Business Planning Team	Revising the mission statement	
Pre-K students		
11th grade students		
Clerical staff	Emergency planning/training	
3rd grade students	Completing Math story problems	

Figure 4.2

Worksheet 4.2:
The Big6™ in Everyday Contexts

- Buying a birthday gift
- Deciding what movie to attend
- Finding out if somebody likes you
- Choosing a college
- Making a banana split
- Starting a band
- Getting directions
- Learning how to use a new cell phone
- Making a budget
- Winning in sports
- _____
- _____
- _____
- _____

Theme #3: Technology skills have meaning within the Big6 process.

Notes:

_____

_____

_____

_____

_____

_____

_____

Technology – Out of Context

Online Electronic indexing HTML PDAs
catalogs Programming VOIP Statistical blog
wiki Schematics analysis Multimedia
Web search Twitter
Instant Word processing software production
Web browsing Web page design Web Publishing
Messaging Graphics CAD/CAM
Upload/download Mind mapping
HTML Algorithms Char check
nload Tagging e-mail ftp. Chat
Games Cell phones Operating systems
Spell/grammar course Web page XML Network
check Online authoring Graphics
Telnet management Virtual worlds COPY/PASTE

Better, But Still Out of Context

- E-Mail
- Word processing
- Group discussion
- Online catalogs
- Article databases
- Web browsing
- Web searching
- Electronic spreadsheets
- Upload/download
- HTML
- Spell/grammar check
- Brainstorming software
- PDAs
- Video production
- Algorithms
- Instant Messaging
- Video production
- Photo editing
- Games
- Tagging
- Video conferencing

- Multimedia production
- Presentation software
- CAD/CAM
- Telnet
- Programming
- ftp
- Chat
- Graphics
- Database management
- Mind mapping
- Operating systems
- Web page design
- Copy/paste
- Statistical analysis
- Blog
- Social Network
- Virtual worlds
- Cell phones
- Course management
- XML
- Web publishing

Technology in Context

Big6 Stage	Technology
Task Definition	Brainstorming software; Email
Info Seeking Strategies	Search engines, article databases, indexes, online library catalogs; Blogs
Location & Access	Search engines, article databases, online library catalogs
Use of Information	Presentation Software; Blogs
Synthesis	Presentation Software
Evaluation	Spell/grammar check; Email

Figure 4.3

Theme #4: The Big6 is not always a linear, step-by-step process.

Notes:

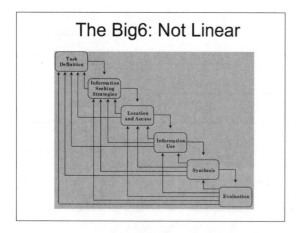

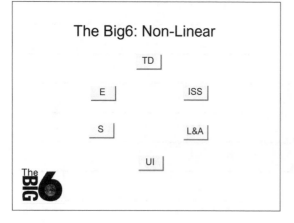

Figure 4.4

Theme #5: The Big6 process is *necessary* and *sufficient* for solving problems and completing tasks.

Consider:
*"What if a particular stage is **not** completely successful?"*

—Mike Eisenberg

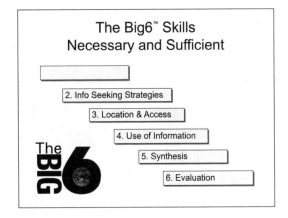

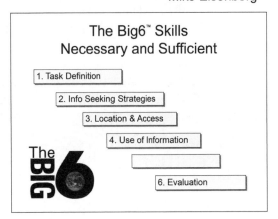

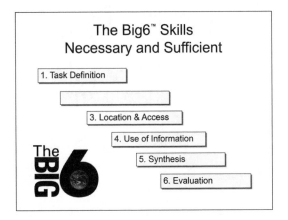

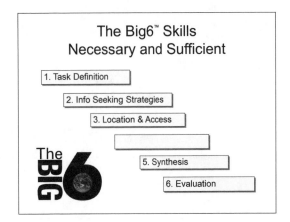

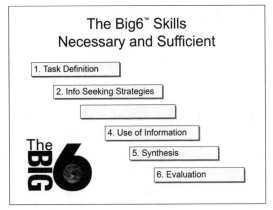

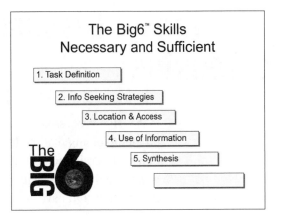

Figure 4.5

Worksheet 4.3: Big6™ Stages

Consider a student working on a writing project: How is global warming affecting the Earth? Imagine if the student does an excellent job on all stages of the Big6 except for the particular stage noted in the chart below. What might be the possible impact on the quality of the project? What evidence might indicate this problem and impact?

Big6 Stage	Impact	Evidence
Use of Information		
Information Seeking Strategy		
Task Definition		
Evaluation		
Location & Access		
Synthesis		

The Big6™ Skills © 1987 Eisenberg & Berkowitz

Sufficiency: Discussion Questions to Consider

- Is the Big6 process complete? Are there any stages of information seeking or problem-solving that the Big6 does not cover?
- Consider "evaluation of information." Someone once proposed that the Big6 expand to the Big7—with a separate stage for evaluation of information. Why doesn't the Big6 have an explicit evaluation of information stage?

Theme #6: The Big6 is an ideal approach for integrating information literacy learning with all subject area curricula at all grade levels.

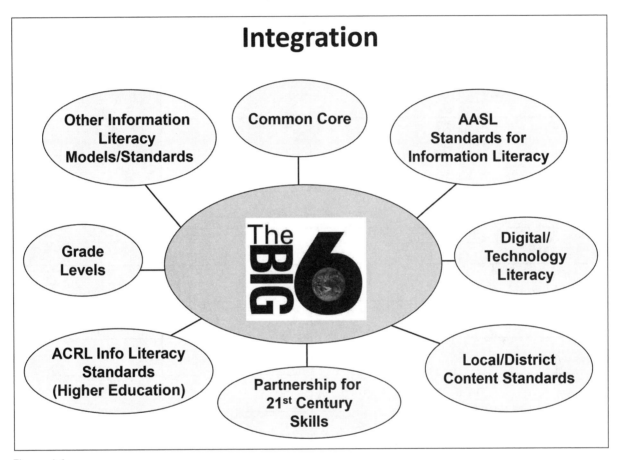

Figure 4.6

Worksheet 4.4:
The Curriculum Connection

Curriculum Unit/ Topic/Standard	Grade	Big6™ Connection	Possible Action(s) (Activity, Lesson, Assignment)

Theme #7: The Big6 provides a common vocabulary for "metacognition"— that helps students (and teachers and parents) talk about how they learn and solve problems.

Big6™ Skills

1. **Task Definition**
   1.1 Define the problem.
   1.2 Identify the information needed.

2. **Information Seeking Strategies**
   2.1 Determine all possible sources.
   2.2 Select the best source.

3. **Location & Access**
   3.1 Locate sources.
   3.2 Find information within sources.

4. **Use of Information**
   4.1 Engage (e.g., read, hear, view).
   4.2 Extract relevant information.

5. **Synthesis**
   5.1 Organize information from multiple sources.
   5.2 Present the result.

6. **Evaluation**
   6.1 Judge the result (effectiveness).
   6.2 Judge the process (efficiency).

The Big6™ Skills © 1987 Eisenberg & Berkowitz

Secondary Poster
Copyright (c) 1994 Michael B. Eisenberg/Robert E. Berkowitz

Elementary Poster
Copyright (c) 1994 Michael B. Eisenberg/Robert E. Berkowitz

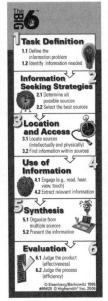

Figure 4.7

⚡ *Think Sheet*

Part 5:
Technology and the Big6™

▶ 5.0 Introduction: Opening Activity—Worksheets 5.1–5.3 95

▶ 5.1 Technology Today and Tomorrow 98

▶ 5.2 Web Resources for the Big6™ and Technology (updated Oct. 2009) 107

The Big6 Technology and the Big6™

5.0 Introduction: Opening Activity

Technology is not an add-on!

Educators and schools (K-20) increasingly recognize the value and importance of using technology and teaching technology skills in the context of classroom curriculum and assignments. It just isn't effective to teach specific computer skills in isolation (as skills to apply at a later time) or in lab settings (independent from the classroom).

Students need to be prepared to use a range of information and communications technologies (ICT) flexibly, creatively, and purposefully. Today, educators at all levels seek ways to move from teaching isolated computer skills to teaching information and communications technology skills within the context of the information problem-solving process. For us, that means integrating various technology tools and strategies within the Big6 or Super3 scaffold.

Individual information and communications skills take on a new meaning when they are learned as part of the Big6 process. Students develop true "information literacy" because they genuinely apply various computer, communication, and technology skills as part of the learning process. Considering technology within the Big6 process provides the necessary structure and framework for this to happen.

To integrate information and communication technology skills effectively, learning has two requirements: (1) the skills must directly relate to the content area curriculum and to classroom assignments; and (2) the skills themselves need to be tied together in a logical and systematic information process model.

This section includes a series of worksheets and PowerPoint handouts for teachers to learn, conceptually and practically, how to integrate information and communications technology options and skills into the Big6 process.

The Opening Activity (Worksheets 5.1) sets the scene by having us reflect on current technology goals, impact, and approaches in schools through answering and sharing a series of questions. This exercise is followed by PowerPoint handouts that display the slides Mike uses to present his thoughts on the current and immediate future state of technology. As noted previously, we encourage you to adapt and supplement these PowerPoint slides with your own slides. See other examples of our slides on the Big6 Web site: www.big6.com.

The slides are followed by two similar exercises (Worksheets 5.2–5.5) designed to demonstrate the connection between technology and the Big6. Technology skills are easy to integrate into the Big6 Skills process.

In Worksheet 5.2, the first column—Baseline Technologies—is for the non-electronic tools that students use. A crayon and paper, for example, is a baseline technology that can be entered on the top line of the first column. Now, consider which Big6 Skills are related to using a crayon and paper? Where in the Big6 does a crayon and paper prove valuable? The answer is Synthesis, and that answer can be entered into the second column. Finally, what are the related electronic technologies that provide a similar boost to crayon and paper, only more so? The answer should include such software as Paint or Draw, graphics programs, or even video or multimedia production. These responses can be entered into the third column.

Baseline Technologies	Related Big6™ Skills	Related Electronic Technology Options
The yellow pages A highlighter Books and magazines A pen and paper The telephone A face-to-face meeting	Location & Access Use of Information Information Seeking Strategies Use of Information/Synthesis Location & Access Task Definition/Information Seeking Strategies, Location & Access, Use of Information, Synthesis, and Evaluation.	Search engines; article search tools; indexes Copy and paste Full-text electronic resources; blogs Word processing; desktop publishing; presentation software; multimedia production E-mail E-mail, chat, IM, audio or video conferencing, 3-D virtual worlds; social networking

After the exercise, the relationship can be turned around—using Worksheet 5.3. That is, for each Big6 stage, indicate the related electronic technologies. This chart forms the basis of the Big6-technology connection.

For example, word processing, desktop publishing, PowerPoint, and other presentation or production software programs are used for Synthesis (to organize and present information). Word processing is also important for Use of Information (note-taking, citation saving). Online databases, encyclopedias, and other full-text electronic resources are part of an effective Information Seeking Strategy and provide Location & Access capabilities. Various Internet communications capabilities are also included in information problem-solving. E-mail is highly useful to link students with their teachers or student-to-student for Task Definition activities and later for Evaluation. Web search engines (e.g., Google, Yahoo) are used in Information Seeking Strategies and as tools for location and access. Word functions like copy and paste, highlighting, bold, and track changes all help students to Use (i.e., engage and extract) information. When technological capabilities are integrated into the information problem-solving process, they become powerful information tools for students.

There is a second Technology-Big6 exercise—see Worksheets 5.4 and 5.5. Similar in approach, the second exercise focuses on very specific technologies (e.g., PowerPoint, Google, Blogs) and asks you to identify the matching Big6 stages.

The Big6-Technology connection concludes with the Technology within the Big6 Framework Chart, a listing of relevant web resources, and an updated integrated technology and Big6 Curriculum written by Mike Eisenberg, Doug Johnson, and Bob Berkowitz.

5.1 Technology: Today and Tomorrow

Technology – Out of Context

© Eisenberg & Berkowitz 2009

Better, But Still Out of Context

- E-Mail
- Word processing
- Group discussion
- Online catalogs
- Electronic indexes
- Web browsing
- Web searching
- Electronic spreadsheets
- Upload/download
- HTML
- Spell/grammar check
- Brainstorming software
- PDAs
- Video production
- Algorithms
- Instant Messaging
- Video production
- Photo editing
- Games
- Tagging
- Video conferencing

- Multimedia production
- Presentation software
- CAD/CAM
- Telnet
- Programming
- ftp
- Chat
- Graphics
- Database management
- Mind mapping
- Operating systems
- Web page design
- Copy/paste
- Statistical analysis
- Blog
- Social Network
- Virtual worlds
- Cell phones
- Course management
- XML
- Web publishing

© Eisenberg & Berkowitz 2009

Technology in Context

TASK DEFINITION	Students use e-mail, chat, audio-, video-, and web-conferencing, txt messaging, group e-mail; Twitter, and other online communication methods to clarify assignments and brainstorm options. Students also use software to generate timelines, charts, mind maps, etc. to plan and organize complex problems.
INFO SEEKING STRATEGIES	Students identify and assess electronic resources (e.g., article databases, online encyclopedias, websites, blogs) as they develop information seeking strategies to address their problem.
LOCATION & ACCESS	Students use article search engines, Web search engines, online catalogs, and other electronic searching tools to find sources and identify information within sources.
USE OF INFORMATION	Students engage information in online or locally stored electronic information sources; view, download, and decompress files; and use copy-and-paste features to extract relevant information. Students also use presentation or word processing software to take notes and document citation information.
SYNTHESIS	Students organize and communicate their results using appropriate media production and presentation software (e.g., word processing, database management, spreadsheet, presentation, graphics, multimedia editing and production) and distribute their projects via e-mail, Web publishing or hosting, or other media.
EVALUATION	Students evaluate their technology-based products as well as the impact, effectiveness, and efficiency of the technology systems they used. Students use a range of communication technologies to share their assessments with teachers, parents, and each other.

© Eisenberg & Berkowitz 2009

Figure 5.1

Worksheet 5.1:
Technology in Context—Opening Activity

Answer these questions being as specific as possible. Be prepared to share your answers with others in the workshop.

1. Describe the impact of technology on student learning in your school.

2. My description of technology integration is:

3. Describe some specific ways your school uses technology in various settings (classrooms, library, labs, home, or community access).

Worksheet 5.1: (*continued*)

Complete these statements being as specific as possible. Be prepared to share your answers with others in the workshop.

4. Describe your ideas about how to use technology as a tool for learning.

5. Describe how the perception of technology integration by a classroom teacher, teacher-librarian, or technology specialist influences student learning.

6. Describe which technology applications most appeal to you and how you implement them within instruction.

Worksheet 5.1: (*continued*)

Complete these statements being as specific as possible. Be prepared to share your answers with others in the workshop.

7. What problems do classroom teachers, teacher-librarians, technology teachers, and others face when managing technology-based instructional units and/or lessons.

8. What challenges do you face using technology for teaching and learning? What resources are available to address the challenge?

Worksheet 5.2:
Technology within the Big6™ Framework I

Baseline Technology	Related Big6™ Skill(s)	Related Electronic Technologies

The Big6™ Skills © 1987 Eisenberg & Berkowitz

Worksheet 5.3:
Technology within the Big6™ Framework II

Use	Technology	Notes
1. Task Definition 1.1 Define the problem. 1.2 Identify the information needed.		
2. Information Seeking Strategies 2.1 Determine all possible sources. 2.2 Select the best source.		
3. Location & Access 3.1 Locate sources. 3.2 Find information within sources.		
4. Use of Information 4.1 Engage (e.g., read, hear, view). 4.2 Extract relevant information.		
5. Synthesis 5.1 Organize information from multiple sources. 5.2 Present the result.		
6. Evaluation 6.1 Judge the result (effectiveness). 6.2 Judge the process (efficiency).		

The Big6™ Skills © 1987 Eisenberg & Berkowitz

Technology in a Big6 Context

TASK DEFINITION	Students use e-mail, chat, audio-, video-, and web-conferencing, text messaging, group e-mail; Twitter, and other online communication methods to clarify assignments and brainstorm options. Students also use software to generate timelines, charts, mind maps, etc., to plan and organize complex problems.
INFO SEEKING STRATEGIES	Students identify and assess electronic resources (e.g., article databases, online encyclopedias, websites, blogs) as they develop information seeking strategies to address their problem.
LOCATION & ACCESS	Students use article search engines, Web search engines, online catalogs, and other electronic searching tools to find sources and identify information within sources.
USE OF INFORMATION	Students engage information in online or locally stored electronic information sources; view, download, and decompress files; and use copy-and-paste features to extract relevant information. Students also use presentation or word processing software to take notes and document citation information.
SYNTHESIS	Students organize and communicate their results using appropriate media production and presentation software (e.g., word processing, database management, spreadsheet, presentation, graphics, multimedia editing and production) and distribute their projects via e-mail, Web publishing or hosting, or other media.
EVALUATION	Students evaluate their technology-based products as well as the impact, effectiveness, and efficiency of the technology systems they used. Students use a range of communication technologies to share their assessments with teachers, parents, and each other.

© Eisenberg & Berkowitz 2010

Figure 5.2 Technology within the Big6 Framework

Worksheet 5.4:
Technologies and the Big6™

Technologies & Big6

Technologies	Big6 Stage
Word processing	
Google	
Spelling/grammar check	
Kidspiration	
Blogs	
Online Library Catalog	
PowerPoint	
E-mail	
Twitter	
ProQuest. EBSCO Host, NewsBank	

The Big6™ Skills © 1987 Eisenberg & Berkowitz

Worksheet 5.5:
The Big6™ and Technologies

Big6 & Technologies

Big6 Stage	Technologies
1. Task Definition	
2. Info Seeking Strategies	
3. Location & Access	
4. Use of Information	
5. Synthesis	
6. Evaluation	

The Big6™ Skills © 1987 Eisenberg & Berkowitz

5.2 Web Resources for the Big6™ and Technology (updated Oct. 2009)

This list contains websites selected from *Websites Organized by Big6 Stages*, from the Big6 Wiki http://big6.wikispaces.com. Compiled by Rob Darrow and reprinted with permission. Last accessed 10/13/09. For the complete annotated list of these websites visit: http://big6.wikispaces.com/

1. Task Definition—Define the problem and identify the information needed

Questioning Toolkit—http://questioning.org/Q7/toolkit.html
GO: Graphic Organizer—http://www.graphic.org/
Reference interview—http://www.olc.org/ore/2interview.htm
Thesis—http://owl.english.purdue.edu/workshops/hypertext/ResearchW/thesis.html
What is a Thesis?—http://www.sdst.org/shs/library/thesis.html
Univ of WA Research Process—http://www.lib.washington.edu/uwill/research101/
Ask an Expert—http://www.refdesk.com/expert.html
Ask Earl—Yahoo Kids—http://kids.yahoo.com/ask_earl
Asking Questions—http://www.askkids.com/

2. Information Seeking Strategies—Determine all possible sources and select the best ones

A+ Research and Writing—Information Search: Learning to Research in the Library—
    http://www.ipl.org/div/teen/aplus/
Basic Library Skills—http://ollie.dcccd.edu/library/BasicSkills.htm
Big6 Web Guide—http://calonline.cusd.com/infolit/big6/big6webguide.htm
Boolean Machine—http://kathyschrock.net/rbs3k/boolean
Choose the Best Search—http://www.noodletools.com/debbie/literacies/information/5locate/
    adviceengine.html
Do We Really Know Dewey?—http://tqjunior.thinkquest.org/5002/index.shtml
Filamentality—www.kn.pacbell.com/wired/fil
Infopeople's Search Tools Chart—http://www.infopeople.org/search/chart.html
ultimedia Tour of the Dewey Decimal System—http://www.oclc.org/dewey/about/ddctour/
    ddc1.html
QUICK: the Quality Information Checklist (K-6)—
    http://www.avon.k12.ct.us/enrichment/Enrich/quickgr4-0.htm
Using the Web for Research—http://ljhs.sandi.net/faculty/SGrant/UsingtheWeb.htm
Using the Parts of a Book—http://www.teach-nology.com/worksheets/research/book/basic/
    index.html
Using an Index for Information—http://www.teach-nology.com/worksheets/research/book/basket/1/
Using the Table of Contents—http://www.teach-nology.com/worksheets/research/book/contents/

3. Location and Access—Locate sources and find information within sources (includes evaluating content of Web sources)

TUTORIALS
    University of Albany (NY) Internet Tutorials—http://www.internettutorials.net/
    UC Berkeley Library: Finding Information on the Internet: A Tutorial
    http://www.lib.berkeley.edu/TeachingLib/Guides/Internet/FindInfo.html

WEBQUESTS for Searching Skills
>   Search the Web Webquest—http://calonline.cusd.com/infolit/
>   SearchQuest: A Webquest about Search Tools—http://www.sdst.org/shs/library/sqstu.html
OTHER RESOURCES
>   Infopeople's Best Search Tools—http://www.infopeople.org/search/tools.html
>   Kid's Search Tools—http://www.rcls.org/ksearch.htm
>   Search Engine Watch—http://www.searchenginewatch.com/
>   Selected and subject arranged Web sites:
-    Fresno County Public Library Homework Help for
-    Children—http://www.fresnolibrary.org/child/hwch/index.html, and
-    Teens—http://www.fresnolibrary.org/teen/hc/index.html
-    Kathy Schrock's Guide for Educators—http://school.discovery.com/schrockguide/
-    Multnomah County Library Homework Center—http://www.multcolib.org/homework/
-    Teaching Search Strategies—http://www.yahooligans.com/content/tg/search.html
WEBQUESTS Evaluating Content of Web Sources
>   Evaluating Web Sites—http://www.sdst.org/shs/library/evalwebstu.html
>   Atlantis WebQuest—http://drb.lifestreamcenter.net/Lessons/Atlantis/index.htm

4. Use of Information—Engage—read, hear, view and extract relevant information, including copyright and plagiarism issues

Big6 WebGuide—http://calonline.cusd.com/infolit/big6/big6webguide.htm

The Cornell Note Taking System—This widely used system for taking notes is explained in a straightforward style.
-    Bucks County Community College "Learning Center" in Pennsylvania—http://www.bucks.edu/~specpop/Cornl-ex.htm
-    Brigham Young University Center for Learning and Teaching—http://ccc.byu.edu/learning/note-tak.php

Improving Note Taking with Mind Maps—http://www.mindtools.com/pages/article/newISS_01.htm

Note Taking Skills—http://www.arc.sbc.edu/notes.html

Oral History Guidelines—http://www.memory.loc.gov/learn/lessons/oralhist/ohguide.html

Smithsonian Center for Folklife and Cultural Heritage -http://www.folklife.si.edu/education_exhibits/resources/guide/introduction.aspx

WEBQUESTS Copyright and Plagiarism
>   The Copyright Webquest—http://edtech.boisestate.edu/elearn/internet/copyright/copyrightwq.htm

OTHER RESOURCES AND ACTIVITIES
>   Copyright Tutorial—http://www.lib.utsystem.edu/copyright/
>   Cyber Ethics for Kids—http://www.usdoj.gov/criminal/cybercrime/rules/cybercitizen.htm

Plagiarism: What it is and How to Recognize and Avoid it—http://www.indiana.edu/~wts/wts/plagiarism.html#original

What is Plagiarism—http://www.plagiarism.org/plag_article_educational_tips_on_plagiarism_prevention.html

5. Synthesis—Organize information from multiple sources and present the result, including citing sources

A+ Research and Writing—for college and high school students—http://www.ipl.org/div/aplus/step6.htm

Create—A—Graph—http://nces.ed.gov/nceskids/graphing/

How to Write a Term Paper—http://www.galegroup.com/free_resources/term_paper/index.htm

Infopeople's How to Create Web Pages: A Webliography—http://infopeople.org/resources/htmlnote.html

Library of Congress Performance Task Idea Generator (pdf)—http://memory.loc.gov/learn//educators/workshop/design01/idea.pdf

Using Primary Sources—http://www.loc.gov/teachers/usingprimarysources/

Pathfinders for Constructing Pathfinders http://home.wsd.wednet.edu/wsd/Instructional/learnteach/libraries_media/Pathfinders/path.htm

Technology Tutorials on the Web—http://www.internet4classrooms.com/on-line2.htm

Timelines: Timeless Teaching Tools—http://www.educationworld.com/a_lesson/lesson044.shtml

WebQuest—http://webquest.sdsu.edu/

Citation Game—http://depts.washington.edu/etriouw/gameindex.htm

Citation Machine—http://citationmachine.net/

Citing Electronic Resources from Internet Public Library—http://www.ipl.org/div/aplus/linkciting.htm

Easybib.com—http://www.easybib.com/

Preparing a bibliography—http://teenlink.nypl.org/bibliography.html

Using MLA Format—http://owl.english.purdue.edu/handouts/research/r_mla.html

6. Evaluation—Judge the result—effectiveness; Judge the process—efficiency

An Assessment Plan for Information Literacy Assessment Plan—http://www.indiana.edu/~libinstr/Information_Literacy/assessment.html

Ideas for Information Literacy Assessment—http://jonathan.mueller.faculty.noctrl.edu/infolitassessments.htm

Kathy Schrock's Guide for Educators: Assessment and Rubric—http://school.discovery.com/schrockguide/assess.html

Project Based Checklists—http://pblchecklist.4teachers.org/

Rubistar—http://rubistar.4teachers.org/

TRAILS—*Tool for Real-time Assessment of Information Literacy Skills*—http://www.trails-9.org/about.php?his

Article 5.3—Information, Communications, and Technology (ICT) Skills Curriculum Based on the Big6 Skills Approach to Information Problem-Solving

By Mike Eisenberg, Doug Johnson and Bob Berkowitz

Revised February 2010

Permission is granted for educational use or reprint of all or parts of this curriculum as long as the authors and Big6™ are properly and prominently credited.

There is clear and widespread agreement among the public and educators that all students need to be proficient technology users. Technology literacy is among the attributes that appear in nearly every set of "21st Century skills." However, while districts spend a great deal of money on technology, there seems to be only a vague notion of what technology literacy really means. Can the student who uses technology well enough to play a game, send e-mail or browse the Web be considered technology literate? Will a student who uses technology in school only for running tutorials or an integrated learning system have the skills necessary to survive in our society? Is the ability to do basic word processing sufficient for students entering the workplace or post-secondary education?

Certainly not. Recent publications by educational associations advocate for a more meaningful use of technology in schools (Partnership for 21st Century Skills, 2008.) Educational technologists clearly describe what students should know and be able to do with technology. They advocate integrating technology skills into the content areas, recognize that technology skills should not be taught in isolation, and affirm that separate "computer classes" do not allow students to apply technology skills in meaningful ways. There is increasing recognition that the end result of technology literacy is not knowing how to operate technology, but rather to use technology as a tool for organization, communication, research, and problem solving. This revised focus on technology as a tool is an important shift in conceptual approach and instructional emphasis.

Moving away from teaching isolated technology skills and thereby moving toward an integrated approach is an important step that takes a great deal of planning and effort. Fortunately, we have a model for doing so. Over the past 30 years, library information and technology professionals have worked hard to move from teaching isolated "library skills" to teaching integrated "information skills." They found that information skills can be integrated effectively when the skills (1) directly relate to the content area curriculum and to classroom assignments, and (2) are tied together in a logical and systematic information process model.

Schools that seek to move away from isolated information technology skills instruction will also need to focus on both of these requirements. Successful integrated information skills programs are designed around collaborative projects jointly planned and taught by teachers and library information and technology professionals. Information technology skills instruction can and should be embedded in such a curriculum. Teacher-librarians, technology teachers, and classroom teachers need to work together to develop units and lessons that will include technology skills, information skills, and content-area curriculum outcomes.

A meaningful, unified information technology literacy curriculum must be more than a "laundry list" of isolated skills, such as knowing the parts of the computer, writing drafts and final products with a word processor, and searching for information on the Internet.

While specific, articulated skills are important for students to learn, the "laundry list" approach does not provide an adequate model for students to transfer and apply skills from situation to situation. These curricula address the "how" of technology use, but rarely the "when" or "why." Students may learn isolated skills and tools, but they would still lack an understanding of how those various skills fit together to solve problems and complete tasks. Students need to be able to use technology tools with flexibility, creativity and a genuine purpose. All learners should be able to recognize what goals they need to accomplish, determine whether technology will help them to do so, and then be able to use the technology as part of the process to accomplish their task. Individual technology skills take on a new meaning when they are integrated within this type of information problem-solving process, and students develop true "information technology literacy" because they have genuinely applied various information technology skills as part of the learning process.

The curriculum outlined in this document demonstrates how technology literacy skills can fit within an information literacy skills context [American Association of School Librarians, (1998), (2007); Association of College and Research Libraries (2000)]. The baseline information literacy context is the Big6 process (see sidebar and Eisenberg & Berkowitz, 1988, 1992, 1999, 2000, 2010). The various technology skills are adapted from the International Society for Technology in Education's National Educational Technology Standards for Students (2007) and the Mankato Schools Information Literacy Curriculum Guideline. Students might reasonably be expected to authentically demonstrate these basic technology skills before graduation.

Additional technology literacy competencies that may be relevant in some situations include knowing: (1) the basic operation, terminology, and maintenance of equipment, (2) how to use technology-assisted instructional programs, (3) the impact of technology on careers, society, and culture (as a direct instructional objective), and (4) computer programming.

Defining and describing technology skills is only a first step to assure all our children become proficient information and technology users. Other critical elements will include a teacher-supported scope and sequence of skills, well designed projects, and effective assessments. Equally essential is fruitful collaboration among classroom teachers, teacher librarians, and technology teachers in order to present students with a unified and integrated approach to ensure that all children master the skills they will need to thrive in an information-rich future (Eisenberg & Lowe, 1999).

The **Information, Communications, and Technology (ICT) Skills for Information Problem Solving** curriculum presented below defines technology capabilities and identifies associated skills based on the Big6 Skills Approach. The Curriculum describes levels of technology proficiency, and in so doing, promotes the skills and concepts basic to information and technology. In an information society, it is essential that students are technologically productive and able to solve information problems effectively and efficiently.

This curriculum requires more than teaching computer skills, technology hardware, and software programs in an isolated approach. An effective technology curriculum must be integrated across content areas and grade levels to improve the learning process. Technology is successfully integrated when it seamlessly supports curricular goals. Students learn and refine their technology skills when they work on projects that require them to solve problems and make decisions.

Information, Communications, and Technology (ICT) Skills for Information Problem Solving: A Curriculum Based on the Big6 Approach

By Mike Eisenberg, Doug Johnson, and Bob Berkowitz

1. Task Definition

The first part in the information problem-solving process involves the ability to recognize that an information need exists, to define the problem, and to identify the types and amount of information needed. In terms of technology, students will be able to:

> A.   Communicate with teachers regarding assignments, tasks, and information problems using e-mail; online discussions (e.g., listservs, threaded Web-based discussions, newsgroups); real-time communications (e.g., instant messaging services, chat rooms, IP telephony); desktop teleconferencing; and shared work spaces on the Internet, intranets, and local area networks.
> B.   Generate topics, define problems, and facilitate cooperative activities among groups of students locally and globally using e-mail, online discussions, real-time communications, desktop teleconferencing, and shared work spaces on the Internet and local area networks.
> C.   Generate topics, define problems, and facilitate cooperative activities with subject area experts locally and globally using e-mail, online discussions, real-time communications, desktop teleconferencing, and shared work spaces on the Internet and local area networks.

> D.   Define or refine the information problem using graphic organizing, brainstorming or idea generating software. This includes developing a research question or perspective on a topic.

> E.   Use a general online information source such as Wikipedia to read a topic overview and clarify the research subject.

2. Information Seeking Strategies

Once the student formulates the information problem, he or she must consider all possible information sources and develop a plan to find the sources. Students will be able to:

> A.   Assess the relevance and credibility of various types of electronic resources for data gathering including databases, commercial and Internet online resources, electronic reference works, community and government information, or other forms of electronic resources (e.g., resources in various media or graphics formats).

> B.   Assess the need for and relevance of primary resources including interviews, surveys, experiments, and documents that are accessible through electronic means.

> C.   Identify and apply specific criteria to evaluate computerized electronic resources.

> D.   Identify and apply specific criteria to construct meaningful original data gathering tools such as online surveys, electronic interviews; or scientific data gathering tools such as probes, meters, and timers.

E. Assess the value of e-mail, online discussions, real-time communications, desktop teleconferencing, and collaborative writing, production, and editing tools on the Internet and local area networks as part of a search of the current literature or in relation to the information task.

F. Use systems to generate modifiable flow charts, time lines, organizational charts, project plans (such as Gantt charts), and calendars that will help the student plan and organize complex or group information problem-solving tasks.

G. Use handheld devices such as personal digital assistants (PDAs), smart phones, electronic slates or tablet PCs to track contacts and create to-do lists and schedules.

H. Use a blog, wiki or other collaborative productivity tool to track the research process in real time.

3. Location and Access

After students determine their priorities for information seeking, they must locate information from a variety of resources and access specific information found within individual resources. Students will be able to:

A. Locate and use appropriate technology resources and technology available within the school library information and technology center, including resources on the library information and technology center's local area network (e.g., online catalogs, periodical indexes, full-text sources, multimedia technology stations, online terminals, scanners or digital cameras).

B. Locate and use appropriate information technology resources and systems available throughout the school including resources and technology available through intranets or local area networks (e.g., full-text resources, productivity software, scanners, or digital cameras).

C. Locate and use appropriate information technology resources and systems available beyond the school through the Internet (e.g., newsgroups, mail lists, WWW sites, ftp sites, online public access library catalogs, blogs, wikis, Nings, social networking sites, commercial article databases and online services, and other community, academic, and government resources).

D. Know the roles and technology expertise of people who work in the school information and technology program and elsewhere who might provide information or assistance. Know how to access that assistance both in person and virtually.

E. Use electronic reference materials (e.g., electronic encyclopedias, ebooks, dictionaries, biographical reference sources, atlases, geographic databanks, thesauri, almanacs, fact books) available through intranets or local area networks, stand-alone workstations, commercial online vendors, or the Internet.

F. Use the Internet or commercial technology networks to contact experts and help and referral services.

G. Conduct self-initiated electronic surveys through e-mail, listservs, newsgroups and online data collection tools.

H. Use search engines, tools and commands for searching commercial databases and services, (e.g., Web-based, online, networked or stand-alone services).

I. Use search engines, tools and commands for searching the Internet, e.g., meta search tools, bots, directories, jump pages, and specialized resources such as those that search the Invisible Web.

J. Use organizational systems and tools specific to electronic information sources that assist in finding specific and general information (e.g., indexes, tables of contents, user's instructions and manuals, legends, boldface and italics, graphic clues and icons, cross-references, Boolean logic strategies, time lines, hypertext links, knowledge trees, URLs, and so forth).

K. Use specialized Web sites and search tools and commands that limit searches by date, location, format, collection of evaluated sites or other criteria.

4. Use of Information

After finding potentially useful resources, students must engage (read, view, listen) the information to determine its relevance and then extract the relevant information. Students will be able to:

A. Connect and operate the technology devices and networks needed to access information; and read the guides and manuals associated with such tasks.

B. Know and be able to use the software and hardware needed to view, download, decompress and open documents, files, and programs from Internet sites and archives.

C. Copy and paste information from an electronic source into a personal document complete with proper citation.

D. Take notes and outline with a word processor, database, presentation or similar productivity program.

E. Record electronic sources of information and gather the URL locations of those sources in order to properly cite and credit sources in footnotes, endnotes, and bibliographies. Include any online sites designed to track and store online resources.

F. Use electronic spreadsheets, databases, and statistical software to process and analyze statistical data.

G. Analyze and filter electronic information in relation to the task, and reject information that is not relevant or credible.

H. Save and backup gathered data to secure locations (e.g. to an external memory device or online/cloud storage).

5. Synthesis

Students must organize and communicate the results of the information problem-solving effort. Students will be able to:

A. Classify and group information using a word processor, database or spreadsheet.

B. Use word processing and desktop publishing software to create printed documents, and apply keyboard skills equivalent to at least twice the rate of handwriting speed.

C. Create and use technology-generated graphics and art in various print and electronic presentations.

D. Use electronic spreadsheet software to create original spreadsheets.

E.   Generate charts, tables and graphs using electronic spreadsheets and other graphing programs.

F.   Use database software to create original databases.

G.   Use presentation software to create slide shows and multi-media presentations. Use websites and online services to create and share multi-media products.

H.   Create media-rich presentations and use projection devices to show hypermedia and multimedia productions that include digital video, audio files and active links to HTML documents or other programs.

I.   Create Web pages and websites using hypertext markup language (HTML) in a text document or by using Web page creation tools; and know the procedure to upload these pages to a Web server.

J.   Use e-mail, ftp, shared documents, and other telecommunications capabilities to publish the results of the information problem-solving activity. Know specialized sites for sharing photographs, slide shows, and multi-media presentations.

K.   Use specialized technology applications as appropriate for specific tasks (e.g., music composition software, computer-assisted drawing and drafting programs, mathematics modeling software, scientific measurement instruments).

L.   Properly cite and credit electronic sources (e.g. text, graphics, sound and video) of information within the product as well as in footnotes, endnotes, and bibliographies.

6. Evaluation

Evaluation focuses on how well the final product meets the original task (effectiveness) and the process of how well students carried out the information problem-solving process (efficiency). Students may evaluate their own work and process or be evaluated by others (e.g. classmates, teachers, library information and technology staff, parents). Students will be able to:

A.   Evaluate electronic presentations in terms of the content and format; and design self-assessment tools to help them evaluate their own work for both content and format.

B.   Use the spelling and grammar checking functions of word processing; and use other software to edit and revise their work.

C.   Apply legal principles and ethical conduct related to information technology, copyright, and plagiarism.

D.   Understand and abide by telecomputing etiquette when using e-mail, newsgroups, listservs and other Internet functions.

E.   Understand and abide by acceptable use policies and other school rules related to using the Internet and other electronic technology.

F.   Use e-mail, real-time communications (e.g., listservs, newsgroups, instant messaging services, chat rooms, IP telephony) desktop teleconferencing, and collaborative spaces on the Internet and local area networks to communicate with teachers and others regarding their performance on assignments, tasks, and information problems.

G.   Thoughtfully reflect on the use of electronic resources and tools throughout the process.

H.   Use online resources in ways that guard privacy and increase users online safety and security.

The Big6 Skills Approach to Information Problem Solving © Eisenberg and Berkowitz 1987

The Big6 is an information literacy curriculum, an information problem-solving process, and a set of skills which provide a strategy for effectively and efficiently meeting information needs. The Big6 Skills approach can be used whenever students are in a situation, academic or personal, which requires information to solve a problem, make a decision or complete a task. This model is transferable to school, personal, and work applications, as well as all content areas and the full range of grade levels. When taught collaboratively with content area teachers in concert with content-area objectives, it serves to ensure that students are information literate.

The Big6
1. Task Definition
1.1 Define the task (the information problem).
1.2 Identify information needed in order to complete the task (to solve the information problem).
2. Information Seeking Strategies
2.1 Brainstorm all possible sources.
2.2 Select the best sources.
3. Location and Access
3.1 Locate sources.
3.2 Find information within the sources.
4. Use of Information
4.1 Engage in the source (read, hear, view, touch).
4.2 Extract relevant information.
5. Synthesis
5.1 Organize information from multiple sources.
5.2 Present the information.
6. Evaluation
6.1 Judge the process (efficiency).
6.2 Judge the product (effectiveness).

References and Suggested Readings

American Association of School Librarians. (2007). *Standards for the 21st-century learner*. Chicago: American Library Association.

Association of College and Research Libraries.(2000) *Information literacy competency standards for higher education*. Chicago: American Library Association, http://www.ala.org/acrl/ilcomstan.Html.

Andrew, T. (2008, March 30). *Teaching with web 2.0: benefits interactive web technology bring to education*. Retrieved from http://teachingtechnology.suite101.com/article.cfm/teaching_with_web_20

Armstrong, S., & Warlick, D. (2004, September 15). The new literacy. *Tech & Learning*, Retrieved from http://www.techlearning.com/article/2806

Beldarrain, Y. (2006). Distance education trends: Integrating new technologies to foster student interaction and collaboration. *Distance Education, 27*(2), 139.

Benzinger, B. (2007). *Back to school with the class of web 2.0.* Retrieved from http://www.solutionwatch.com/515/back-to-school-with-the-class-of-web-20-part-2/

Borgman, C.L. (2007). *Scholarship in the digital age: Information, infrastructure, and the Internet.* Cambridge, MA: MIT Press.

Brabek, K., Fisher, K., & Pitler, H. (2004). Building better instruction: how technology supports nine research-proven instructional strategies. *Learning & Leading with Technology, 31*(5), 6-11.

Brown, D., & Warschauer, M. (2006). From the university to the elementary classroom: Students' experiences in learning to integrate technology in instruction. *Journal of Technology and Teacher Education, 14*(3), 599.

Cambre, M., & Hawkes, M. (2004). *Toys, tools & teachers: The challenges of technology.* Lanham, MD: Scarecrow Education.

Caruso, J.B. & Kvavik, R.B. (2005). *Students and information technology: Convenience, connection, control, and learning.* Educause Center for Applied Research.

Cavanaugh, C., & Blomeyer, R. L. (2007). *What works in K-12 online learning* (1st ed.).Eugene, OR: International Society for Technology in Education.

Cavanaugh, T. W. (2006). *The digital reader: Using e-books in K-12 education.* Eugene, OR: International Society for Technology in Education.

Christel, M. T., & Sullivan, S. (2007). *Lesson plans for creating media-rich classrooms.*Urbana, IL: National Council of Teachers of English.

Coppola, E. M. (2004). *Powering up: Learning to teach well with technology.* New York: Teachers College Press.

Crane, B. E. (2000). *Teaching with the internet: Strategies and models for K-12 curricula.* New York: Neal-Schuman Publishers.

Cuban, S., & Cuban, L. (2007). *Partners in literacy: Schools and libraries building communities through technology.* New York; ALA Editions: Teachers College Press; Chicago, IL.

Eisenberg, M. & Berkowitz, R. with B. Jansen and T. Little (1999). *Teaching information and technology skills" The Big6 in elementary schools.* Columbus, OH: Linworth Publishing.

Eisenberg, M. & Berkowitz, R. with R. Darrow and K Spitzer (2000). *Teaching Information Teaching information and technology skills" The Big6 in secondary schools.* Columbus, OH: Linworth Publishing.

Eisenberg, M. & Robinson, L. (2007). *The Super3: Information skills for young learners.* Columbus, OH: Linworth Publishing.

Ely, D. P., & Plomp, T. (1996). *Classic writings on instructional technology.* Englewood, CO: Libraries Unlimited.

Gordon, D. T. (2000). *The digital classroom: How technology is changing the way we teach* and learn. Cambridge, MA: Harvard Education Letter.

Guerrero, S., N. Walker, et al. (2004). "Technology in support of middle grade mathematics: what have we learned? (Third International Mathematics and Science Study) (National Council of Teachers of Mathematics)." *Journal of Computers in Mathematics and Science Teaching, 23*(1): 5(16).

Head, A.J., & Eisenberg, M.B. (2009). *Finding context: what today's college students say about conducting research in the digital age. project information literacy progress report.* Informally published manuscript, Information School, University of Washington, Seattle, WA.

International Society for Technology in Education, (ISTE) (2009). *The ISTE national educational technology standards (NETS•A), and performance indicators for administrators,* http://www.iste.org/Content/NavigationMenu/NETS/ForAdministrators/2009Standards/NETS-A_2009.pdf ISTE

International Society for Technology in Education, (ISTE) (2007). *The ISTE national educational technology standards (NETS•S), and performance indicators for students,* http://www.iste.org/Content/NavigationMenu/NETS/ForStudents/2007Standards/NETS_for_Students_2007_Standards.pdf ISTE

International Society for Technology in Education, (ISTE) (2008). *The ISTE national educational technology standards (NETS•T), and Performance Indicators for Teachers,* http://www.iste.org/Content/NavigationMenu/NETS/ForTeachers/2008Standards/NETS_T_Standards_Final.pdf ISTE

International Technology Education Association. (1996, 2003). *Technology for all americans: a rationale and structure for the study of education.* Reston, VA: ITEA.

Iowa Department of Education. (2006). *The essential skills of a world-class core curriculum.* Retrieved from http://www.iowa.gov/educate/index2.php?option=com_docman&task=doc_view&gid=2375&Itemid=99999999

Iowa Department of Education. (2009). *Iowa core curriculum: 21st century skills.* Retrieved from http://www.core curriculum.iowa.gov/ContentArea.aspx?C=21st+Century+Skills

Johnson, D. (2003). *Learning right from wrong in the digital age: An ethics guide for parents, teachers, librarians, and others who care about computer-using young people.* Columbus, OH: Linworth Publishing.

Library Research Service. (2005). *School library impact studies.* Retrieved from http://www.lrs.org/impact.php

Loertscher, D. V., C. Koechlin, and S. Zwaan. (2005). *Ban those bird units: 15 models for teaching and learning in information-rich and technology-rich environments.* Salt Lake City: Hi Willow Research and Publishing.

Monroe, B. J. (2004). *Crossing the digital divide: Race, writing, and technology in the classroom.* New York: Teachers College Press.

NCTE. (2008). *The NCTE definition of 21st century literacies.* NCTE. Retrieved from www.ncte.org/positions/statements/21stcentdefinition.

Oklahoma State Dept. of Education. (2003). (2009). *Oklahoma state department of education priority academic student skills: Instructional technology.* Retrieved from http://sde.state.ok.us/Curriculum/PASS/default.html

Partnership for 21st Century Skills (2008). *A framework for 21st century learning.* Retrieved from http://www.21stcenturyskills.org/

Partnership for 21st Century Skills. (2008). *21st century skills, education & competitiveness: A resource and policy guide.* Retrieved from http://www.21stcenturyskills.org/documents/21st_century_skills_education_and_competitiveness_guide.pdf

Pitler, H. (2007). *Using technology with classroom instruction that works.* Alexandria, VA; Denver, CO: Association for Supervision and Curriculum Development; Mid-continent Research for Education and Learning.

Pletka, B. (2007). *Educating the net generation: How to engage students in the 21st century.* Santa Monica, CA: Santa Monica Press.

Renzulli, J. S., Leppien, J. H., & Hays, T. S. (2000). *The multiple menu model: A practical guide for developing differentiated curriculum.* Mansfield Center, CT: Creative Learning Press.

Richardson, W. (2006). *Blogs, wikis, podcasts, and other powerful web tools for classrooms.* Thousand Oaks, CA: Corwin Press.

Rogers, Patricia L. (Ed). (2002). *Designing instruction for technology-enhanced learning.* Hershey, PA: Idea Group Publishing.

Rose, D. H., & Meyer, A. (2002). *Teaching every student in the digital age: Universal design for learning.* Alexandria, VA: Association for Supervision and Curriculum Development.

Rose, D. H., Meyer, A., & Hitchcock, C. (2005). *The universally designed classroom: Accessible curriculum and digital technologies.* Cambridge, MA: Harvard Education Press.

Seitzinger, J. (2006). Be constructive: Blogs, podcasts, and wikis as constructivist learning tools. *Learning Solutions.* Retrieved from http://www.elearningguild.com/pdf/2/073106des.pdf

Staudt, C. (2005). *Changing how we teach and learn with handheld computers.* Thousand Oaks, CA: Corwin Press.

Trilling, B., & Hood, P. (1999). Learning, technology, and education reform in the knowledge age. *Educational Technology, 39*(3), 5-18.

Warschauer, M. (2006). *Laptops and literacy: Learning in the wireless classroom.* New York: Teachers College Press.

Washington State Department of Education. *Technology essential conditions. Rubric for K-12 schools.* Retrieved from http://www.k12.wa.us/EdTech/TechLiteracy/TechEssCondRubric.aspx

Wisconsin Department of Public Instruction. (1997). Office of Educational Accountability. *Final summary report of the proficiency score standards for the Wisconsin student assessment system (WSAS) knowledge & concepts examinations for elementary, middle and high school at grades 4, 8 and 10.* Madison, WI: WDPI. Retrieved from http://dpi.wi.gov/oea/hist/proficfnlsumrpt.html

Zucker, A. A. (2008). *Transforming schools with technology: How smart use of digital tools helps achieve six key education goals.* Cambridge, MA: Harvard Education Press.

The Authors

Mike Eisenberg is Dean Emeritus and Professor, University of Washington Information School, Seattle, WA.

Bob Berkowitz is Library Media Specialist, Wayne Central Schools, Ontario Center, NY.

Doug Johnson is Director of Media and Technology, Mankato Public Schools, Mankato, MN.

Think Sheet

Part 6:
Standards, Tests, and the Big6™

▶ 6.0 Introduction 123

▶ 6.1 Standards 124

▶ 6.2 Information Literacy and Information Technology Standards 125

▶ 6.3 Subject Area Content Standards 125

▶ 6.4 Tests 128

▶ **6.5 Article—It's All About Learning: Ensuring That Students Are effective Users of Information on Standardized Tests by Mike Eisenberg.** **159**

▶ **6.6 Article—Testing Information Literacy Skills (Grades K–12) by: Janet Murray** **174**

The BIG6™ Standards, Tests, and the Big6™

6.0 Introduction

This material on standards and tests is a new part to the *Big6 Workshop Handbook*. In the past, we included standards in the material on planning—both macro and micro, and we discussed test tips as part of micro, lesson, and unit planning. In recent presentations and handouts, we provided supplemental handouts on these topics. These handouts and much more are now included here.

The topic of standards is crucial to effective information and technology skills programs at all levels (school, district, and state). We now devote considerable time and effort in workshops and presentations to the connection between the Big6 and standards and tests for meaningful student learning. This new part includes major new resources related to standards and tests.

The goals of Part 6 are to:

■ Make connections between various information literacy standards and the Big6 process and specific Big6 Skills.

■ Identify information and technology-focused standards within various subject area standards and make connections to the Big6 process and specific Big6 Skills.

■ Emphasize how the Big6 process approach provides valuable context for teachers to help their students learn essential information and technology skills.

■ Provide practice opportunities to develop expertise in making Big6-standards connections and to improve instruction in any school environment.

6.1 Standards

Educational standards—sometimes called frameworks, benchmarks, essential learnings, or grade level expectations—seek to define the goals and objectives of instruction in various subject areas and across grade levels.

Developed by professional associations, state education departments, and the U.S. Department of Education with good intentions, the quantity and complexity of standards can overwhelm educators on the front lines.

The challenge for classroom teachers, teacher-librarians, and other educators is to identify all the standards relevant to their students and to weave together a meaningful, coordinated curriculum and instructional program. For example, some questions facing teachers include:

- What are the relevant standards for a specific class of students, grade level, or subject area?

- Are the standards mandated, recommended, or suggested?

- How up-to-date and relevant are the standards? Are revisions planned in the near future?

- Are there recommended strategies for implementing the standards?

- How are the standards assessed—locally or at the state level?

Even if we narrow our immediate focus to information literacy or information and technology skills, the situation can be confusing because:

1. Standards on information and technology skills learning are found throughout the standards documents for various subjects and levels.

2. Many organizations and states also have separate information or information & technology standards.

This is where the Big6 approach can help. From experience, we know that information skills standards listed and explained in various documents and publications (information-literacy-specific or subject-area-specific) can be easily and successfully linked to the Big6 Skills and the Big6 process. Linking specific and sometimes isolated standards to the Big6 process is crucial because it:

1. Provides educators with an easy way to connect specific and seemingly isolated standards together.

2. Offers a process context for teachers and students.

3. Makes it relatively easy to tie the skills/process standards to subject area standards.

4. Combines learning and assessment of subject area content with learning and assessment of information and technology skills.

In this part of the *Big6 Workshop Handbook*, we look at two sets of standards:

- Information literacy/information technology standards
- Subject area content standards

6.2 Information Literacy and Information Technology Standards

The major sources of information literacy and information, communications, and technology (ICT) standards come from subdivisions of the American Library Association (the Association for College and Research Libraries, ACRL, and the American Association of School Librarians, AASL), and the International Society for Technology in Education (ISTE).

Mike likes to begin his presentations on standards with PowerPoint slides that provide brief summaries of the key elements of standards from various organizations, for example, AASL, ACRL. These are presented here under the heading, Information Literacy–ICT Standards. Since various states also provide information literacy or ICT standards, the slides also include standards from one representative state, Montana.

We then move on to exercise worksheets (see Worksheets 6.1 and 6.2) designed to help make the standards-Big6 connection. Curriculum standards are entered in the left side columns of Worksheet 6.1 (the Standards—Big6 Worksheet), and the exercise requires identifying corresponding Big6 stages and sub-stages.

We call this "Big6-ing" the standards, and it is important because the Big6 provides a process-context for the standards—a common vocabulary that links from one state or organization to another, as well as to the various Big6 lessons and techniques for teaching and learning the standards. We find that focusing on process rather than lists of skills helps teachers to design better instruction and provides a context for students to better learn the skills. Use Worksheet 6.2, the Big6—Standards Worksheet to "invert" the information in the completed Worksheet 6.1—to put the various skills in the order of the Big6 process.

Figure 6.2 is a useful example of how to align various information literacy and information technology standards in a Big6 process context. This was developed by Janet Murray and Colet Bartow for use in Montana.

Figure 6.3, also by Janet Murray, takes this comparison one step further by linking the Big6, AASL, and ISTE/NETS standards to basic and advanced specific student actions. For example, Big6 Stage #1 Task Definition is linked to AASL 1.1.3 and 1.2.1, NETS 3a, 4a, and 4b, and can be specifically accomplished by students using graphic organizers. Big6 Stage #3, Location and Access, is linked to AASL 1.1.8 and 1.3.2, and NETS 3b, and more specifically to keyword searching actions. Big6 Stage #6 Evaluation, is linked to AASL 3.4.1 and 3.4.2, NETS 1a and 5b, and assessment rubrics. All these connections are live links on Janet's Web site, so we encourage you to check out and use the matrix at http://www.janetsinfo.com/big6info.htm.

Last of all, on the topic of information literacy/information technology standards, we include (with permission and thanks) Janet Murray's complete article from *Library Media Connection* (April/March 2008) explaining why and how to make the standards-Big6 connection: "Looking at ICT Literacy Standards through the Big6 Lens."

6.3 Subject Area Content Standards

Every school district, state, and professional organization seeks to define the nature and scope of its content domain through some form of standards document. Fortunately, almost all are available for open and easy access through the World Wide Web. There are also some useful compilations of standards across states and organizations. Below are links to some of these:

States

- Florida Department of Education: http://www.floridastandards.org/Standards/FLStandardSearch.aspx
- Michigan Department of Education: http://www.michigan.gov/mde/0,1607, 7–140–28753—-,00.html
- Missouri Department of Elementary & Secondary Education: http://dese.mo.gov/standards/
- Montana Office of Public Instruction: http://opi.mt.gov/Curriculum/
- New York State Education Department: http://www.emsc.nysed.gov/ciai/standards.html
- North Carolina Department of Public Instruction: http://www.ncpublicschools.org/curriculum
- South Carolina Department of Education: http://ed.sc.gov/topics/curriculumstds/
- Texas Education Agency http://www.tea.state.tx.us/index.aspx?id=3427&menu_id=720&menu_id2=785
- Washington Office of Superintendent of Public Instruction: http://www.k12.wa.us/CurriculumInstruct/EALR_GLE.aspx

Organizations

- American Alliance for Health, Physical Education, Recreation, and Dance: http://www.aahperd.org/whatwedo/nationalStandards.cfm
- National Council for the Social Studies: http://www.socialstudies.org/standards/curriculum
- National Council of Teachers of English/International Reading Association: http://www.ncte.org/standards
- National Council of Teachers of Mathematics: http://www.nctm.org/standards/default.aspx?id=58
- National Science Teachers Association: http://www.nap.edu/openbook.php?isbn=0309053269

Compilations

Education World: http://www.educationworld.com/standards/

McREL (the Mid-continent Research for Education and Learning) Compendium of Content Standards and Benchmarks: http://www.mcrel.org/Standards-benchmarks/

Common Core State Standards Initiative (CCSSI): The National Governors Association is also sponsoring an effort to create a common core of standards across states. This is a collaboration among 48 states, 2 territories, and the District of Columbia: http://www.corestandards.org/

We emphasize continually in the handbook, Big6 information skills learning is best accomplished in context—that is, as part of the overall Big6 process and integrated with classroom, subject area curriculum. The following exercises show the pervasiveness of the Big6 process within subject area content standards. The exercises also help you to gain proficiency in linking specific standards statements to appropriate Big6 stages. Note that some standards statements match more than one Big6 stage. This occurs because some standards statements include multiple student actions and therefore represent more than one Big6 stage. For example, the standard statement "Review and revise communications to improve accuracy and clarity" requires the student to review communications (equivalent to Big6 stage 6—Evaluation) as well as to revise communications (equivalent to Big6 Stage 5—Synthesis).

Standards can also match more than one stage, because the specific student action represented by the standard can take place at more than one stage in the Big6 process. For example, determining the value and reliability of content on Web sites can take place when determining which Websites to use (part of Big6 Stage #2—Information Seeking Strategies) or when engaging with the information on the Web sites, part of Big6 Stage #4—Use of Information.

In these and other cases, it is appropriate to link the standard to multiple Big6 stages. In practice, we are likely to know a great deal more about the actual context (e.g., topic, assignment, objectives) , so the relevant Big6 stage will become clearer.

Worksheets 6.3 through 6.6 provide practice examples from various state standards in different subject areas in order to sharpen your Big6 perspective and place the standards in a Big6 context.[1] After completing the exercises, you should be able to review and "Big6" any local, state, or subject curriculum. Figures 6.4–6.6 present our matching of the standards to the Big6. Finally, in Figures 6.7–6.9, we invert the table—using the same matches as in the previous set of figures, but sorting the information in Big6 process order and then by grade level. Worksheets 6.6 and 6.7 (duplicates of Worksheets 6.1 and 6.2) are blank worksheets provided so that you can analyze your own local or state standards and make the standards-Big6 connection.

The Content Standards section concludes with two summary figures:

"Figure 6.10—Big6 Skills Aligned with National Academic Content Standards and ICT Literacy Standards" is a chart created by Janet Murray in her book, *Achieving Educational Standards Using the Big6* (Murray, Linworth, 2008). This multi-page chart demonstrates the connections and alignment across standards with different central focuses (e.g., information literacy, ICT literacy, English/Language Arts, Science, Social Studies, and Math.

Lastly, "Figure 6.11: Big6 Skills Aligned with Montana Content Standards" is an impressive multi-page chart compiled by Janet Murray and Colet Bartow that aligns the

---

1. Note that Figure 3.3 in Part 3 also involved matching student actions derived from curriculum standards to the Big6 process.

Big6 process to Montana content standards in Communication Arts (equivalent to English/Language Arts), Social Studies, Science, Technology, and Workplace Competencies.

6.4 Tests

While Bob and I are not necessarily enthusiastic proponents of standardized, "high stakes" testing, we recognize that success in K-12 education today is generally measured by student achievement. Furthermore, around the globe, student achievement is defined and measured by standard tests of one form or another. In the United States, national, state, and local educational priorities all focus on student performance as measured on standard tests.

In earlier sections, we made direct connections between information and information technology standards, state content standards, and the Big6. It is essential to establish these connections, but it is not the end of the story. The final part of the plan is to extend the connection to your state tests. This step requires the following activities:

- Become familiar with your state tests (including the nature, format, and content of the tests).

- Analyze the state tests and individual test questions from an information perspective (i.e., identify relevant information skills standards or skills within models such as the Big6 that would help students to succeed on specific test questions).

- Offer opportunities for students to learn and apply the relevant information skills to specific state test questions.

- Design and deliver lessons that help students learn and apply the relevant information skills to specific test questions.

- Document actions taken to connect information skills instruction to tests, test questions, and standards.

- Assess success by looking at the test results (as provided in the various state "report cards").

- Revise and plan for future instruction.

This approach clearly requires a long-term commitment and effort. One-shot lessons and interventions will probably not result in any measurable improvement in student performance. Over time, however, the Big6 information and technology literacy instructional programs can make a difference by helping students to apply learned information skills to subject area content performance as assessed on standardized tests. This approach is not "teaching to the test." It is "teaching skills that allow students to perform better on tasks that are measured by standardized tests."

Information on standardized state and national tests is readily available on the Web. The National Assessment of Educational Progress (NAEP), for example, is sponsored by the U.S. Department of Education's National Center for Educational Statistics (NCES). NAEP includes standard assessments for students in mathematics, reading, science, writing, the arts, civics, economics, geography, and U.S. history (see nces.ed.gov/nationsreportcard/).

NAEP and other Web sites provide sample exam questions across subject areas and grade levels. Some samples also include references to the related state or national content standards. These references provide useful insights into how standards are translated into test items, as well as the style and format of test questions.

Due to copyright restrictions, we cannot republish sample tests here. In Big6 workshop settings, we will provide examples relevant to the location and grade levels of audiences. If you are reading this *Workshop Handbook* on your own, we recommend that you search for examples of exams from your own state or region, or look at the NAEP examples (nces.ed.gov/nationsreportcard/itmrlsx/default.aspx)

The section below on tests includes a series of PowerPoint slides that Mike and Bob use to present practical approaches to integrating Big6 instruction with subject area content exams. The slides include:

■ Approaches to tests

■ Information-oriented attributes of exams

■ Sample Big6 lessons and activities to help students learn to apply information skills to subject area content and exam-taking

Again, this is not simply "teaching to the test." This is teaching students to learn information skills that can be applied to subject area content and tasks that are assessed via standardized tests.

We conclude the section with two articles that further explain and provide specific examples of Big6 test-taking approaches:

■ Mike Eisenberg's March 2004 article in *Library Media Connection*, "It's All About Learning: Ensuring That Students Are Effective Users of Information on Standardized Tests," and

■ Janet Murray's 2008 article in the Big6 eNewsletter, "Testing Information Literacy Skills (Grades K–12)."

ACRL 2000: Information Literacy
Competency Standards for Higher
Education

1. The information literate student determines the
   nature and extent of the information needed.

2. The information literate student accesses
   needed information effectively and efficiently.

3. The information literate student evaluates
   information and its sources critically and
   incorporates selected information into his or
   her knowledge base and value system.

www.ala.org/ala/mgrps/divs/acrl/standards/standards.pdf

* Eisenberg & Berkowitz

ACRL 2000: Information Literacy
Competency Standards for Higher
Education

4. The information literate student, individually or as a
   member of a group, uses information effectively to
   accomplish a specific purpose.

5. The information literate student understands many of
   the economic, legal, and social issues surrounding the
   use of information and accesses and uses information
   ethically and legally.

www.ala.org/ala/mgrps/divs/acrl/standards/standards.pdf

* Eisenberg & Berkowitz

ISTE – NETS
2007

"What students should know and be able to do to learn effectively
and live productively in an increasingly digital world …"

1. Creativity and Innovation
2. Communication and Collaboration
3. Research and Information Fluency
4. Critical Thinking, Problem-Solving & Decision-Making
5. Digital Citizenship
6. Technology Operations and Concepts

www.iste.org/inhouse/nets/cnets/students/pdf/NETS_for_Students_2007.pdf

* Eisenberg & Berkowitz

AASL - 2007

Learners use skills, resources, and tools to:

1. Inquire, think critically, and gain knowledge.
2. Draw conclusions, make informed decisions, apply
   knowledge to new situations, and create new knowledge.
3. Share knowledge and participate ethically and productively
   as *members* of our democratic society.
4. Pursue personal and aesthetic growth.

www.ala.org/ala/mgrps/divs/aasl/guidelinesandstandards/learningstandards/standards.cfm

www.ala.org/ala/mgrps/divs/aasl/guidelinesandstandards/learningstandards/AASL_
Learning_Standards_2007.pdf

* Eisenberg & Berkowitz

Figure 6.1: Information Literacy and ICT Standards

Worksheet 6.1:
Standards to Big6 Connection

Source/Subject	ID	Level	Standard/Framework/Benchmark	Big6	Notes

The Big6™ Skills © 1987 Eisenberg & Berkowitz

Worksheet 6.2:
Big6 to Standards Connection

Big6	Source/Subject	ID	Level	Standard/Framework/Benchmark	Notes

The Big6™ Skills © 1987 Eisenberg & Berkowitz

Content Standard	Big6™	AASL Standards for the 21st C. Learner	ISTE NETS for Students	Benchmark at Grade 4	Benchmark at Grade 8	Benchmark Upon Graduation
1. Students identify the task and determine the resources needed.	1	1.1.3	3a, 4a,	Define the problem	Analyze the parts of the problem to be solved	Evaluate the purpose and scope of the problem
		1.2.1	4b	Identify the types of information needed	Identify information resources needed	Determine the nature and extent of information needed
	2	1.1.4 1.1.5	3c	Choose from a range of resources	Evaluate and select appropriate resources	Evaluate and select appropriate resources
2. Students locate sources, use information and present findings.	3.1	1.1.8 1.3.2	3b	Locate a resource needed to solve the problem	Locate multiple resources using search tools	Locate multiple resources using a variety of search tools
	2.2	1.1.4 1.1.5	3c	Evaluate resources	Evaluate resources	Evaluate resources
	3.2	1.1.8 1.3.2	3b	Locate information within the source	Locate information within multiple resources	Locate information within a wide variety of resources
	4.2	1.1.8 1.3.2	3b	Extract information from resources needed to solve problems	Extract information from multiple resources needed to solve the problem	Extract information from a wide variety of resources needed to solve the problem
	5.1	2.1.4 3.1.4	2a, 2b	Organize information to solve problems	Organize and manage information to solve the problem	Organize and manage information from a wide variety of sources to solve the problem
	5.2	2.1.4 3.1.4		Create a product that presents findings	Create a product that presents findings	Create and defend a product that presents findings
3. Students evaluate their product and learning process.	6.1	3.4.1 3.4.2	1a, 5b	Assess the quality of the product	Assess the quality and effectiveness of the product	Assess the quality and effectiveness of the product
	6.2			Describe the process	Evaluate how the process met the need for information	Evaluate the process in order to revise strategies
4. Students use information safely, ethically and legally.	3, 4	1.1.7 2.1.1 1.3.3	4c, 5a	Legally obtain and use information	Legally obtain, store and disseminate text, data, images or sounds	Legally obtain, store and disseminate text, data, images or sounds
	1, 4, 5	1.1.7 2.1.1 1.3.3	4c, 5a, 2a, 2b	Identify the owner of ideas and information	Appropriately credits ideas and works of others	Follow copyright laws and fair use guidelines when using the intellectual property of others
	1, 4, 5	1.1.7 2.1.1 1.3.3	4c, 5a	Participate and collaborate in intellectual and social networks following safe and effective practices	Participate and collaborate in intellectual and social networks following safe and accepted practices	Participate and collaborate in intellectual and social networks following safe and accepted practices
5. Students pursue personal interests through literature and other creative expressions.	1, 4, 5	1.1.7 2.1.1 1.3.3		Use a variety of digital and print formats for pleasure and personal growth	Use and respond to a variety of print and digital formats for pleasure and personal growth	Use and critique a variety of print and digital formats for pleasure and personal growth
	1, 4, 5	1.1.7 2.1.1 1.3.3	4c, 5a	Use a variety of genres for pleasure and personal growth	Use and respond to a variety of genres for pleasure and personal growth	Use and critique a variety of genres for pleasure and personal growth
	3, 4	1.1.7 2.1.1 1.3.3		Access and understand multiple resources from diverse cultures including Montana American Indians	Analyze and respond to multiple resources and creative expressions from diverse cultures, including Montana American Indians	Evaluate multiple resources and other creative expressions from diverse cultures, including Montana American Indians
	2, 3, 4, 5	1.1.8 1.3.2 1.1.7 2.1.1 1.3.3	3b, 4c, 5a	Access libraries to seek information for personal interest	Access and use libraries and other information environments to find information for personal use and to make connections to resources beyond the school library	Access and use resources and information from all types of information environments to pursue personal and creative interests

Please see Murray, Janet R. *Achieving Educational Standards Using the Big6* , Linworth Books: Columbus, OH, 2008 pages 25-26 figure 3-2 for Big6, AASL, NETS-S Alignment

Figure 6.2 Montana Content and Performance Standards, p. 124

Source: Janet Murray Article—reprint—Library Media Connection article—Apr/Mar '08 "Looking at ICT Literacy Standards Through the Big6™ Lens"

The BIG 6 Skill	AASL Standards	NETS	Basic Activities	Advanced Activities
1 Task Definition	1.1.3 1.2.1	3a 4a 4b	Concept Mapping Graphic Organizers	Ask Essential Questions
2 Information Seeking Strategies	1.1.4 1.1.5	3c	Subject Directories Evaluating Web Sites	Web Site Evaluation
3 Location and Access	1.1.8 1.3.2	3b	Keyword Searching Search Strategies	Advanced Search Strategies
4 Use of information	1.1.7 2.1.1 1.3.3	4c 5a	Extract Information Analyze Sources Bibliographic Citations	Identify Point of View
5 Synthesis	2.1.4 3.1.4	2a 2b	Critical Thinking Appropriate Product	Classroom Applications
6 Evaluation	3.4.1 3.4.2	1a 5b	Assessment Rubrics	RubiStar

Figure 6.3 Applying Big6™ Skills, AASL Standards and ISTE NETS to Internet Research by Janet Murray, Author, *Achieving Educational Standards Using the Big6*. Linworth Publications. 2008.

Worksheet 6.3:
Standards Examples I—ELA

Standard Examples I - ELA

Source/ Subject	ID	Level	Standard/Framework/ Benchmark	Big6	Notes
ME/ELA	p. 16 A1	7	f. Demonstrates comprehension by summarizing, generating, drawing, conclusions, making judgments, and making connections between prior knowledge and multiple texts.		
ME/ELA	p. 21 A3	5	d. Distinguish between facts and opinions in text and/or draw conclusions from text.		
ME/ELA	p. 24 B1	preK-2	a. Select a focus for writing and develop an idea, including a beginning, middle, and end.		
SC/ELA	RS1.1	6-8	Demonstrate the ability to ask questions to guide his or her research inquiry.		
SC/ELA	RS3 2	7	Demonstrate the ability to present his or her research findings in a variety of formats.		
TX/E-LA-R	110 15	4	(13) (B) explain factual information presented graphically (e.g., charts, diagrams, graphs, illustrations)		
TX/E-LA-R	110.18	6	(b) (22) (B) generate a research plan for gathering relevant information about the major research question.		
TX/E-LA-R	110.20	8	(12) (B) evaluate graphics for their clarity in communicating meaning or achieving a specific purpose.		
TX/E-LA-R	110.31	High school	(10) (A) analyze the relevance, quality, and credibility of evidence given to support or oppose an argument for a specific audience.		

The Big6™ Skills © 1987 Eisenberg & Berkowitz

Worksheet 6.4:
Standards Examples II—Math

Standard Examples II - Math

Source/ Subject	ID	Level	Standard/Framework/ Benchmark	Big6	Notes
ME/Math	p. 63 1a	7	a. Create tables, pictograms, bar graphs, line graphics, pie charts, stem and leaf plots, box and whiskers plots, and histograms using pencil and paper and electronic technologies		
MO/Math	NCTM St 1; MO 2.2, 3.6, 3.7, 3.8	k-4	I e verify, interpret, and evaluate whether a solution addresses the original problem		
MO/Math	NCTM St 2; MO 3.5, 4.1	5-8	II e draw mathematical ideas and conclusions from reading, listening, and viewing		
TX/Math	111.14 Mathematics	2	(b) (2.12) (A) identify the mathematics in everyday situations		
TX/Math	111.17 Mathematics	5	(b) (5.14) (B) use a problem-solving model that incorporates understanding the problem, making a plan, carrying out the plan, and evaluating the solutions for reasonableness;		
TX/Math	111.23 Mathematics	7	(b) (7.2) (G) determine the reasonableness of a solution to a problem.		
TX/Math	111.31 Algebra	High School	(b) (1) (B) gather and record data and use data sets to determine functional relationships between quantities;		
TX/Math	111.33 Algebra II	High School	(b) (11) (D) determine solutions of exponential and logarithmic equations using graphs, tables, and algebraic methods;		
TX/Math	111.36 Models with Applications	High School	(c) (2) (A) interpret information from various graphs, including line graphs, bar graphs, circle graphs, histograms, scatterplots, line plots, stem and leaf plots, and box and whisker plots to draw conclusions from the data;		

The Big6™ Skills © 1987 Eisenberg & Berkowitz

Worksheet 6.5:
Standards Examples III—Various

Standard Examples I - ELA Linked to Big6

Source/ Subject	ID	Level	Standard/Framework/ Benchmark	Big6	Notes
ME/ELA	p. 16 A1	7	f. Demonstrate comprehension by summarizing, generalizing, drawing conclusions making judgments, and making connections between prior knowledge and multiple texts.	#1 – Task Definition #5 = Synthesis	"Comprehension" = Use of Information; summarizing, etc. = Synthesis to demo the ability to comprehend.
ME/ELA	p. 21 A3	5	d. Distinguish between facts and opinions in text and/or draw conclusions from text.	#4 – Use of information #5 – Synthesis	Distinguish between is use; draw conclusions is synthesis.
ME/ELA	p.24 B1	preK-2	a. Select a focus for writing and develop an idea, including a beginning, middle, and end.	#1 – Task Definition #5 = Synthesis	Writing and developing the idea is synthesis.
SC/ELA	RS1.1	6-8	Demostrate the ability to ask questions to guide his or her research inquiry	#1 – Task Definition	Questions guide the research
SC/ELA	RS3.2	7	Demostrate the ability to present his or her research finding in a variety of formats.	#5 – Synthesis	
TX/E-LA-R	110.15	4	(13) (B) explain factual information presented graphically (e. g., charts, diagrams, graphs, illustrations)	#4 – Use of information #5 – Synthesis	"Explaining" is to demonstraite the ability to comprehend graphic information.
TX/E-LA-R	110.18	6	(b) (22) (B) generate a research plan for gathering relevant information about the major research question.	#2 – Info Seek Strategies #3 – Location & Access	Selection 23 is labled research/Gathering sources.
TX/E-LA-R	110.20	8	(12) (B) evaluate graphics for their clarity in communicating meaning or achieving a specific purpose.	#6 – Evaluation	
TX/E-LA-R	110.31	High school	(10) (A) analyze the relavance, quality, and credibility of evidence given to support or oppose an argument for a specific audience.	#4 – Use of Information	Analyzing the information in a source, not the source.

The Big6™ Skills © 1987 Eisenberg & Berkowitz

Standard Examples I – ELA Linked to Big6

Source/Subject	ID	Level	Standard/Framework/Benchmark	Big6	Notes
ME/ELA	p. 16 A1	7	f. Demonstrate comprehension by summarizing, generalizing, drawing conclusions, making judgements, and making connections between prior knowledge and multiple texts.	#1 - Task Definition #5 = Synthesis	"Comprehension" = Use of Information; summarizing, etc. = Synthesis to demo the ability to comprehend.
ME/ELA	p. 21 A3	5	d. Distinguish between facts and opinions in text and/or draw conclusions from text.	#4 - Use of Information #5 - Synthesis	Distinguish between is use; draw conclusions is synthesis.
ME/ELA	p.24 B1	preK-2	a. Select a focus for writing and develop an idea, including a beginning, middle and end.	#1 - Task Definition #5 - Synthesis	Writing and developing the idea is synthesis.
SC/ELA	RS1.1	6-8	Demonstrate the ability to ask questions to guide his or her research inquiry.	#1 - Task Definition	Questions guide the research
SC/ELA	RS3.2	7	Demonstrate the ability to present his or her research findings in a variety of formats.	#5 - Synthesis	
TX/E-LA-R	110.15	4	(13) (B) explain factual information presented graphically (e.g., charts, diagrams, graphs, illustrations).	#4 - Use of Information #5 - Synthesis	"Explaining" is to demonstrate the ability to comprehend graphic information.
TX/E-LA-R	110.18	6	(b) (22) (B) generate a research plan for gathering relevant information about the major research question.	#2 - Info Seek Strategies #3 - Location & Access	Section 23 is labeled Research/Gathering Sources.
TX/E-LA-R	110.20	8	(12) (B) evaluate graphics for their clarity in communicating meaning or achieving a specific purpose.	#6 - Evaluation	
TX/E-LA-R	110.31	High school	(10) (A) analyze the relevance, quality and credibility of evidence given to support or oppose an argument for a specific audience.	#4 - Use of Information	Analyzing the information in a source, not the source.

The Big6™ Skills © 1987 Eisenberg & Berkowitz

Figure 6.4 Standards Examples I—ELA Linked to Big6™

Standard Examples II – Math Linked to Big6

Source/Subject	ID	Level	Standard/Framework/Benchmark	Big6	Notes
ME/Math	p. 63 1a	7	a. Create tables, pictograms, pie charts, bar graphs, line graphs, stem and leaf plots, box and whiskers plots, and histograms using pencil and paper and electronic technologies	#5 - Synthesis	
MO/Math	NCTM St 1; MO 2.2, 3.6, 3.7, 3.8	K-4	I e. Verify, interpret, and evaluate whether a solution addresses the original problem	#6 - Evaluation	Formative evaluation
MO/Math	NCTM St 2; MO 3.5, 4.1	5-8	II e. Draw mathematical ideas and conclusions from reading, listening, and viewing	#4 - Use of information #5 - Synthesis	
TX/Math	111.14 Mathematics	2	(b) (2.12) (A) identify the mathematics in everyday situations;	#1 - Task Definition	
TX/Math	111.17 Mathematics	5	(b) (5.14) (B) use a problem-solving model that incorporates understanding the problem, making a plan, carrying out the plan, and evaluating the solution for reasonableness;	#1, 2, 3, 4, 5, 6 - the entire Big6 process	In every Math grade level
TX/Math	111.23 Mathematics	7	(b) (7.2) (G) determine the reasonableness of a solution to a problem	#6 - Evaluation	
TX/Math	111.31 Algebra	High School	(b) (1) (B) gather and record data and use data sets to determine functional relationships between quantities;	#4 - Use of information #5 Synthesis	A compound standard
TX/Math	111.33 Algebra II	High School	(b) (11) (D) determine solutions of exponential and logarithmic equations using graphs, tables, and algebraic methods	#5 - Synthesis	
TX/Math	111.36 Models with Applications	High School	(c) (2) (A) interpret information from various graphs, including line graphs, bar graphs, circle graphs, histograms, scatterplot, line plots, stem and leaf plots, and box and whisker plot to draw conclusions from data;	#4 - Use of information #5 Synthesis	Synthesis relates to drawing conclusion, beyond comprehensions.

The Big6™ Skills © 1987 Eisenberg & Berkowitz

Figure 6.5 Standards Examples II—Math Linked to Big6™

Standard Examples I – ELA Linked to Big6

Source/ Subject	ID	Level	Standard/Framework/ Benchmark	Big6	Notes
TX/ Science	111.6	4	(b) (4.3) Scientific processes… (B) draw inferences based on information related to promotional materials for products and services;	#5 - Synthesis	
TX/ Science	112.23	7	(b) (7.3) (D) evaluate the impact of research on scientific thought, society, and the environment;	#1 - Task Definition #6 - Evaluation	Evaluate impact can be a task or a criteria for evaluating the product
ME/ Health	p. 43 F2	3-5	b. Identify resources to assist in achieving the health goal.	#2 - Information Seeking Strategies	Linked to the task
ME/ Soc St	p. 40 A1	6-8	f. Evaluate and verify the credibility of the information found in print and non-print sources.	#4 - Use of information #2 - Information Seeking Strategies	Depends on whether focus on sources or info.
ME/Soc St	p. 108 A1	PreK-2	c. Locate and collect information for a specific purpose from sources including maps, photographs, charts, and graphs.	#3 - Location & Access #4 - Use of Information	Collecting = extraction = use.
ME/ Sci&Tech	p. 86 B1	9 - Diploma	a. Identify questions, concepts, and testable hypotheses that guide scientific investigations.	#1 - Task Definition	
WA/ Soc St	CBA Causes of Conflict	6	History 1.1.1a Group personal, local, state, and national events in terms of past, present, and future, and place in proper sequence on a timeline.	#5 - Synthesis	CBA = classroom based assessments
WA/ Soc St	CBA Causes of Conflict	6	Social Studies 1.1.f Create a product that demonstrates understanding of information and responds to central questions; present product to a meaningful audience.	#5 - Synthesis	CBA = classroom based assessments
WA/ The Arts	2.3 The Arts	K-12	Evaluates using supporting evidence and criteria	#6 - Evaluation	

The Big6™ Skills © 1987 Eisenberg & Berkowitz

Figure 6.6 Standards Examples III—Various Linked to Big6™

Standard Examples I – ELA In Order By Big6 & Grade Level

Big6	Level	Source subject	ID	Standard/Framework/Benchmark	Notes
#1- Task Definition	preK-2	ME/ELA	p. 24 B1	a. Select a focus for writing and develop an idea, including a beginning, middle, and end.	
#1- Task Definition	6-8	SC/ELA	RS 1.1	Demonstrate the ability to ask questions to guide his or her research inquiry	Questions guide the research
#2 - Info SS #3 - L&A	6	TX/E-LA-R	110.18	(b) (22) (B) generate a research plan for gathering relevant information about the major research question	Section 22 - Research/Gathering Sources.
#4 - Use of Information	4	TX/E-LA-R	110.15	(13) (B) explain factual information presented graphically (e.g., charts, diagrams, graphs, illustrations).	"Explain" here refers to comprehend information.
#4 - Use of Information	5	ME/ELA	p. 21 A3	d. Distinguish between facts and opinions in text and/or draw conclusions from text.	2 part standard
#4 - Use of Information	7	ME/ELA	p. 16 A1	f. Demonstrate comprehension by summarizing, generalizing, drawing conclusions, making judgements, and making connections between prior knowledge and multiple texts.	"Comprehension" = Use of Information;
#4 - Use of Information	High school	TX/E-LA-R	110.31	(10) (A) analyze the relevance, quality, and credibility of evidence given to support or oppose an argument for a specific audience	Analyzing the information in a source, not the source.
#5 - Synthesis	preK-2	ME/ELA	p. 24 B1	a. Select a focus for writing and develop an idea, including a beginning, middle, and end.	Writing and developing the idea is synthesis.
#5 - Synthesis	4	TX/E-LA-R	110.15	(13) (B) explain factual information presented graphically (e.g., charts, diagrams, graphs, illustrations).	"Explain" here refers to comprehend information.
#5 - Synthesis	5	ME/ELA	p. 21 A3	d. Distinguish between facts and opinions in text and/or draw conclusions from text.	2 part standard
#5 - Synthesis	7	SC/ELA	RS3.2	Demonstrate the ability to present his or her research findings in a variety of formats.	
#5 - Synthesis	7	ME/ELA	p. 16 A1	f. Demonstrate comprehension by summarizing, generalizing, drawing conclusion, making judgments, and making connections between prior knowledge and multiple texts.	summarizing, etc. = Synthesis to demo the ability to comprehend.
#6 - Evaluation	8	TX/E-LA-R	110.20	(12) (B) evaluate graphics for clarity in communicating meaning or achieving a specific purpose	

The Big6™ Skills © 1987 Eisenberg & Berkowitz

Figure 6.7 Standards Examples I—ELA in Order by Big6™ & Grade Level

Standard Examples I – ELA In Order By Big6 & Grade Level

Big6	Level	Source/Subject	ID	Standard/Framework/Benchmark	Notes
#1, 2, 3, 4, 5, 6 the entire Big6 process	5	TX/Math	111.17 Mathematics	(b) (5.14) (B) use a problem-solving model that incorporates understanding the problem, making a plan, carrying out the plan, and evaluating the solution for reasonableness;	
#1 - Task Definition	2	TX/Math	111.14 Mathematics	(b) (2.12) (A) identify the mathematics in everyday situations;	
#4 - Use of Information	5-8	MO/Math	NCTM St 2; MO 3.5, 4.1	II e. draw mathematical ideas and conclusion from reading, listening, and viewing	
#4 - Use of Information	High School	TX/Math	111.31 Algebra	(b) (1) (B) gather and record data and use data sets to determine functional relationships between quantities;	A compound standard
#4 - Use of Information	High School	TX/Math	111.36 Models with Applications	(c) (2) (A) interpret information from various graphs, including line graphs, bar graphs, circle graphs, histograms, scatterplots, line plots, stem and leaf plots, and box and whisker plots to draw conclusions from the data;	Synthesis relates to drawing conclusions, beyond comprehension
#5 - Synthesis	5-3	Mo/Math	NCTM St 2; MO 3.5, 4.1	II e. draw mathematical ideas and conclusions from reading, listening, and viewing	
#5 - Synthesis	7	ME/Math	p. 63 1a	a. Create tables, pictograms, bar graphs, line graphs, pie charts, stem and leaf plots, and box and whisker plots and histograms using pencil and paper and electronic technologies	
#5 - Synthesis	High School	TX/Math	111.31 Algebra	(b) (1) (B) gather and record data and use data sets to determine functional relationships between quantities;	A compound standard
#5 - Synthesis	High School	TX/Math	111.36 Models with Applications	(c) (2) (A) interpret information from various graphs, including line graphs, bar graphs, circle graphs, histograms, scatterplots, line plots, stem and leaf plots, and box and whisker plots to draw conclusions from the data;	Synthesis relates to drawing conclusions, beyond comprehension
#5 - Synthesis	High School	TX/Math	111.33 Algebra II	(b) (11) (D) determine solutions of exponential and logarithmic equations using graphs, tables, and algebraic methods;	
#6 - Evaluation	K-4	MO/Math	NCTM St 1, MO 2.2, 3.6, 3.7, 3.8	I e. verify, interpret, and evaluate whether a solution addresses the original problem	Formative evaluation
#6 - Evaluation	7	TX/Math	111.23 Mathematics	(b) (7.2) (G) determine the reasonableness of a solution to a problem.	

The Big6™ Skills © 1987 Eisenberg & Berkowitz

Figure 6.8 Standards Examples II—Math in Order by Big6™ & Grade Level

Standard Examples III – Various In Order By Big6 & Grade Level

Big6	Level	Source/Subject	ID	Standard/Framework/Benchmark	Notes
#1 - Task Definition	7	TX/Science	112.23	(b) (7.3) (D) evaluate the impact of research on scientific thought, society, and the environment;	Evaluate impact can be a task or a criteria for evaluating the product
#1 - Task Definition	9 - Diploma	ME/Sci&Tech	p. 86 B1	a. Identify questions, concepts, and testable hypotheses that guide scientific investigations.	
#2 - Info Seeking Strategies	3-5	ME/Health	p. 43 F2	b. Identify resources to assist in achieving the health goal.	Linked to the task
#2 - Info Seeking Strategies	6-8	ME/Soc St	p. 40 A1	f. Evaluate and verify the credibility of the information found in print and non-print sources.	Depends on whether focus on sources or info.
#3 - Location & Access	PreK-2	ME/Soc St	p. 108 A1	c. Locate and collect information for a specific purpose from sources including maps, photographs, charts, and graphs.	
#4 - Use of Information	PreK-2	ME/Soc St	p. 108 A1	c. Locate and collect information for a specific purpose from sources including maps, photographs, charts, and graphs.	Collecting = extraction = use.
#4 - Use of Information	6-8	ME/Soc St	p. 40 A1	f. Evaluate and verify the credibility of the information found in print and non-print sources.	Depends on whether focus on sources or info
#5 - Synthesis	4	TX/Science	111.6	(b) (4.3) Scientific processes... (B) draw inferences based on information related to promotional materials for products and services:	
#5 - Synthesis	6	WA/Soc St	CBA Causes of Conflict	History 1.1.1a Group personal, local, state, and national events in terms of past, present, and future, and place in proper sequence on a timeline.	
#5 - Synthesis	6	WA/Soc St	CBA Causes of Conflict	Social Studies 1.1.f Create a product that demonstrates understanding of information and responds to central questions;present product to a meaningful audience.	
#6 - Evaluation	K-12	WA/The Arts	2.3 The Arts	Evaluates using supporting evidence and criteria	
#6 - Evaluation	7	TX/Science	112.23	(b) (7.3) (D) evaluate the impact of research on scientific thought, society, and the environment;	Evaluate impact can be a task or a criteria for evaluating the product

The Big6™ Skills © 1987 Eisenberg & Berkowitz

Figure 6.9 Standards Examples III—Various in Order by Big6™ & Grade Level

Worksheet 6.6:
Standards to Big6™

Source/Subject	ID	Level	Standard/Framework/Benchmark	Big6	Notes

The Big6™ Skills © 1987 Eisenberg & Berkowitz

Worksheet 6.7:
Big6™ to Standards

Big6	Source/ Subject	ID	Level	Standard/Framework/ Benchmark	Notes

The Big6™ Skills © 1987 Eisenberg & Berkowitz

Big6™ Skills Aligned with National Academic Content Standards and ICT Literacy Standards

Reprinted from *Achieving Educational Standards Using the Big6™* (Murray, Linworth, 2008)

Big6™ Skill	Information Literacy Standards (AASL/A ECT 1998)	NETS-S (ISTE 2000)	Content Standards	
1. Task Definition	1.1 recognizes the need for information 1.3 formulates a question based on information needs	6.1 use technology resources for solving problems and making informed decisions.	**E/LA:** conduct research on issues and interests by generating ideas and questions, and by posing problems.	**Sci:** Identify questions that can be answered through scientific investigations.
2. Information Seeking Strategies	1.4 identifies a variety of potential sources of information 2.4 selects information appropriate to the problem or question at hand	5.3 evaluate and select new information resources . . . based on the appropriateness for specific tasks.	**E/LA:** gather, evaluate, and synthesize data from a variety of sources.	**SS:** identify and use processes important to reconstructing and reinterpreting the past, such as using a variety of sources, providing, validating, and weighing evidence for claims, checking credibility of sources, and searching for causality.
3. Location and Access	1.5 develops and uses successful strategies for learning information 7.1 seeks information from diverse sources, contents, disciplines, and cultures	5.1 use technology to locate, evaluate, and collect information from a variety of sources.	**SS:** locate, access, organize, and apply information about an issue of public concern from multiple points of view.	**Math:** formulate questions that can be addressed with data and collect, organize, and display relevant data to answer them.
4. Use of Information	2.1 determines accuracy, relevance, and comprehensiveness 2.2 distinguishes among facts, point of view, and opinion 8.2 respects intellectual property rights 8.3 uses information technology responsibly	2.2 practice responsible use of technology systems, information, and software.	**E/LA:** gather, evaluate, and synthesize data from a variety of sources.	**Sci:** Use appropriate tools and techniques to gather, analyze, and interpret data.
5. Synthesis	3.1 organizes information for practical application 3.4 produces and communicates information and ideas in appropriate formats 9.1 shares knowledge and information with others	3.2 use productivity tools to collaborate in constructing technology-enhanced models, prepare publications, and produce other creative works. 4.2 use a variety of media and formats to communicate information and ideas effectively to multiple audiences.	**E/LA:** write and use different writing process elements appropriately to communicate with different audiences for a variety of purposes.	**SS:** explore causes, consequences, and possible solutions to persistent, contemporary, and emerging global issues.
6. Evaluation	6.1 assesses the quality of the process and products of one's own information-seeking	3.1 use technology tools to enhance learning, increase productivity, and promote creativity.		

Reprinted with permission from "What is the Big6?" <http://www.big6.com/showarticle.php?id=415> The "Big6™" is copyright © (1987) Michael B. Eisenberg and Robert E. Berkowitz. For more information, visit: www.big6.com.

Information Literacy Standards for Student Learning: Standards and Indicators (excerpt from Chapter 2, "Information Literacy Standards for Student Learning," of *Information Power: Building Partnerships for Learning*) © 1998, American Library Association. Reprinted with permission.

Reprinted with permission from *National Educational Technology Standards for Students: Connecting Curriculum and Technology*, © 2000, ISTE ® (International Society for Technology in Education), iste@iste.org, www.iste.org and from Curriculum and Content Area Standards <www.iste.org/inhouse/nets/cnets/currstands/index.html>. All rights reserved. Permission does not constitute an endorsement by ISTE.

Figure 6.10 Big6™ Skills Aligned with National Academic Content Standards and ICT Literacy Standards

Montana Content Standards: Information Literacy/Library Media	Benchmark (Grade 4)	Big6™ Skill	Montana Content Standards: Communication Arts	Montana Content Standards: Social Studies, Science	Montana Content Standards: Technology, Workplace Competencies
1. Students identify the task and determine the resources needed.	Define the problem.	**1. Task Definition** 1.1 Define the information problem.	5.2 select appropriate topics and generate topic sentences that indicate the writer's purpose for writing 5.10 use information problem solving process to research a topic	SS 1.1 identify and practice the steps of an inquiry process (i.e., identify question or problem, ...) Sc 1 Students, through the inquiry process, demonstrate the ability to design ... scientific investigations. Sc 5.3 simulate scientific collaboration by sharing and communicating ideas to identify and describe problems	T 1.1 identify and investigate a problem and generate possible solutions WC 5.2 solve problems both individually and with others
	Identify the types of information needed.	1.2 Identify information needed.	5.10 use information problem solving process to research a topic	SS 1.1 identify and practice the steps of an inquiry process (i.e. ... locate ... potential resources, ...) Sc 1 (Rationale): Students must understand the process of science—how information is gathered ...	WC 5.1 identify and select information sources using technology
	Choose from a range of resources.	**2. Information Seeking Strategies** 2.1 Determine all possible sources.	5.10 use information problem solving process to research a topic	SS 1.1 identify and practice the steps of an inquiry process (i.e. ... locate and evaluate potential resources, ...)	T 1.2 collect data and information using digital tools WC 3.1 identify a variety of sources that provide workplace information

Janet Murray, *Achieving Educational Standards Using the Big6™* (Linworth, 2008).
Reprinted with permission from "What is the Big6?" The "Big6™" is copyright © (1987) Michael B. Eisenberg and Robert E. Berkowitz. For more information, visit: http://www.big6.com
Montana Content and Performance Standards: Information Literacy/Library Media Alignment Matrix. *http://www.opi.mt.gov/PDF/llbmedia/ILLM_Big6_Align.pdf*
Montana Content Standards and Performance Descriptors. *http://www.opi.mt.gov/Curriculum/index.html?gpm=1_8#p7GPc1_8*

Figure 6.11 Big6™ Skills Aligned with Montana Content Standards

Montana Content Standards: Information Literacy/Library Media	Benchmark (Grade 4)	Big6™ Skill	Montana Content Standards: Communication Arts	Montana Content Standards: Social Studies, Science	Montana Content Standards: Technology, Workplace Competencies
2. Students locate sources, use information and present findings.	Locate a resource needed to solve the problem.	**3. Location and Access** 3.1 Locate sources (intellectually and physically).	5.10 use information problem solving process to research a topic	SS 1.1 identify and practice the steps of an inquiry process (i.e. ... locate and evaluate potential resources, ...).	WC 3.4 access and organize information from print and electronic sources
	Evaluate resources.	2.2 Select the best sources.	5.10 use information problem solving process to research a topic	SS 1.2 evaluate information quality (e.g., accuracy, relevance, fact or fiction) Sc 1 Students, through the inquiry process, demonstrate the ability to ... evaluate ... the results ... of scientific investigations.	T 1.4 identify the accuracy, diversity and point of view, including Montana American Indians, of digital information WC 5.1 identify and select information sources using technology
	Locate information within the source.	3.2 Find information within sources.	2.9 identify main ideas and supporting details 5.10 use information problem solving process to research a topic	SS 1.1 identify and practice the steps of an inquiry process (i.e. ... gather and synthesize information, ...)	T 4.1 show skills needed to use communication, information and processing technologies WC 3.4 access and organize information from print and electronic sources
	Extract information from resources needed to solve problems.	**4. Use of Information** 4.2 Extract relevant information.	2.7 generate and answer questions to clarify meaning by locating specific information in text 5.10 use information problem solving process to research a topic	SS 1.1 identify and practice the steps of an inquiry process (i.e. ... gather and synthesize information, ...)	T 3.3 use technology to discover connections between facts
	Organize information to solve problems.	**5. Synthesis** 5.1 Organize information from multiple sources.	2.12 identify the organizational structure of a selection, including sequential, problem-solution and cause-effect 5.4 organize writing using a logical progression of ideas 5.10 use information problem solving process to research a topic	SS 1.1 identify and practice the steps of an inquiry process (i.e. ... gather and synthesize information, ...) Sc 1 Students, through the inquiry process, demonstrate the ability to ... communicate the results and form reasonable conclusions of scientific investigations.	T 1.3 organize collected data and information using a variety of digital tools T 4.1 show skills needed to use communication, information and processing technologies WC 3.2 organize information using systematic methods

Janet Murray, *Achieving Educational Standards Using the Big6™* (Linworth, 2008).
Reprinted with permission from "What is the Big6?" The "Big6™" is copyright © (1987) Michael B. Eisenberg and Robert E. Berkowitz. For more information, visit: http://www.big6.com
Montana Content and Performance Standards: Information Literacy/Library Media Alignment Matrix. http://www.opi.mt.gov/PDF/libmedia/ILLM_Big6_Align.pdf
Montana Content Standards and Performance Descriptors. http://www.opi.mt.gov/Curriculum/Index.html?gpm=1_8#p7GPc1_8

Figure 6.11 Big6™ Skills Aligned with Montana Content Standards (*continued*)

Montana Content Standards: Information Literacy/Library Media	Benchmark (Grade 4)	Big6™ Skill	Montana Content Standards: Communication Arts	Montana Content Standards: Social Studies, Science	Montana Content Standards: Technology, Workplace Competencies
2. Students locate sources, use information and present findings. (continued)	Create a product that presents findings.	5.2 Present the information.	4.6 create a media message for specific audiences and purposes (e.g., inform, entertain, or persuade) 5.10 use information problem solving process to research a topic	SS 1.1 identify and practice the steps of an inquiry process (i.e. … create a new product, …) Sc 5.4 use scientific knowledge to make inferences and propose solutions for simple environmental problems	T 2.3 communicate the results of research and learning with others using digital tools
3. Students evaluate their product and learning process.	Assess the quality of the product.	**6. Evaluation** 6.1 Judge the product (effectiveness).	5.10 use information problem solving process to research a topic 5.13 recognize and use writing as a means of clarifying thinking and reflecting	SS 1.1 identify and practice the steps of an inquiry process (i.e. … evaluate product …) Sc 1 Students, through the inquiry process, demonstrate the ability to … form reasonable conclusions of scientific investigations.	
	Describe the process.	6.2 Judge the process (efficiency).	5.10 use information problem solving process to research a topic 5.13 recognize and use writing as a means of clarifying thinking and reflecting	SS 1.1 identify and practice the steps of an inquiry process (i.e. … evaluate … process).	WC 6.6 describe and demonstrate the importance of personal goal setting and planning

Janet Murray. *Achieving Educational Standards Using the Big6™* (Linworth, 2008).
Reprinted with permission from "What is the Big6?" The "Big6™" is copyright © (1987) Michael B. Eisenberg and Robert E. Berkowitz. For more information, visit: http://www.big6.com
Montana Content and Performance Standards: Information Literacy/Library Media Alignment Matrix. *http://www.opi.mt.gov/PDF/libmedia/ILLM_Big6_Align.pdf*
Montana Content Standards and Performance Descriptors. *http://www.opi.mt.gov/Curriculum/Index.html?gpm=1_8#p7GPc1_8*

Figure 6.11 Big6™ Skills Aligned with Montana Content Standards (*continued*)

Montana Content Standards: Information Literacy/Library Media	Benchmark (Grade 4)	Big6™ Skill	Montana Content Standards: Communication Arts	Montana Content Standards: Social Studies, Science	Montana Content Standards: Technology, Workplace Competencies
4. Students use information safely, ethically and legally.	Legally obtain and use information.	**3. Location and Access** **4. Use of Information**	4.4 recognize the norms, rules, laws and etiquette that govern the use and creation of media messages		T 1.5 share information ethically and note sources WC 5.4 discriminate between responsible and irresponsible use of technology
	Identify the owner of ideas and information.	**1. Task Definition** **4. Use of Information** **5. Synthesis**	4.2 identify the sources of media messages 5.11 identify the owner of ideas and information, with respect to all forms of information (e.g., oral resources), including Montana American Indians		T 3.4 understand ownership of digital media
	Participate and collaborate in intellectual and social networks following safe and effective practices.	**1. Task Definition** **4. Use of Information** **5. Synthesis**	4.4 recognize the norms, rules, laws and etiquette that govern the use and creation of media messages 4.5 recognize consequences to self and others when using and creating media messages		T 2.2 identify and explore safe, legal, and responsible use of digital collaboration and communication tools

Janet Murray, *Achieving Educational Standards Using the Big6™* (Linworth, 2008).
Reprinted with permission from "What is the Big6?" The "Big6™" is copyright © (1987) Michael B. Eisenberg and Robert E. Berkowitz. For more information, visit: http://www.big6.com
Montana Content and Performance Standards: Information Literacy/Library Media Alignment Matrix. *http://www.opi.mt.gov/PDF/libmedia/ILLM_Big6_Align.pdf*
Montana Content Standards and Performance Descriptors. *http://www.opi.mt.gov/Curriculum/Index.html?gpm=1_8#p7GPc1_8*

Figure 6.11 Big6™ Skills Aligned with Montana Content Standards (*continued*)

Montana Content Standards: Information Literacy/Library Media	Benchmark (Grade 4)	Big6™ Skill	Montana Content Standards: Communication Arts	Montana Content Standards: Social Studies, Science	Montana Content Standards: Technology, Workplace Competencies
5. Students pursue personal interests through literature and other creative expressions.	Use a variety of digital and print formats for pleasure and personal growth.	**1. Task Definition** **4. Use of Information** **5. Synthesis**	3.6 express and justify personal responses to literature		T 3.1 use digital tools for personal expression T 3.5 use digital tools and skills to construct new personal understandings WC 6.6 describe and demonstrate the importance of personal goal setting and planning
	Use a variety of genres for pleasure and personal growth.	**1. Task Definition** **4. Use of Information** **5. Synthesis**	3.3 identify the characteristics of select literary genres		
	Access and understand multiple resources from diverse cultures including Montana American Indians.	**3. Location and Access** **4. Use of Information**	2.14 recognize author's purpose, point of view, and language use in culturally diverse texts, including those by and about Montana American Indians 3.4 identify how culture and history are represented in literary works, including works of Montana American Indians	SS 6.4 identify characteristics of American Indian tribes and other cultural groups in Montana. Sc 5.2 describe a scientific or technological innovation that impacts communities, cultures, and societies	T 1.4 identify the accuracy, diversity and point of view, including Montana American Indians, of digital information

Janet Murray, *Achieving Educational Standards Using the Big6™* (Linworth, 2008).
Reprinted with permission from "What is the Big6?" The "Big6™" is copyright © (1987) Michael B. Eisenberg and Robert E. Berkowitz. For more information, visit: http://www.big6.com
Montana Content and Performance Standards: Information Literacy/Library Media Alignment Matrix. *http://www.opi.mt.gov/PDF/libmedia/ILLM_Big6_Align.pdf*
Montana Content Standards and Performance Descriptors. *http://www.opi.mt.gov/Curriculum/Index.html?gpm=1_8#p7GPc1_8*

Figure 6.11 Big6™ Skills Aligned with Montana Content Standards (*continued*)

Montana Content Standards: Information Literacy/Library Media	Benchmark (Grade 4)	Big6™ Skill	Montana Content Standards: Communication Arts	Montana Content Standards: Social Studies, Science	Montana Content Standards: Technology, Workplace Competencies
5. Students pursue personal interests through literature and other creative expressions. (continued)			3.5 identify similarities and differences between personal experiences and literary works, including the works of Montana American Indians 4.7 recognize that media messages embed values and influences individuals, cultures and societies		
	Access libraries to seek information for personal interest.	**2. Information Seeking Strategies** **3. Location and Access** **4. Use of Information** **5. Synthesis**	3.6 express and justify personal responses to literature		

Janet Murray, *Achieving Educational Standards Using the Big6™* (Linworth, 2008).
Reprinted with permission from "What is the Big6?" The "Big6™" is copyright © (1987) Michael B. Eisenberg and Robert E. Berkowitz. For more information, visit: http://www.big6.com
Montana Content and Performance Standards: Information Literacy/Library Media Alignment Matrix. *http://www.opi.mt.gov/PDF/llbmedia/ILLM_Big6_Align.pdf*
Montana Content Standards and Performance Descriptors. *http://www.opi.mt.gov/Curriculum/Index.html?gpm=1_8#p7GPc1_8*

Figure 6.11 Big6™ Skills Aligned with Montana Content Standards (*continued*)

Content Standards

**Big6™ Skills Aligned with National Academic
Content Standards and ICT Literacy Standards**

Reprinted from *Achieving Educational Standards Using the Big6™* (Murray, Linworth, 2008)

Big6™ Skill	Standards for the 21st-Century Learner (AASL, 2007)	NETS-S (ISTE 2007)	Content Standards	
1. Task Definition	1.1.3 Develop and refine a range of questions to frame the search for new understanding. 1.2.1 Display initiative and engagement by posing questions and investigating the answers beyond the collection of superficial facts.	3a. plan strategies to guide inquiry. 4a. identify and define authentic problems and significant questions for investigation. 4b. plan and manage activities to develop a solution or complete a project.	**E/LA:** conduct research on issues and interests by generating ideas and questions, and by posing problems.	**Sci:** Identify questions that can be answered through scientific investigations.
2. Information Seeking Strategies	1.1.4 Find, evaluate, and select appropriate sources to answer questions. 1.1.5 Evaluate information found in selected sources on the basis of accuracy, validity, appropriateness for needs, importance, and social and cultural context.	3c. evaluate and select information sources and digital tools based on the appropriateness to specific tasks.	**E/LA:** gather, evaluate, and synthesize data from a variety of sources.	**SS:** identify and use processes important to reconstructing and reinterpreting the past, such as using a variety of sources, providing, validating, and weighing evidence for claims, checking credibility of sources, and searching for causality.

Figure 6.12 Janet Murray's Big6™ Skills Aligned with National Academic Content Standards and ICT Literacy Standards

3. Location and Access	1.1.8 Demonstrate mastery of technology tools for accessing information and pursuing inquiry. 1.3.2 Seek divergent perspectives during information gathering and assessment.	3b. locate, organize, analyze, evaluate, synthesize, and ethically use information from a variety of sources and media.	**SS:** locate, access, organize, and apply information about an issue of public concern from multiple points of view.	**Math:** formulate questions that can be addressed with data and collect, organize, and display relevant data to answer them.
4. Use of Information	1.1.7 Make sense of information gathered from diverse sources by identifying misconceptions, main and supporting ideas, conflicting information, and point of view or bias. 2.1.1 Apply critical-thinking skills (analysis, synthesis, evaluation, organization) to information and knowledge. 1.3.3 Follow ethical and legal guidelines in gathering and using information.	4c. collect and analyze data to identify solutions and/or make informed decisions. 5a. advocate and practice safe, legal, and responsible use of information and technology.	**E/LA:** gather, evaluate, and synthesize data from a variety of sources.	**Sci:** Use appropriate tools and techniques to gather, analyze, and interpret data.

Figure 6.12 Janet Murray's Big6™ Skills Aligned with National Academic Content Standards and ICT Literacy Standards (*continued*)

			E/LA: write and use different writing process elements appropriately to communicate with different audiences for a variety of purposes.	SS: explore causes, consequences, and possible solutions to persistent, contemporary, and emerging global issues.
5. Synthesis	2.1.4 Use technology and other information tools to analyze and organize information. 3.1.4 Use technology and other information tools to organize and display knowledge and understanding in ways that others can view, use, and assess.	2a. interact, collaborate, and publish with peers, experts or others employing a variety of digital environments and media. 2b. communicate information and ideas effectively to multiple audiences using a variety of media and formats.		
6. Evaluation	3.4.1 Assess the processes by which learning was achieved in order to revise strategies and learn more effectively in the future. 3.4.2 Assess the quality and effectiveness of the learning product.	1a. apply existing knowledge to generate new ideas, products, or processes. 5b. exhibit a positive attitude toward using technology that supports collaboration, learning, and productivity.		

Reprinted with permission from "What is the Big6?" <http://www.big6.com/showarticle.php?id=415> The "Big6™" is copyright © (1987) Michael B. Eisenberg and Robert E. Berkowitz. For more information, visit: www.big6.com.
"AASL Standards for the 21st-Century Learner." © 2007. American Association of School Librarians. <http://www.ala.org/aasl/standards> Reprinted with permission.
Reprinted with permission from *National Educational Technology Standards for Students, Second Edition,* © 2007, ISTE® (International Society for Technology in Education), www.iste.org, and from *Curriculum and Content Area Standards* <www.iste.org/inhouse/nets/cnets/currstands/index.html>. All rights reserved. Permission does not constitute an endorsement by ISTE.

Figure 6.12 Janet Murray's Big6™ Skills Aligned with National Academic Content Standards and ICT Literacy Standards (*continued*)

Test and Testing

Approach to Tests

1. Analyze test items to determine direct connections to Big6 instruction.

2. Target Big6 instruction to specific test items (connected to standards).

3. Document your lessons on a Big6 x Unit matrix.

4. Evaluate the impact of these interventions on student performance on test items.

M. Eisenberg

English/LA Reading Comprehension Tests
Things I Noticed

- Instructions – Almost every exam includes instructions such as these:

  "Read the passage below. Then answer questions 1-6."

  "Read the story and then answer Numbers 9 through 16 in the Answer Section."

  "Read the article and then answer question numbers 1 through 5 in your Answer Booklet."

  "Read each of the passages. Then read the questions that follow and decide on the BEST answer."

- Big6 Reaction: No! Read the questions first and then read the passage. Then answer then questions.

- Big6 Lessons:
  - Read the questions first.
  - Highlight/underline key words in the questions.
  - Skim/read the text.
  - Highlight key words/sentences related to the questions
  - Go back and answer the questions.

M. Eisenberg

English/LA Reading Comprehension Tests
Things I Noticed

- Typical questions:
  - The last sentence of the passage says that orcas are endangered. What does this mean and why may this happen?
  - Read this sentence from the passage: "They prefer to eat sea grasses and aquatic plants." What does the word "aquatic" mean?
  - Look at the websites below. Which would most likely be the best site if you wanted to find out how to help the orcas?

- Big6 Reaction: Tests often ask the same types of questions from year to year.

- Big6 Lesson:
  - Learn to identify certain types of questions.
  - Learn how to answer each type of question.

M. Eisenberg

Figure 6.13 The Big6™ and Standard Tests

English/LA Reading Comprehension Tests
Things I Noticed

- Typical questions:
  - The last sentence of the passage says that orcas are endangered. What does this mean and why may this happen?
  - Read this sentence from the passage: "They prefer to eat sea grasses and aquatic plants." What does the word "aquatic" mean?
  - Look at the websites below. Which would most likely be the best site if you wanted to find out how to help the orcas?
- There are often a lot of extra, non-essential instructions on the test booklet (sometimes even "test tips.')
- Big6 Reaction: Tests often ask the same types of things from year to year.
  - What "best describes" ...narrator's tone, character, feelings.
  - What is the purpose of?
  - What does a word mean?
  - Which websites…
- Big6 Lessons:
  - Be familiar with the test format and instructions.
  - Recognize the instructions, but don't spend time on the hints or suggestions.
  - Learn to identify certain types of questions.
  - Learn how to answer each type of question.

M. Eisenberg

Sample Big6/Comprehension Lessons

- Task Definition:
  - What is the question?
  - Learn to identify key words in questions:
    - ✓ Highlight and define the key words in questions.
    - ✓ Students make flash cards to help them study and remember terms.
    - ✓ Some terms tell the students what they are to do (usually the verbs). Other terms tell the students what they should be looking for (usually nouns).
    - ✓ Highlight key words "to do" and key words "to look for."
- Use of Information:
  - How to read for a purpose.
  - Skim and scan a text.
  - highlight relevant parts of a reading passage.
- Synthesis:
  - Put it all together.
  - Match key parts of questions to key parts of readings.

M. Eisenberg

Writing Tests – Things I Noticed

- Instructions are similar from year to year.
- The types of writings are predictable.
- Learn how to create an outline or graphic organizer for the writing.
- Don't dwell on non-essential instructions or suggestions, for example:
  - "Remember to:
    - ▢ Focus on ….
    - ▢ … the purpose, audience, and context ….
    - ▢ Organize your [writing] so that your ideas progress logically.
    - ▢ Include relevant details to clearly develop your [writing].
    - ▢ Edit your article for standard grammar and language usage.

M. Eisenberg

Figure 6.13 The Big6™ and Standard Tests (*continued*)

Sample Big6/Writing Lessons

- Task Definition –
    - To expect the instructions.
    - What all the words in the instructions mean.
- Synthesis
    - 5.1: organize – create a graphic organizer based on the question (e.g., Bob's boxes).
    - 5.2: present – practice writing from a "perfect box."
    - 5.1/5.2 – put it all together.
- Evaluation
    - Process: what is the hardest part of the writing test?
    - Process: where in the process can you improve?
    - Product: what makes a good writing piece?

M. Eisenberg

Math Tests – Things I Noticed

- Instructions are similar from year to year.
- Students are often required to show their work.
- There are usually questions that ask students to "describe their process for solving the problem."
- Big6 Lessons
    - Be familiar with the test format and instructions.
    - Recognize the instructions, but don't spend time on the hints or suggestions.
    - Learn to identify certain types of questions.
    - Learn how to answer each type of question.

M. Eisenberg

Evaluation
Learning to Explain Process

- Students should be able to reflect on their process and communicate what they did.
- Use the terms of the Big6 stages to describe their process.
- Learn to break down their thoughts and actions into steps:
    - List actions and thoughts - one at a time - on index cards or PowerPoint slides.
    - Review the order and revise until satisfied.
    - Add actions or thoughts if necessary.
    - Look at the result as a "process with steps."
    - Be able to describe the process orally and verbally.
- Practice written self-reflection on various assignments, classwork, and tests.

M. Eisenberg

Summary

- Remember
    - Students won't "get it" from just one lesson. Repeat!
    - Use the same format and instructions as on the state exams.
    - It's all about context – the Big6 process.
- If standards and tests are the district or school priority, then we should:
    - Fully link the Big6 information and technology skills instructional program to standards, curriculum, and tests.
    - Offer a comprehensive, predictable, and accountable program.

M. Eisenberg

Figure 6.13 The Big6™ and Standard Tests (*continued*)

6.5 Article

"It's All About Learning: Ensuring That Students Are Effective Users of Information on Standardized Tests," by Mike Eisenberg. Gale/Linworth Education Issues in Education Forum at AASL conference, *Library Media Connection*, March 2004, p. 22.

It's All About Learning: Ensuring That Students Are Effective Users of Information on Standardized Tests

by Mike Eisenberg

This article describes and advocates for taking the next step in connecting school library media programs to student learning and academic achievement. It's time to get specific and detailed in terms of the examining and documenting the relationship between library media program services, particularly information skills instruction, and student performance as measured on standardized tests. Making this connection is crucial if school library media programs are to thrive in an educational system increasingly focused on accountability and measured achievement through examination by standardized testing.

Where the Action Is

It's pretty obvious. The bottom line in K-12 education today is student achievement, and, like it or not, increasingly that achievement is defined by standardized testing and the "No Child Left Behind" act. For example, an August 2003 poll on the Big6.org website asked, "Starting the 2003-04 school year, what is the new initiative in your district?" Of the almost 700 responses, 86% indicated No Child Left Behind/Standardized Testing! Standardized testing is the overwhelming educational focus around the country. We as educators need to take action to ensure success for all students.

"No Child Left Behind," President Bush's education agenda, is designed to improve student achievement in all schools across the United States. The Act is intended to guarantee quality education for all children—with an emphasis on increased funding for poor school districts, higher achievement for poor and minority students, and new measures to hold schools accountable for their students' progress. The Act significantly expands the role of standardized testing in American public education.

The bill mandates that states develop and implement "challenging" academic standards in reading and math, set annual statewide progress objectives to ensure that all groups of students reach proficiency within 12 years, and then test children annually in Grades 3 through 8, in reading and math, to measure their progress. The bill specifically prohibits any "national testing" or "federally controlled curriculum." It is up to the states to select and/or design their own tests, and to make sure that the tests are aligned with the state curriculum standards. (U.S. Department of Education 2003; Public Broadcasting System, 2003) The test results are made public in annual "report cards" on how schools are performing and how states are progressing overall toward their proficiency objectives.

Before continuing, let me be very clear about one thing: I am not a proponent of standardized testing. Standardized testing has its place, but the "testing movement" seems overboard to me. As library and information professionals, it is our job to fight for true education reform (e.g., focusing on higher-level thinking skills) rather than simply testing. At the same time, we need to help students succeed at whatever has been set before them. Today, that means focusing on standardized tests and the relationship between information literacy skills instruction and student performance on these standard tests.

What This Means for Library Media Programs

In considering a more direct connection between library media programs and standardized tests, it's important to remind ourselves of our ultimate purpose and goal: "the mission of the library media program is to ensure that students . . . are effective users of ideas and information." (Information Power, 1998) Our work is founded on a fundamental conviction—the more skilled that students are in gathering, processing, evaluating, and applying information, the more they will be able to achieve on any task. Thus, it is essential that we direct our attention to student success as measured by standardized tests.

The school library media field appears to be increasingly aware of this need to focus on achievement and standards. Over the past 10 years, much progress has been made in focusing programs on student performance and the connection to state and subject area standards. Teacher-librarians recognize that the key to providing a meaningful program is the direct connection to curriculum and the classroom.

The library media field has also made progress in recognizing that it's not enough to simply "say" that we are important and make a difference. Ross Todd nailed it on the head in his August/September 2003 article in LIBRARY MEDIA CONNECTION. It's right on the cover, "It's not enough to say that school libraries contribute to learning. Now you have to prove it." Exactly, and as Todd implies, we need to focus on what it all means for students—how does an effective school library media program help students? What does it enable them to do and to become? What does it mean in terms of student learning? (p. 13).

Among the research that Todd reviews are the well-cited studies conducted by Keith Curry Lance and colleagues. (Lance 2001) These studies empirically analyzed the connection between student achievement and school library media programs. As recently reported in an Association of Supervision and Curriculum Development Research Brief (ASCD 2003), the Lance studies confirmed a correlation between the presence of a library or librarian and higher student achievement, especially in reading. Among other findings, studies in Alaska, Colorado, Oregon, and Pennsylvania found that professionally trained and credentialed teacher-librarians have a positive effect on student achievement.

The Smith (2001) study of Texas school library media programs looked specifically on the effects of school libraries on student achievement as measured by the reading portion of the Texas standardized test, the Texas Assessment of Academic Skills (TAAS). The study found that school library media programs do have a measurable effect on student achievement. At the elementary and middle school levels, library media programs could account for approximately 4% of the variance in TAAS scores; at the high school level, 8.2% of variance.

Furthermore, at the middle school level, two variables stood out, including "providing information skills instruction to students." At the high school level, seven variables were noted including "units planned with teachers."

This is great news, right? Isn't this the evidence that we've all be waiting for? We should be shouting the news from roof-tops and on street corners! Better yet, the eyes of administrators and school boards should be finally opened and the money and support for library media programs should be flowing.

Well, not so fast. While these results are encouraging, they are not overwhelming in any sense. First, these studies are correlational, not causal. It appears that effective library media programs have a positive impact on student performance, but there are no studies that demonstrate a direct causal effect. Second, we are talking potential impact in the 4–8% range, and that pales before the strongest predictor of academic success, socioeconomic factors. Lastly, as the ASCD piece asks, how much does a 4–8% variance cost a district? What is the cost-benefit analysis, and what specific aspects of the library media program account for the variance?

A missing element is a direct connection between core library media functions (specifically information skills and reading advocacy) and performance on standardized tests. We do have valuable and important studies on the nature and impact of information skills instruction. Kuhlthau (2001, 1993), Todd (2003), and others investigate student performance on papers, projects, and reports. These are certainly important pieces of the evidence puzzle. But, we need to go one step further; we need to address the specific questions of performance on standardized tests.

Therefore, I propose that we complete the picture by taking the next, bold step—to get detailed and specific in focusing our attention on state standards and tests and the connection to core library media functions. I propose that we move from broad, sometimes vague correlations to specific and direct connections.

Specifically, that means:

■ Analyzing state standards and test items to determine direct connections to information skills instruction.

■ Targeting information skills instruction actions to specific standards and test items.

■ Evaluating the impact of these interventions on student performance on test items.

Today's library media program encompasses three important functions: reading advocacy, information skills instruction, and information management. While there are direct connections between all of these functions and standardized tests, we are limited as to what can be covered because of time and space constraints.

Therefore, the focus for the remainder of this article will be on information skills instruction and testing.

Information Skills Instruction

There's an extensive body of literature on the information skills instruction and information literacy (see Eisenberg, Lowe, and Spitzer, 2004) including the empirical work of Carol Kuhlthau (1993), various state standards (e.g., Wisconsin 1998), the national AASL/AECT standards (AASL/AECT 1998), and my Big6 problem solving skills approach, developed in conjunction with Bob Berkowitz. (Eisenberg and Berkowitz, 1990)

I have previously written on a number of occasions about the commonalities among these models. (see Figure 1, based on Eisenberg and Lowe 1996; also in Spitzer, Eisenberg, and Lowe, 1998). From this side-by-side view, we see a process unfold—that information skills are connected activities that flow from identifying a task through gathering, evaluating, use, synthesis, and assessment of information.

More recently, Janet Murray went even further, matching the Big6 model, the AASL/AECT national standards, Information Literacy Standards, and the National Educational Technology Standards for Students (NETS) developed by ISTE. Murray documented the relationship between the Big6 and specific state information and technology skills standards, with examples from Washington, North Carolina, Colorado, and Missouri. (see Murray, 2002)

Comparison of Information Skills Process Models

Kuhlthau Information Seeking		Eisenberg/Berkowitz Information Problem Solving (The Big6 Skills)	AASL/AECT Information Literacy Standards	Pitts/Stripling Research Process	New South Wales Information Process
1. Initiation 2. Selection		1. Task definition 1.1 Define the problem 1.2 Identify info requirements		1. Choose a broad topic 2. Get an overview of the topic	Defining
	4. Formulation (of focus)			3. Narrow the topic 4. Develop thesis/purpose statement	
3. Exploration (investigating info on the general topic)	5. Collection (gather info on the focused topic)	2. Information seeking 2.1 Determine range sources 2.2 Prioritize sources	1. Accesses information efficiently and effectively.	5. Formulate questions to guide research 6. Plan for research and production	Locating
		3. Location and access 3.1 Locate sources 3.2 Find info		7. Find, analyze, evaluate resources	Selecting
		4. Information use 4.1 Engage (read, view, etc.) 4.2 Extract info	2. Evaluates information critically and competently.	8. Evaluate evidence, take notes/compile bib	Organizing
6. Presentation		5. Synthesis 5.1 Organize 5.2 Present	3. Uses information accurately and creatively.	9. Establish conclusions/ organize info into an outline 10. Create and present final product	Presenting
7. Assessment (of outcome process)		6. Evaluation 6.1 Judge the product 6.2 Judge the process		(Reflection point—is the paper/project satisfactory	Assessing

M. Eisenberg 2003

Figure 1 Comparison of Information Skills Process Models

(Adapted from Eisenberg, M. and Brown, M.,1992 and Spitzer, Eisenberg, and Lowe, 1998)

1. Task Definition:	4. Use of Information:
1.1 Define the problem.	4.1 Engage (e.g., read, hear, view).
1.2 Identify the information needed.	4.2 Extract relevant information.
2. Information Seeking Strategies:	5. Synthesis:
2.1 Determine all possible sources.	5.1 Organize information from multiple sources.
2.2 Select the best sources.	5.2 Present information.
3. Location and Access:	6. Evaluation:
3.1 Locate sources.	6.1 Judge the result (effectiveness).
3.2 Find information within sources.	6.2 Judge the process (efficiency).

Figure 2 The Big6

What all this means is that, regardless of the information skills curriculum, model or standards used, you can make the connection to other models and standards, including the AASL/AECT framework and the Big6 approach. Because it is the most widely used approach to information literacy instruction in K-12 schools and because of my familiarity with it, I will use the Big6 process to explore the relationship of information skills instruction and standardized tests. The Big6 is a process model of how students solve an information problem. From practice and study, we found that successful information problem-solving encompasses six stages with two sub-stages under each (see Figure 2).

Students go through these Big6 stages—consciously or not—when they seek or apply information to solve a problem or make a decision—both on a personal level and with school work. It's not necessary to complete these stages in a linear order, and a given stage doesn't have to take a lot of time. We have found that in almost all successful problem-solving situations, all stages are addressed.

Content Area Standards and the Information Skills Connection

State and subject area standards are now part of the fabric of K-12 education and define the goals of education across the United States. McREL, the Mid-Central Regional Education Lab, has compiled content for K-12 curriculum (see McREL 2003, www.mcrel.org/standards-benchmarks). According to McREL, in the 1980s and 1990s, most national subject-matter organizations sought to establish standards in their respective areas, including mathematics, science, civics, dance, theater, music, art, English/language arts, history, and social studies. "Since 1990 the movement has acquired considerable momentum at the state level as well. As of 1999, the District of Columbia, Puerto Rico, and every state except Iowa have set or are setting common academic standards for students." (American Federation of Teachers, 1999 quoted on the McREL website).

Much has been written about the importance of connecting library media programs to school and classroom curriculum. We talk about context and collaboration, and one important tangible way to do this is to make the connection between information skills instructional programs to state content area standards. Furthermore, this connection is essential when we turn to focusing on standardized tests. Tests are developed to assess student performance on state standards, and individual test questions are referenced to the state standards (this is explained in more detail in the next section). The connection between information skills standards and state content standards allows us to make the necessary connection and target information skills instruction to student achievement as measured on the standardized tests.

Fortunately, we have a number of excellent models of how to make the connection between state content standards and information skills. Wisconsin (1998) was one of the first states to develop combined information and technology skills standards. The heart of these standards, "Information and Inquiry" is based directly on the Big6 approach. Wisconsin also led the way in fully integrating information and technology skills standards with content area standards and offers an extensive set of matrices connecting information technology literacy standards to content area standards. (Wisconsin 2000). See Figure 3 for more information on these connections.

The state of Missouri also fully documents the relationship between state information and technology literacy skills standards and the state content standards, as well as more general process/performance standards. (Missouri 2001) Figure 4 illustrates how, under the broad information skill of "Access of Information," the specific skill of "Determine purpose" links to Process/Performance Standards 1.1 and 3.1. The even more detailed sub-skill "Brainstorm" links to Process/Performance Standards 3.6 and Science Content/Knowledge Standards SC 7. Figure 4 illustrates the similarities between the Missouri program and the Show-Me Standards.

If your state does not have a linking document, it is relatively easy to do so. Sue Wurster and I (Eisenberg and Wurster 2002) created a matrix aligning the Florida Language Arts Standards with the Big6 Skills. We paid particular attention to Language Arts Standards that are tested on the Florida FCAT exams (see Figure 5)

A. Mathematical Processes

Students in Wisconsin will draw on a broad body of mathematical knowledge and apply a variety of mathematical skills and strategies, including reasoning, oral and written communication, and the use of appropriate technology, when solving mathematical, real-world and nonroutine problems.

ITL Performance Indicators

- formulate initial questions to define what additional information is needed—B.4.1
- determine a specific focus for the information search questions—B.4.1
- recognize that materials in the school library media center are organized in a systematic manner—B.4.3
- locate materials using the classification system of the school library media center—B.4.3
- identify new information and integrate it with prior knowledge—B.4.6
- determine if information is relevant to the information question—B.4.6
- select information applicable to the information question—B.4.6
- seek additional information if needed—B.4.6
- apply the information gathered to solve the information problem or question—B.4.6
- recognize the three common types of communication or presentation modes (written, oral, visual)—B.4.7
- choose a presentation format (e.g., speech, paper, web page, video, hypermedia)—B.4.7
- develop a product or presentation to communicate the results of the research—B.4.7

Figure 3 Wisconsin 4th Grade Examples of Connections: Mathematics

(From Combined Matrix, Model 2, B. Information and Inquiry ITL Content Standard: p. 179–180)

Access of Information			Process/Performance Standards	Content/Knowledge Standards
Determine purpose			1.1; 3.1	
■ Identify personal interest			4.1; 4.8	
■ Assess				
Prior knowledge			3.2; 3.3	
Knowledge needed			3.4	
■ Brainstorm			3.6	SC 7

COMPONENT	PROCESS	DETAILS/ SKILLS

PROCESS/PERFORMANCE GOALS/STANDARDS
(Show-Me Standards)

2.6=Goal 2 Standard 6
3.5=Goal 3 Standard 5

CONTENT/KNOWLEDGE STANDARDS
(Show-Me Standards)

CA=Communication Arts
FA= Fine Arts
HP=Health/Physical Education
MA=Mathmatics
SC=Science
SS=Social Studies

Figure 4 Missouri (2001) Information and Technology Literacy: A Comparison to the Show-Me Standards (p. 7)

3rd grade – 5th grade	Big6 Skill #2: Information Seeking Strategies
LA.A.2.2.8: The student selects and uses a variety of appropriate reference materials, including multiple representations of information, such as maps, charts and photos, to gather information for research projects. *(Tested on FCAT)*	2.1 Determine the range of possible resources 2.2 Select the best sources **Big6 Skill #3 Location and Access** 3.1 Locate sources (intellectually and physically) 3.2 Find information within sources **Big6 Skill #4: Use of Information** 4.1 Engage (e.g., read, hear, view) the information in a source 4.2 Extract information from a source
6th grade - 8th grade LA.A.2.3.5: The student locates, organizes, and interprets written information for a variety of purposes, including classroom research, collaborative decision making, and performing a school or real-world task. *(Tested on FCAT)*	**Big6 Skill #3 Location and Access** 3.1 Locate sources (intellectually and physically) 3.2 Find information within sources **Big6 Skill #4: Use of Information** 4.1 Engage (e.g. read, hear, view) the information in a source 4.2 Extract relevant information from a source **Big6 Skill #5: Synthesis** 5.1 Organize information from multiple sources 5.2 Present information

Figure 5 Sample Florida Language Arts Standards and the Big6

The Final Chapter: Making the Connection to Standardized Tests

Making the connection between information skills standards to state content standards is essential to the task of making library media programs relevant to educational priorities, but it is not the end of the story. The last part of the plot is extending the connection to the state tests themselves. This requires:

- Becoming familiar with various state tests (including the nature, format, and content of the tests)

- Analyzing the tests and individual test questions from an information perspective (i.e., identifying relevant information skills standards or skills within models such as the Big6 that would help students to succeed on specific test questions).

- Collaborating with classroom teachers to offer opportunities for students to learn and apply the relevant information skills to specific test questions.

- Designing and delivering lessons that help students to learn and apply the relevant information skills to specific test questions.

- Documenting actions taken to connect information skills instruction to tests, test questions, and standards.

- Assessing success by looking at the test results (as provided in the various state "report cards").

- Revising and planning for future instruction.

This is clearly a long-term commitment and effort. One-shot lessons and interventions will probably not result in any measurable improvement in student performance. However, over time, teacher-librarians can make a difference by working with classroom teachers to integrate information skills instruction into subject area learning that is targeted to performance requirements on standardized tests. This is not "teaching to the test." It is "teaching skills that allow students to perform better on tasks as measured by standardized tests."

Information on tests is readily available from most states on the Web. These include sample exams across subject areas and grade levels. Most samples also include references to the related state content standards. These references provide useful insights into how standards are translated into test items as well as the style and format of test questions.*

Here are three examples of what I am proposing—using sample test questions from three different states, subject areas, and grade levels.

Example 1: Wisconsin 4th Grade Mathematics

Sample test questions for the "Wisconsin Knowledge and Concepts Examinations" are presented by subject, grade, and proficiency category (minimal performance, basic, proficient, and advanced). The questions provided are edited and are intended as samples only. Actual questions are available to Wisconsin educators through the local district or school.

Mathematics Question 9 from the Wisconsin Department of Public Instruction, Office of Educational Accountability (1997, http://www.dpi.state.wi.us/dpi/oea/ math4bas.html) reads:

"The tree in the picture is 10 feet tall. Next to the tree, draw another tree that is 20 feet tall. Explain how you decided how tall to draw your tree."

This question is followed by a picture of a tree with a ruler next to it noting its height as 10 feet. Blank spaces are provided below for students to show and explain their answers.

According to the scoring explanation provided, this item tests two objectives: Measurement and Communication. For Measurement, the student demonstrates an understanding of scale by drawing the second tree twice the height of the first. The student can use the ruler provided or another strategy. Communication objectives include relating daily vocabulary to mathematical terminology and relating models, diagrams, and pictures to mathematics. Students validate their solutions by explaining their decision-making process.

Looking at this question from an information perspective, it appears to relate to two Big6 skills:

Big6 #1: Task Definition—recognizing that the question has two parts to it. It's not enough to just draw a tree, the student must also explain his or her decision-making process.

Big6 #6: Evaluation—reflect on decision-making process. "Explain how you decided how tall to draw your tree" is asking students to describe and reflect on their decision-making process.

Task Definition lessons may include:

■ Recognizing multiple parts of questions. Assignments and questions frequently have multiple components, and students need to learn to focus on this. Using existing homework, tests, and other assignments, students can be asked to break them down and identify the parts—and the relative importance of each part to the assignment or question.

■ Learning key words in questions. Bob Berkowitz works with high school students to highlight and define the key verbs in questions. Students make flash cards to help them study and remember the terms. For example, in the question above, the key terms are "draw" "explain" and "decided." Most students will understand "draw" but they may have more trouble with knowing what is required for "explain" and also that "decided" means that they are to reflect on their decision-making process.

For Evaluation, students should be able to reflect on their process and communicate what they did:

■ Teacher-librarians and classroom teachers can teach students how to break down their actions into steps, for example, by listing them one-by-one or writing them on cards.

■ Students can practice this type of written self-reflection if they are sometimes required to include an explanation of their work when they turn in assignments.

Example 2: Florida (FCAT) 8th Grade Reading

Florida provides extensive sample information for its FCAT. (Florida's Comprehensive Assessment Test Keys (2002–2003). A series of questions, including #16, follows a 900+ word reading passage, *America's Saltiest Sea: Great Salt Lake* by Angela B. Haight, illustrations from the Utah Division of Wildlife. *Cricket Magazine,* April 1996.

Question 16 (from Florida's Comprehensive Assessment Test FCAT Sample Test Books and Answer Keys (2002–2003) Grade 8 Reading, 2003, p.12):

Question 16: Using details and information from the article, summarize the main points of the article.

For a complete and correct response, consider these points.

- Its history

- Its interesting features

- Why it is a landmark.

A Scoring Rubric for Question 16 is provided in the Grade 8 Answer Key Book (p. 11). It refers to the passage as an "informational text" and references it to the following Language Arts Benchmark:

Benchmark: LA.A.2.3.5 The student locates, organizes, and interprets written information for a variety of purposes, including classroom research, collaborative decisionmaking, and performing a school or real-world task. (Includes LA.A.2.3.6 uses a variety of reference materials, including indexes, magazines, newspapers, and journals, and tools, including card catalogs and computer catalogs, to gather information for research projects; and LA.A.2.3.7 synthesizes and separates collected information into useful components using a variety of techniques, such as source cards, note cards, spreadsheets, and outlines.)

According to the Rubric, "a top-score response will include information about the Great Salt Lake's history, interesting features, and why it is a landmark."

From the Eisenberg/Wurster chart *(see Figure 5)*, we see that Florida Benchmark: LA.A.2.3.5 is linked to Big6 Skills #3, Location and Access, #4, Use of Information, and #5, Synthesis. Therefore, in considering this question and the rubric from an information perspective, and by analyzing the question and information skills required of students more carefully, it seems that students will be successful if they are able to:

- Effectively and efficiently extract relevant information (Big6 4.2, Use of Information).

- Organize and present complete information (Big6 #5, Synthesis)
  Use of Information lessons related to this need might include:

- Teaching students how to skim and scan a text. One key element of this is helping students to learn to read for a purpose (i.e., to look at the questions being asked of them *before* they start reading the text) so that they know what to look for.

- Highlight relevant parts of a reading passage. Again, students should learn to first look at the questions being asked and then how to read a text and highlight key parts.

Another possible approach to this question combines Task Definition, Use of Information, and Synthesis. Devised by Bob Berkowitz, students learn to analyze the parts of question, create a chart that outlines the parts, read the text and take notes on the chart, and finally to write the full answer from the chart.

For example, Question 16 requires three information items about the Great Salt Lake: its history, its interesting features, and why it is a landmark. Before even reading the passage, students can create the following blank chart:

History	
Interesting Features	
Why a Landmark	

Then, if they come across any information on the aspects when reading the passage, they can simply enter the information into the chart, for example:

History	■ In 1847, settlers arrived in Salt Lake City ■ Once, during a swarm of crickets, seagulls saved the settlers' crops
Interesting Features	■ 25 percent salt ■ 75 miles long by 50 miles wide ■ the largest body of water west of the Mississippi River.
Why a Landmark	■ the largest body of water west of the Mississippi River.

With this chart in hand, it's a straightforward matter to write a complete response that directly answers the question. Students are able to draw the relevant facts out of the passage before having to worry about the writing process.

Example 3: Missouri 10th Grade Science
The Missouri State Department of Elementary and Secondary Education provides up-to-date examples of the Missouri Assessment Program (MAP). Question 2 on the 2003 Grade 10 Science test (Missouri State Department of Elementary and Secondary Education 2003 Science Released Items Grade 10, p. 3) asks:

Each of the three main particles that make up a neutral atom has mass and either a positive (+), negative (–), or neutral (0) charge.

List the three main particles found in a neutral atom.

1. _____

2. _____

3. _____

Show the charge on each of these three particles by writing a symbol (+, −, or 0) to the right of its name.

Circle the name of the particle that has the least mass.

The Scoring Guide for Question 2 notes that this relates to Missouri Standard: III.A.4 (Std 1) Goals: 1.10. The answer should include the following elements:

■ Electron, proton, neutron (in any order)

■ − with electron, + with proton, 0 with neutron

■ Electron is circled.

Students receive the following scoring points:

3 points	three key elements
2 points	two key elements
1 point	one key element
0 points	other

Analyzing this question from an information perspective, we again see that a key to this question is Big6 #1, Task Definition as well as Big6 #6, Evaluation, for which students are able to judge and score answers themselves.

For question 2, Students must include all three elements to receive the 3 maximum possible points. Teacher-librarians can work with classroom teachers to design learning experiences that help students learn to recognize the requirements of a complete answer and to make sure that students do, in fact, include all of the requirements in their answer. These learning experiences can include:

■ Lessons that teach students how to analyze questions and identify the requirements.

■ Exercises and homework that have students practice analyzing questions and identifying requirements.

■ Having students create their own rubrics for questions, homework, and assignments.

Summary: Putting It All Together

The three examples presented in the previous section demonstrate how it is possible to not only link information skills standards to content area standards, but to get much more specific in providing meaningful information skills instruction that helps students to succeed on standardized tests. I recognize that one lesson here and there will not have much of an impact on student performance. However, over time, repeated lessons that focus on the same information skills—targeted to questions in the same format and style that appear on statewide tests, taught collaboratively by the teacher—librarian and classroom teacher—can make a difference.

To review the recommended approach:

- Become familiar with various state tests.

- Analyze and break down the tests and individual test questions from an information perspective.

- Collaborate with classroom teachers to offer opportunities for students to learn and apply the relevant information skills to specific test questions.

- Design and deliver lessons that help students to learn and apply the relevant information skills to specific test questions.

- Document actions taken to connect information skills instruction to tests, test questions, and standards.

- Assess success by looking at the test results.

- Revise and plan for future instruction.

While not discussed in detail in this article, these last three bullets—document, assess, and plan—are as important as the others to overall success. Documentation (through charts, schedules, or reports) of specific information skills instructional efforts provides evidence of the involvement of the library media program in the effort to improve student achievement.

Documentation also provides a baseline for assessing any potential impact on test scores. In addition to assessing success, examining test results will point to problem areas for student performance, and future information instructional efforts can be targeted to the most problematic areas. Lastly, revisions in the instructional efforts should be systematically planned and communicated to administrators and school decision makers.

The targeting of library media information skills instructional programs to standardized testing is not an add-on to existing programs. Rather, it is a long-term commitment to targeting the focus of instruction to school and district priorities. It is fully consistent with the mission and goals of the library media program as it takes a systematic approach to "ensuring that students are effective users of ideas and information."

The potential result is for library media programs to make a difference in student performance and to finally gain the deserved recognition that library media programs are vital to education in an information society.

> "Targeting library media information skills instructional programs to standardized testing is not an add-on to existing programs. Rather, it is a long-term commitment to targeting the focus of instruction to school and district priorities "

BIBLIOGRAPHY

American Library Association and Association for Educational Communications and Technology (1998). "Information Literacy Standards for Student Learning," In *Information Power: Building Partnerships for Learning* (Chapter 2).

Association for Supervision and Curriculum Development (ASCD) (2003). *School Libraries and Their Impact on Student Performance.* Research Brief (September 2,

2003, volume 1, number 18), Available online: www.ascd.org/publications/
researchbrief/volume1/v1n18.html

Eisenberg, M. and Berkowitz, R. (1990). *Information Problem-Solving: The Big6™ Skills Approach to Library & Information Skills Instruction.* Norwood, NJ: Ablex.

Eisenberg, M. and Brown, M. (1992). "Current Themes Regarding Library and Information Skills Instruction: Research Supporting and Research Lacking." *School Library Media Quarterly* 20(2): 103–109.

Eisenberg, M., Lowe, C., and Spitzer, K. (In press). *Information Literacy: Essential Skills for the Information Age.* Westport, CT: Libraries Unlimited.

Eisenberg, M. and Wurster, S.L. (2002). Florida State Language Arts Standards Aligned with Big6(tm) Skills. Available online: http://www.big6.com/ showarticle. php?id=151

Florida's Comprehensive Assessment Test FCAT Sample Test Books and Answer Keys (2002–2003). Available online: http://www.firn.edu/doe/sas/ fcat/fcatit02.htm

Florida's Comprehensive Assessment Test FCAT (2002). Grade 8 Reading 2003. Available online: http://www.firn. edu/doe/sas/fcat/pdf/fc8rib2a.pdf p.12

Florida's Comprehensive Assessment Test FCAT (2002). Grade 8 Reading 2003. Grade 8 Answer Key Book. Available online: http://www.firn.edu/doe/sas/fcat/pdf/ fc8rik2a.pdf p. 11

International Society for Technology in Education (2003). National Educational Technology Standards NETS. Available online: http://cnets.iste.org/students/s_stands. html

Kuhlthau, Carol C. (2001). Rethinking libraries for the information age school: vital roles in inquiry learning. Keynote Address, International Association of School Librarianship Conference & International Research, Forum on Research in School Librarianship, July 9, 2001 Auckland, New Zealand. Available online: www.scils. rutgers.edu/~kuhlthau/Presentations.htm

Kuhlthau, Carol C. (1993). *Seeking meaning: a process approach to library and information services.* Norwood, NJ: Ablex, 1993.

Lance, K. (2001). *Proof of the power: Recent research on the impact of school library media programs on the academic achievement of U.S. public school students.* Syracuse, NY: ERIC Digest: ERIC Clearinghouse on Information & Technology. Available online: http://ericit.org/digests/EDO-IR-2001-05.shtml

McREL. (2003). *Content Knowledge.* 3rd Edition. Available online: http://www.mcrel. org/standards-benchmarks/

Missouri State Department of Elementary and Secondary Education (2001). Information and Technology Literacy: A Comparison to the Show-Me Standards. Available online: http://dese.mo.gov/divimprove/curriculum/literacy/document.pdf

Missouri State Department of Elementary and Secondary Education (2003). Missouri Assessment Program Spring 2003 Science Released Items Grade 10. Available online: http://www.dese.state.mo.us/divimprove/assess/science/releaseditems/2003/ sc10released2003.pdf

Murray, J. (2002). Big6™ and State Standards. *Big6 eNewsletter* 3(2). Available online: http://www.big6.com/showarticle.php?id=339

Murray, J. (2003). Apply Big6™ Skills to Integrate Content Standards in the Curriculum, *Big6 eNewsletter* 4(1). Available online: http://www.big6.com/showarticle.php?id=325

U.S. Department of Education (2003). No Child Left Behind. Available online: www.ed.gov/nclb/landing.jhtml

Public Broadcast System (2003). *Frontline: The New Rules.* Available online: www.pbs.org/wgbh/pages/frontline/shows/schools/nochild/nclb.html)

Smith, E. G. (2001). Texas school libraries: Standards, resources, services, and students' performance. Austin, TX: Texas State Library and Archives Commission. Available online: http://www.tsl.state.tx.us/ld/pubs/ schlibsurvey/survey.pdf

Spitzer, K., Eisenberg, M., and Lowe, C. (1998). "Information Literacy: Essential Skills for the Information Age." *ERIC Clearinghouse on Information & Technology* ED427780.

Todd, Ross (2003). "School Libraries & Evidence: Seize the Day, Begin the Future" *Library Media Connection* 22(1): 12–18.

Wisconsin Department of Public Instruction, Office of Educational Accountability (1997). Sample Test Questions, MATHEMATICS Proficiency Category: BASIC Elementary School Level at Grade 4. Available online: http://www.dpi.state.wi.us/ dpi/oea/math4bas.html

Wisconsin Department of Public Instruction (2002). Curriculum Alignment Resources for Wisconsin's Model Academic Standards An Information Technology Literacy (ITL) Resource http://www.waunakee.k12.wi.us/DPI_Standards/index.htm

Wisconsin Department of Public Instruction (2000), "B. Information and Inquiry ITL Content Standard: Information and Inquiry, Combined Matrix, Model 2," Curriculum Alignment Resources for Wisconsin's Model Academic Standards An Information Technology Literacy (ITL) Resource p. 179–180. Available online: http://www.waunakee.k12.wi.us/DPI_Standards/ITL%20Standards%20Matrix/ Matrix%20Model%202.doc

Wisconsin Department of Public Instruction (1998). Model Academic Standards for Information and Technology Literacy, Available online: http://www.waunakee.k12. wi.us/DPI_Standards/Academic%20Standards/Info%20Tech%20Literacy.doc

*Unfortunately, I have not found any references to state information skills standards. It is up to us—the library media field—to begin to make and communicate these connections.

Michael B. Eisenberg is Dean of the Information School of the University of Washington. Prior to his role as Dean, Mike Eisenberg worked for many years as Professor of Information Studies at Syracuse University and as Director of the Information Institute of Syracuse (including the ERIC Clearinghouse on Information & Technology, AskERIC, and GEM). Mike and his co-author Bob Berkowitz created the Big6 approach to information problem solving, and he has worked with thousands of students (preK through higher education) as well as people in public schools, business, government, and communities to improve their information and technology skills. Mike has written numerous books and articles on aspects of information science and librarianship, information literacy, library media work, and information technology. He can be reached at mbe@u.washington.edu; www.ischool.washington.edu/mbe. Visit www.linworth.com for Big6™ titles, posters, and bookmarks.

6.6 Article

"Testing Information Literacy Skills (Grades K-12)," by Janet Murray. *Big6 eNewsletter*, June 8, 2005. Available online: http://www.big6.com/2005/06/08/testing-information-literacy-skills-grades-k-12/

Testing Information Literacy Skills (Grades K–12)
by: Janet Murray 2005 Big6 eNewsletter

The Educational Testing Service (ETS) recently "announced the launch of the ETS ICT (Information and Communication Technology) Literacy Assessment, a simulation-based testing program that measures postsecondary students' ability to define, access, manage, integrate, evaluate, create and communicate information in a technological environment" (Barrish, 2005). The test measures "not just knowledge of technology, but the ability to use critical-thinking skills to solve problems within a technological environment" (ETS, 2005).

The test was administered for the first time to participating beta institutions between January and March, 2005. In a related article on the ETS web site, President & CEO Kurt M. Landgraf labels technology as "the fourth basic literacy . . . teaching children about technology is as fundamental as teaching reading, writing and arithmetic" (Landgraf, 2004).

The ETS ICT literacy assessment requires students to demonstrate competence in five areas by using technology tools to solve problems and design solutions. "It uses scenario-based assignments to assess all the ICT skills required of today's higher education students—not just knowledge of technology, but the ability to use critical-thinking skills to solve problems within a technological environment" (ETS, 2005). The five abilities tested are:

Define: The ability to use ICT tools to identify and appropriately represent an information need.

Access: The ability to collect and/or retrieve information in digital environments.

Manage: The ability to apply an existing organizational or classification scheme for digital information.

Integrate: The ability to interpret and represent digital information.

Evaluate: The ability to determine the degree to which digital information satisfies the needs of the task in ICT environments.

Big6ers will immediately identify these skills in familiar terms!

Define—Task Definition

Access—Information Seeking Strategies, Location & Access

Manage—Synthesis (5.1)

Integrate—Use of Information (4.1) and Synthesis (5.2)

Evaluate—ISS (2.2 evaluate sources) and Evaluation (6.1)

Students who take the test will demonstrate their abilities by using a proctored personal computer to create an academic research topic, locate information in databases and on the web, create concept maps, organization charts and tables, synthesize information in a word processing document, use a spreadsheet to compare and contrast information, rank web pages, sort e-mail, and create presentations. "The market didn't need one more multiple-choice test, and it didn't need another test that proves you know how to use Microsoft Word, et cetera," said Tom Ewing, director of external communications for ETS. "Educators needed to determine that their students had the ability to manage and process information through technology, interpret, then communicate it in [a] way that is meaningful and accurate" (Brumfeld, 2005).

The two-hour exam "presents the test-taker with a challenge and gives him or her the resources to investigate, Ewing said. . .For instance, the test-taker might be asked to perform an advanced search based on the need to find certain information. He or she might then be asked to use that information to put together a graph or compose an E-mail message that summarizes the results of the research and draws subsequent conclusions from the data" (Brumfeld, 2005).

Apply the Big6 Skills to ICT Literacy

Those of us who teach in K-12 schools know that "students can identify . . . thousands of . . . potential resources on the Internet—and, as any teacher will attest, they are not always adept at sorting the wheat from the chaff" (Zeller, 2005). However, we can use the Big6 Skills to guide students in developing the critical thinking skills that will encourage them to *"define, access, manage, integrate, evaluate, create and communicate information in a technological environment."* How does this work?

Students use stage 1, *Task Definition*, to *define* their tasks. They may use a technology tool like Inspiration to create a graphic organizer identifying the aspects of the information problem they need to research. Then they use the skills they've learned in stage 2, *Information Seeking Strategies*, to *evaluate* sources of information. Is a particular web site credible? Is the author an expert on the topic? Is the information reliable?

In Big6 stage 3, *Location and Access*, students learn to use subject directories, subscription databases, and Internet search engines to access reliable sources of information appropriate for use in schools. They *manage* and *integrate* the information they've found through stage 4, *Use of Information*. Finally, they use technology tools like word processors, desktop publishing, PowerPoint and web pages to *create* and *communicate* in stage 5, *Synthesis*. The ETS test doesn't ask students to *Evaluate* their product and process, but it's that critical Big6 stage 6 that helps them improve their information literacy skills.

Karen Bruett, board chair of the Partnership for 21st Century Skills, observed, "It's not enough for students to master PowerPoint and Excel. They need to think critically about how they translate data and information into effective communication" (Warlick, 2005).

Information Literacy Standards

Look at the Information Literacy Standards for Student Learning developed by the American Association of School Librarians (AASL) and the Association for Educational Communications and Technology (AECT) and the National Educational Technology Standards for Students (NETS-S) developed by the International Society for Technology in Education (ISTE). Can you see how closely they align with the expectations of the ETS ICT Literacy assessment? For example, according to AASL:

"The student who is information literate

■ Accesses information efficiently and effectively

■ Evaluates information critically and competently

■ Uses information accurately and creatively"

and four of the six NETS for Students emphasize using technology as a tool for productivity, communications, research and problem-solving.

One way to see the relationship between the standards and the Big6 is in a matrix I use to teach teachers: Applying Big6 Skills, Information Literacy Standards and ISTE NETS to Internet Research. The Big6 course offered through the University of Washington's Online Learning also emphasizes using the Big6 Skills to achieve information literacy and NETS standards.

Personally, I've been directing my Big6 Skills instruction toward these standards since they were first announced, because I believe that these skills are essential for our students. David Warlick, author of *Redefining Literacy for the 21st Century*, concludes, "We live in a time when the very nature of information is changing: in what it looks like, what we use to view it, where and how we find it, what we can do with it, and how we communicate it. If this information is changing, then our sense of what it means to be literate must also change . . . If we can establish an expanded sense of what it means to be literate in this new information environment, then we may achieve more progress, in terms of better preparing children for the 21st century, by integrating contemporary literacy, instead of integrating technology" (Warlick, 2005).

The Bottom Line

According to Robert B. Reich, author of *Work of Nations: Preparing Ourselves for 21st Century Capitalism*, "Critical thinking is a central aspect of the new economy." The 2004–2005 edition of the *Occupational Outlook Handbook* asserts that "The long-term shift from goods-producing to service-providing employment is expected to continue . . . Employment growth will be driven by the increasing reliance of businesses on information technology . . . Employment in the information supersector is expected to increase by 18.5 percent, adding 632,000 jobs by 2012" (U.S. Bureau of Labor, 2004).

Marjorie Bynum, vice president of workforce development for the Information Technology Association of America, also involved in the [ETS ICT Literacy] test's development, said, "These kinds of logical reasoning tests speak to employability skills. Increasingly, we're looking at the growing importance of non-technical skills—what we call employability skills" (Brumfeld, 2005).

Helping our students achieve information literacy and critical thinking skills is an important goal, regardless of what ETS chooses to test or NCLB mandates. Today's students must be able to purposefully access information from a variety of sources, analyze and evaluate the information, and then integrate it to solve problems in life and work as well as school. They need to learn information problem-solving skills, integrated with technology research and productivity tools, in order to be employable in the 21st century. Using the Big6 Skills can help them acquire and develop these important abilities.

Sources Cited

Barrish, Todd. 2004. "ETS Launches ICT Literacy Assessment, an Online Measure of Student Information and Communication Technology Proficiency." *ETS News & Media* (November 8).

Brumfeld, Robert. 2005. "New Test Gauges ICT Literacy." *eSchool News Online* (Feb. 9), http://www.eschoolnews.com/news/PFshowstory.cfm?ArticleID=5504.

ICT Literacy Assessment: An Issue Paper from ETS. 2004. . Educational Testing Service. http://www.ets.org/Media/Tests/Information_and_Communication_Technology_Literacy/0202heapaper.pdf

St. Lifer, Evan. 2005. "Literacy Skills Are in Vogue." *School Library Journal,* 51 (2): 11.

"Tomorrow's Jobs." June 2, 2004. *Occupational Outlook Handbook.* Washington, DC: U.S. Bureau of Labor Statistics. Office of Occupational Statistics and Employment Projections.

Warlick, David. 2005. "The New Literacy." *Scholastic Administrator* (March/April).

Zeller, Tom Jr. 2005. "Measuring Literacy in a World Gone Digital." *New York Times* (Jan. 17).

Part 7: Micro Planning: Instructional Design

▶ 7.0 Introduction 181

▶ 7.1 Developing Big6™
Understandings 184

▶ 7.2 Unit & Lesson Implementation . . 185

▶ 7.3 Unit Planning Guide 186

▶ 7.4 Big6™ Unit Planning 188

▶ 7.5 Lesson Plan Format 190

▶ 7.6 Generic Lesson Plan Format 191

▶ 7.7 Big6™ Instructional Design
Checklist. 192

▶ 7.8 Big6™ Instructional Strategies. 193

▶ 7.9 Sample Super3™ Lessons. 194

▶ 7.10 Article—Motivation in Instructional
Design by Ruth Small 205

▶ 7.11 Article—Activate a Big6™ Tool to
Improve Learning (Grades 7–12)
by Bob Berkowitz 208

▶ 7.12 Article—Know Your Information Sources
(Grades 7–12) by Susan McMullen. 210

▶ 7.13 Article—Diamond Thinking
by Bob Berkowitz 212

▶ 7.14 Article—Acing the Exam
by Rick Margolis 214

▶ 7.15 Article—Moving Every Child Ahead
by Bob Berkowitz with Ferdi Serim. 218

▶ 7.16 Article—Plagiarism by
Mike Eisenberg 226

The BIG6 Micro Planning

7.0 Introduction

Learning the Big6 is cumulative—that is, students gain proficiency in the process and build skills over time. The Big6 Skills are best learned in connection with three important contexts:

- The context of the overall process itself.
- Technology integrated into the Big6 context.
- Within the context of real needs—curricular or personal.

Teachers need to design meaningful learning activities to ensure students become familiar with the overall Big6 process as well as the individual Big6 Skills. This "systematic instructional design" takes place on two levels:

- The micro level—designing integrated instructional units and lessons.
- The macro level—planning for integrated curriculum on the classroom, grade, subject area, or overall school level.

This chapter, Part 7, will focus on developing the micro level: implementing the Big6 through lessons, units, activities, worksheets, and readings. Part 9 will cover the macro level skill development—for analysis and planning.

The goal in micro instructional planning is to help classroom, library, and technology teachers learn to integrate Big6 strategies within units and lessons. The school- or classroom-defined subject area curriculum contains such units and lessons.

Students must engage in the various Big6 information problem-solving stages as part of any classroom learning experience. Therefore, students use the Big6 whenever a teacher requires them to do the following:

- Listen to a lecture or video
- Conduct an experiment
- Read from a textbook
- Complete a worksheet
- Make a project
- Take a test
- Select a topic for a project
- Do some homework

It is possible and highly desirable to weave Big6 instruction throughout existing or planned classroom instruction. The Big6 is NOT an add on—it is easy to integrate Big6 into current curriculum and classroom practices. Big6 instruction is integral to success in completing subject area goals and objectives.

The activities and worksheets in this part focus attention on the curriculum-to-Big6 connection. One key requirement—educators need to recognize the Big6 Skills within units and lessons. To this end, the questions and forms help all teachers (classroom, library, and technology) to decide upon (1) the important elements of instruction, (2) the key skills for student success—as well as where they may have difficulties, and (3) the specifics of delivering integrated instruction through units and lessons.

Part 7 concludes with a reprint of a number of Super3 and Big6 articles and sample materials. Here is a brief synopsis of each one.

ERIC Digest, "Motivation in Instructional Design," by Ruth Small, Ph.D.
This Digest explains the ARCS Model of Motivational Design. ARCS stands for:

Attention

Relevance

Confidence

Satisfaction

We find that designing integrated units and lessons from an ARCS model guarantees effective Big6 and content area learning.

Super3 Samples, included here are student handouts used in Super3 lessons. The first three handouts are from the book *The Super3: Information Skills for Young Learners* by Michael Eisenberg and Laura Robinson, Linworth 2007. There are handouts for each Super3 Stage: Plan/Beginning, Do/Middle, Review/End. The second set of handouts, "Super3 Animal Project," created by Laura Robinson, are from the *Super3 Discovery Projects: Blackline Masters for Grades K-3*, available from Big6 Associates (http://www.big6.com/product-catalog)

"Activate a Big6 Tool to Improve Learning" (Grades 7–12) by Bob Berkowitz

The tool is the KWHL Chart, a simple, yet effective organizer that students can use for planning and gathering information. Specifically, the KWHL Chart is useful when a student needs to access prior information on a topic or theme, identify needed primary and secondary resources, develop a plan for accessing resources, identify attributes and characteristics to research, and take notes on what the student is learning.

"Know Your Information Sources" (Grades 7–12) by Susan McMullen

The purpose of this article and worksheet is to help students recognize various information sources and apply appropriate criteria for selecting the best information source(s) for their particular research need. The lesson is applicable for tasks that involve any type of information seeking, research, or report writing in secondary and higher education settings.

"Diamond Thinking" by Bob Berkowitz

In this activity, students associate their ideas with the information they find. Designed for grades 6–12, Diamond Thinking is an Information Use strategy **to help** students become divergent thinkers. This **graphic organizer** activity **worksheet** encourages students to expand their ideas as they engage and extract information from material they read, hear, or view.

Worksheet 7.1:
Developing Big6™ Understandings Integrated Curriculum Situation

Create a typical, integrated curriculum situation. Describe one or two activities that relate to each of the Big6™ Skills.

Big6™ Skills	Activities
1. Task Definition 1.1 Define the problem. 1.2 Identify the information needed.	
2. Information Seeking Strategies 2.1 Determine all possible sources. 2.2 Select the best source.	
3. Location & Access 3.1 Locate sources. 3.2 Find information within sources.	
4. Use of Information 4.1 Engage (e.g., read, hear, view). 4.2 Extract relevant information.	
5. Synthesis 5.1 Organize information from multiple sources. 5.2 Present the result.	
6. Evaluation 6.1 Judge the result (effectiveness). 6.2 Judge the process (efficiency).	

The Big6™ Skills © 1987 Eisenberg & Berkowitz

Worksheet 7.2:
Unit & Lesson Implementation (Integrated Big6™-Unit Planning Guide A)

Collaborative Instructional Unit Planning: Key Questions to Ask and Answer

1. What do we want students to know, do, and be like when they finish this unit of study?

2. What are the content area objectives?

3. What are the Big6™ skills objectives?

4. Where does this fit into the overall curriculum? Note relevant local or state standards.

5. What relevant technologies might or should be used?

6. What will students do to demonstrate their new knowledge or skill?

7. How will the instructional unit be managed? (grouping, time frame, materials, etc.)

The Big6™ Skills © 1987 Eisenberg & Berkowitz

Worksheet 7.3:
Unit Planning Guide (Integrated Big6™-Unit Planning Guide B)

Unit Title	
Teacher	**Grade Level**
Subject/Topic Area	**Number of periods**
Key Words:	**Level**
Evaluation Method	**Calendar Quarter**
Primary Teaching Method	**School**

The Big6™ Skills © 1987 Eisenberg & Berkowitz

Worksheet 7.3: (*continued*)

Rationale: What do you students to know, do and be like when they finish this unit of study:

Overview: A brief summary of the nature and scope of the unit.

The BIG question(s) will guide this unit and focus teaching and learning.

Content Objectives:

BIG6 Objectives:

The Big6™ Skills © 1987 Eisenberg & Berkowitz

Worksheet 7.4:
Big6™ Unit Planning

Teacher: Subject:

Unit/Topic:

Big6™ Skills	Collaborative Instructional Planning Guide: Activities	Level of Instruction	LMS and/or Teacher	Focus
1. Task Definition 1.1 Define the problem. 1.2 Identify the information needed.				
2. Information Seeking Strategies 2.1 Determine all possible sources. 2.2 Select the best source.				
3. Location & Access 3.1 Locate sources. 3.2 Find information within sources.				
4. Use of Information 4.1 Engage (e.g., read, hear, view). 4.2 Extract relevant information.				
5. Synthesis 5.1 Organize information from multiple sources. 5.2 Present the result.				
6. Evaluation 6.1 Judge the result (effectiveness). 6.2 Judge the process (efficiency)				

The Big6™ Skills © 1987 Eisenberg & Berkowitz

Worksheet 7.4: (*continued*)

Content Outline: activities, timeframe, product/ performance, standards
How will students demonstrate what they have learned?
Task Overview
Evaluation: What evidence will show that students understand?
Teaching Materials:
Resources:
Follow-Up Activities *Optional*
Learning Activities: Description of the sequence of teaching and learning activities. *Optional*

The Big6™ Skills © 1987 Eisenberg & Berkowitz

Worksheet 7.5:
Lesson Plan Format

Subject:	Teacher:
Lesson Name:	Location:
Class:	Unit Context:
Date:	

Activities	Big6™ Skills	Subject/Area Objectives

Materials/Resources: Evaluation: Notes:

The Big6™ Skills © 1987 Eisenberg & Berkowitz

Worksheet 7.6:
Generic Lesson Plan Format

Title:

Grade Level	Related Big6™ Skills	Purpose

Learning Contexts: **Discussion:**   **Sample in Context:**

The Big6™ Skills © 1987 Eisenberg & Berkowitz

Worksheet 7.7:
Big6™ Instructional Design Checklist

Remember, you can best take advantage of the **Big6 Skills Approach** by designing challenging instructional units and assignments that are problem-solving or decision-making based.

Unit/Topic: Task Definition

_____ The assignment is well defined so students can successfully complete the requirements.

_____ The assignment includes three levels of thinking: literal, interpretive, applied.

Information Seeking Strategies

_____ Does your assignment require multiple sources?

_____ Have you consulted with the teacher-librarian and/or instructional technology teacher to determine the availability of Internet sites, and/or print sources for your students?

_____ Students are expected to use a variety of print and non-print resources (online databases, Internet, and CDROM) sources to successfully complete the assignment.

Location & Access

_____ Students know how to use the OPAC (online public access catalog) to find library resources.

_____ You met with the teacher-librarian to determine that students have been taught search skills or need to learn to locate information in Internet sites and print sources.

Use of Information

_____ Students are expected to use graphic organizers/note sheets that require them to cite their sources.

_____ Students are required to evaluate the sources of information they use.

Synthesis

_____ Does your assignment encourage students to present information in the form of graphs?

Evaluation

_____ Students have a scoring guide or rubric and that will allow them to assess the quality of their work: product and process.

The Big6™ Skills © 1987 Eisenberg & Berkowitz

Worksheet 7.8:
Big6™ Instructional Strategies

Title:

Grade Level	Related Big6™ Skills	Purpose

Learning Contexts: **Discussion:**   **Sample in Context:**

The Big6™ Skills © 1987 Eisenberg & Berkowitz

7.9 Sample Super3™ Lessons

Worksheet 7.9: Sample Super3™—Plan

Name:_____

Plan 3

What will I need to complete my task?

Computer	Art Supplies	Books

Teacher	Family/Friends	Paper/Pencil

Other:	Other:	Other:

Worksheet 7.10:
Sample Super3™—Do

Name:_____

Do 2

Touch (feeling)

Smell (smelling)

Sound (hearing)

Sight (seeing)

Taste (tasting)

Worksheet 7.11:
Sample Super3™—Review

Name:_____

Review 2

I followed all directions. 😊 😠 😢

I found all the information I needed. 😊 😠 😢

I answered all questions. 😊 😠 😢

I did my best work. 😊 😠 😢

I checked my work for mistakes. 😊 😠 😢

Instructor's Guide

Super3 Animal Project

Objective/Purpose:

Students will learn about a specific animal including what it looks like, what it eats, where it lives, and other interesting facts about it.

The educational objective is to establish sound research skills during early elementary learning. This high interest topic will engage learners as they develop research skills.

Context for Use:

Teacher-librarians may use the animal project to teach early library research skills. Students can complete the task in a linear manner, reinforcing the Super3 problem solving stages: beginning, middle, and end.

It's appropriate to use this animal project after teaching a curriculum unit on animal groups.

The animal recording sheet may be used as an assessment tool after the class has learned about a particular animal.

Ideas for Teaching and Learning:

Introduce various animal groups and talk about their similarities and differences. Encourage students to think about what types of animals interest them and might be good subjects for their research, including:

- **Zoo animals**
- **Jungle animals**
- **Farm animals**
- **Animals of Africa**
- **Family pets**
- **Insects**
- **Fish**
- **Birds**
- **Mammals,**
- **Reptiles**
- **Amphibians**

Discuss the different information sources/resources— the internet, animal books, encyclopedias, veterinarians, pet store owners—that students may use throughout this project.

Review relevant vocabulary terms:

Amphibians – cold blooded vertebrates that typically live in the water and breathe using gills. Adult amphibians breathe using lungs and through their moist skin. Amphibians include frogs, toads, and salamanders.

Birds – warm-blooded, egg-laying, feathered vertebrates that have forelimbs modified to form wings.

Fish – cold-blooded, water vertebrates, having gills, fins, and a body covered with scales.

Habitat – the natural area or environment where a person or animal lives.

Insects – small arthropods with three pairs of legs and a body segmented into a head, thorax, and abdomen. Insects include flies, beetles, mosquitoes, and bees.

Mammals – warm-blooded animals with a covering of hair on the skin. Their young are born alive and are nourished with milk from their mother.

Reptiles – egg-laying, cold blooded animals with a covering of scales or horny plates. Reptiles include snakes, lizards, turtles, and crocodiles.

Extension Activities:

Select an animal class mascot and complete the animal project as a whole class for the chosen mascot.

Students may complete the **Do: Middle** stage as a whole class activity where students record information about a specific animal on the recording sheet while the instructor reads aloud from various information sources.

Students may draw their animal and write a fictional story about a day in the life of their animal.

The class could combine their animal projects to create a whole class animal book.

Super3 Animal Project Instructor's Guide, Page 1

Figure 7.1

Eisenberg, M. and Robinson, L. (2010) *Super3 Animal Project Instructor's Guide*, Blackline Masters, B6 Media.

Instructor's Guide

Super3 Animal Project

Project Overview

1. Plan: Beginning

Students will think about their task and will record what they need to do for this project, how they will get their information, and the supplies they will need in order to complete the task.

> For example, "I would like to learn more about sheep. I will look in the *Farm Animals* book and will go to the book's pages about sheep. I will read the details and find three facts to note on my paper.
>
> I will need some paper and a pencil, my animal packet, animal books, and colored pencils."

2. Do: Middle

Students will draw a picture of their animal and will write three facts they learned about their animal, noting where they found their information, with stickers or drawings.

Students can draw their animal in its natural habitat and use the animal recording page to explain and/or draw what their animal looks like, what it eats, where it lives, and other interesting facts about the animal.

Younger students may complete only one **Do: Middle** worksheet, while older students may complete both pages.

3. Review: End

Students will think about and reflect on their work. Students will identify their favorite part and the part of the project that they found to be the hardest.

> For example, "My favorite part was drawing a picture of my animal and the hardest part was finding three new facts about my animal."

New Words/Glossary - In this section, students will identify and define any unfamiliar words. Students may use a dictionary to help define the word. Younger students may write the word and then draw a picture to help define the word.

Resources - To cite a resource, younger students may use citation stickers or draw simple pictures. Older students may write each source's title and publication date.

Super3 Animal Project Instructor's Guide, Page 2

Figure 7.1 (*continued*)

Eisenberg, M. and Robinson, L. (2010) *Super3 Animal Project Instructor's Guide*, Blackline Masters, B6 Media.

Worksheet 7.12:
My Super3™ Animal Project Cover Page

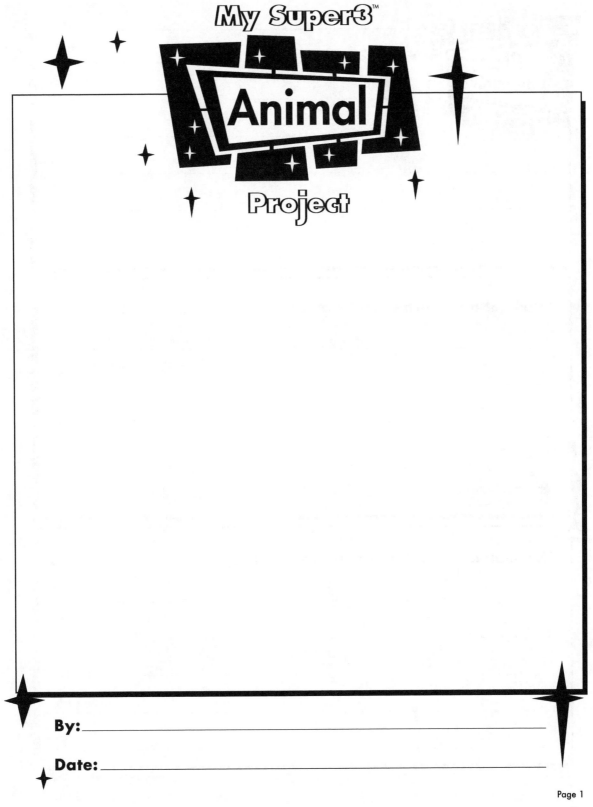

By: _____

Date: _____

Eisenberg, M. and Robinson, L. (2010) *Super3 Animal Project Instructor's Guide*, Blackline Masters, B6 Media.

Worksheet 7.13:
My Super3™ Animal Project—Plan

Plan: Beginning

For this project I need to:_____

_____

_____

_____

_____

I will get my information from:_____

_____

_____

_____

_____

MY PLAN

The supplies I need for my project are:_____

_____

_____

_____

_____

_____

My Super3 Animal Project, Page 2

Eisenberg, M. and Robinson, L. (2010) *Super3 Animal Project Instructor's Guide*, Blackline Masters, B6 Media.

Worksheet 7.14:
My Super3™ Animal Project—Do I

Do:
Middle

My animal: _____

My animal looks like this:

Here are three facts about my animal:

1. _____

_____

2. _____

_____

3. _____

_____

Eisenberg, M. and Robinson, L. (2010) *Super3 Animal Project Instructor's Guide*, Blackline Masters, B6 Media.

Worksheet 7.15:
My Super3™ Animal Project—Do II

Do:
Middle

Animal Recording Sheet

This is the animal I learned about:

_____

The information I gathered is from:

_____

My animal looks like this:	**My animal eats this:**

My animal lives in a place like this:	**One interesting fact about my animal is:**

Eisenberg, M. and Robinson, L. (2010) *Super3 Animal Project Instructor's Guide*, Blackline Masters, B6 Media.

Worksheet 7.16:
My Super3™ Animal Project—Review I

Review: End

My favorite part of this project was:

_____

_____

_____

_____

Sam

The hardest part of this project was:

_____

_____

_____

_____

My Super3 Animal Project, Page 5

Eisenberg, M. and Robinson, L. (2010) *Super3 Animal Project Instructor's Guide*, Blackline Masters, B6 Media.

Worksheet 7.17:
My Super3™ Animal Project—Review II

Review: End

New Words/Glossary

Word	Definition
1. _____	_____
	_____
2. _____	_____
	_____
3. _____	_____
	_____
4. _____	_____
	_____

Resource and Book List

1. _____

2. _____

3. _____

my source

my source

my source

My Super3 Animal Project, Page 6

Eisenberg, M. and Robinson, L. (2010) *Super3 Animal Project Instructor's Guide*, Blackline Masters, B6 Media.

7.10 Article—Motivation in Instructional Design

by Ruth Small

ERIC Digest

Introduction

Developing life-long learners who are intrinsically motivated, display intellectual curiosity, find learning enjoyable, and continue seeking knowledge after their formal instruction has ended has always been a major goal of education. Early motivational research was conducted primarily in the workplace, and centered on ways to motivate industrial workers to work harder, faster, and better.

More recent motivational research focuses on the identification of effective techniques for enhancing instructional design, improving classroom management, and meeting the needs of diverse student populations (Wlodkowski, 1981). Learning-motivation researchers are applying some of the same theories and concepts found to be effective in industry to the development of motivational models that enhance the teaching-learning environment. One such model is the ARCS Model of Motivational Design developed by John M. Keller of Florida State University (Keller, 1983, 1987). ARCS is a systematic model for designing motivating instruction. This digest will describe the ARCS Model, and will outline some of the ways in which ARCS components may be applied to instructional design.

The ARCS Model of Motivational Design

The ARCS Model of Motivational Design is a well-known and widely applied model of instructional design. Simple, yet powerful, the ARCS Model is rooted in a number of motivational theories and concepts (see Keller, 1983), most notably expectancy-value theory (e.g. Vroom, 1964; Porter and Lawler, 1968).

In expectancy-value theory, "effort" is identified as the major measurable motivational outcome. For "effort" to occur, two necessary prerequisites are specified: (1) the person must value the task and (2) the person must believe he or she can succeed at the task. Therefore, in an instructional situation, the learning task needs to be presented in a way that is engaging and meaningful to the student, and in a way that promotes positive expectations for the successful achievement of learning objectives.

The ARCS Model identifies four essential strategy components for motivating instruction:

> [A]ttention strategies for arousing and sustaining curiosity and interest;
>
> [R]elevance strategies that link to learners' needs, interests, and motives;
>
> [C]onfidence strategies that help students develop a positive expectation for successful achievement; and
>
> [S]atisfaction strategies that provide extrinsic and intrinsic reinforcement for effort (Keller, 1983).

Keller (1987) breaks each of the four ARCS components down into three strategy sub-components. The strategy sub-components and instructionally relevant examples are shown below.

Attention

Perceptual Arousal: provide novelty, surprise, incongruity or uncertainty. Ex. The teacher places a sealed box covered with question marks on a table in front of the class.

Inquiry Arousal: stimulate curiosity by posing questions or problems to solve. Ex. The teacher presents a scenario of a problem situation and asks the class to brainstorm possible solutions based on what they have learned in the lesson.

Variability: incorporate a range of methods and media to meet students' varying needs. Ex. After displaying and reviewing each step in the process on the overhead projector, the teacher divides the class into teams and assigns each team a set of practice problems.

Relevance

Goal Orientation: present the objectives and useful purpose of the instruction and specific methods for successful achievement. Ex. The teacher explains the objectives of the lesson.

Motive Matching: match objectives to student needs and motives. Ex. The teacher allows the students to present their projects in writing or orally to accommodate different learning needs and styles.

Familiarity: present content in ways that are understandable and that are related to the learners' experience and values. Ex. The teacher asks the students to provide examples from their own experiences for the concept presented in class.

Confidence

Learning Requirements: inform students about learning and performance requirements and assessment criteria. Ex. The teacher provides students with a list of assessment criteria for their research projects and circulates examples of exemplary projects from past years.

Success Opportunities: provide challenging and meaningful opportunities for successful learning. Ex. The teacher allows the students to practice extracting and summarizing information from various sources and then provides feedback before the students begin their research projects.

Personal Responsibility: link learning success to students' personal effort and ability. Ex. The teacher provides written feedback on the quality of the students' performance and acknowledges the students' dedication and hard work.

Satisfaction

Intrinsic Reinforcement: encourage and support intrinsic enjoyment of the learning experience. Ex. The teacher invites former students to provide testimonials on how learning these skills helped them with subsequent homework and class projects.

Extrinsic Rewards: provide positive reinforcement and motivational feedback. Ex. The teacher awards certificates to students as they master the complete set of skills.

Equity: maintain consistent standards and consequences for success. Ex. After the term project has been completed, the teacher provides evaluative feedback using the criteria described in class.

Motivation Assessment Instruments

Since the ARCS Model was introduced in the early 1980s, several instruments have been developed for assessing the motivational quality of instructional situations. The Instructional Materials Motivation Survey (IMMS) (Keller, 1987) asks students to rate 36 ARCS-related statements in relation to the instructional materials they have just used. Some examples are:

"These materials are eye-catching." (Attention)
"It is clear to me how the content of this material is related to things I already know." (Relevance)
"As I worked on this lesson, I was confident that I could learn the content." (Confidence)
"Completing the exercises in this lesson gave me a satisfying feeling of accomplishment." (Satisfaction)

Keller and Keller (1989) developed the Motivational Delivery Checklist, a 47-item ARCS-based instrument for evaluating the motivational characteristics of an instructor's classroom delivery. Examples of items related to each ARCS component are:

"Uses questions to pose problems or paradoxes." (Attention)
"Uses language and terminology appropriate to learners and their context." (Relevance)
"Provides feedback on performance promptly." (Confidence)
"Makes statements giving recognition and credit to learners as appropriate." (Satisfaction)

The Website Motivational Analysis Checklist (WebMAC) (Small, 1997) is an instrument used for designing and assessing the motivational quality of

World Wide Web sites. WebMAC builds on Keller's work (1987a; 1987b; 1989), Taylor's Value-Added Model (1986), and the research on relevance and information retrieval (e.g. Schamber, 1994). Still in development and testing, WebMAC identifies 60 items that are categorized according to four general characteristics: Engaging, Meaningful, Organized, and Enjoyable. Some examples of items are:

"Eye-catching title and/or visual on home page." (Engaging)
"User-controlled type of information accessed." (Meaningful)
"Logical sequence of information." (Organized)
"Links to other websites of interest." (Enjoyable)

Summary

The ARCS Model of Motivational Design is an easy-to-apply, heuristic approach to increasing the motivational appeal of instruction. ARCS provides a useful framework for both the design and improvement of the motivational quality of a range of informational entities—from classroom instruction to Internet resources—and increases the likelihood that these entities will be used and enjoyed.

References and Related Readings

Chemotti, J. T. 1992, June. "From Nuclear Arms to Hershey's Kisses: Strategies for Motivating Students." *School Library Media Activities Monthly*, 8 (10): 34–36. (EJ 446 223)

Keller, J. M. 1983. "Motivational Design of Instruction." In *Instructional Design Theories and Models: An Overview of Their Current Status,* ed. C. M. Reigeluth. Hillsdale, NJ: Erlbaum, 1983.

Keller, J. M. 1987a, Oct. "Strategies for Stimulating the Motivation to Learn." *Performance and Instruction*, 26 (8): 1–7. (EJ 362 632)

Keller, J. M. 1987b. "IMMS: Instructional Materials Motivation Survey." Tallahassee: Florida State University.

Keller, J. M., and B. H. Keller. 1989. *Motivational Delivery Checklist.* Tallahassee: Florida State University.

Porter, L. W., and E. E. Lawler. 1968. *Managerial Attitudes and Performance.* Homewood, IL: Dorsey Press.

Schamber, L. 1994. "Relevance and Information Behavior." In *Annual Review of Information Science and Technology.* Medford, NJ: Learned Information, Inc. (EJ 491 620)

Small, R. V. 1992, Apr. "Taking AIM: Approaches to Instructional Motivation." *School Library Media Activities Monthly,* 8 (8): 32–34.

Small, R. V. 1997. "Assessing the Motivational Quality of World Wide Websites." ERIC Clearinghouse on Information and Technology. (ED 407 930, IR 018 331)

Taylor, R. S. 1986. "Value-Added Processes in Information Systems." Norwood, NJ: Ablex. (ISBN: 0–89391–273–5)

Vroom, V. H. 1964. *Work and Motivation.* New York: Wiley.

Wlodkowski, R. J. 1981. Making Sense out of Motivation: A Systematic Model to Consolidate Motivational Constructs across Theories. *Educational Psychologist,* 16 (2): 101–10.

. . . . .

This ERIC Digest was prepared by Ruth V. Small, associate professor of Information Studies at Syracuse University, Syracuse, New York.

ERIC Digests are in the public domain and may be freely reproduced and disseminated.

ERIC Clearinghouse on Information & Technology, Syracuse University, 621 Skytop Rd. Suite 160, Syracuse, New York 13244–4100; (315) 443–3640; (800) 464–9107; Fax: (315) 443–5448; E-mail: eric@ericir.syr.edu; URL: http://ericit.org/

This publication was prepared with funding from the Office of Educational Research and Improvement, U.S. Department of Education under contract no. RR93002009. The opinions expressed in this report do not necessarily reflect the positions of OERI or ED.

7.11 Article—Activate a Big6™ Tool to Improve Learning (Grades 7–12)

by Bob Berkowitz

Here is a recipe for improvement. It's a twist on an old idea. Maybe you have used a "KWL" graphic organizer before, but one Big6 modification links a series of questions to your research goal. To the old "KWL" Chart, simply add an "H." That one change can turn an old idea into a new, best strategy when you need to make sense of your task and organize a lot of information—its now a "KWHL" Chart.

K—Stands for what you KNOW about the subject.

W—Stands for determining what you WANT to learn.

H—Stands for HOW you can learn more (sources where additional information on the topic can be found).

L—Stands for identifying what you LEARN as you read.

The KWHL Chart is a simple, yet effective organizer that you can use for planning and gathering information. Specifically, the KWHL Chart is useful when you need to access prior information on a topic or theme, identify needed primary and secondary resources, develop a plan for accessing resources, identify attributes and characteristics to research, and take notes on what you are learning.

The KWHL Chart is an excellent tool you can use as a plan for investigation. A KWHL inquiry chart can include questions about predictions and/or implications. Additionally, these charts can be used as a basis to formulate a hypothesis, or research question, with confirmation or refutation as your research progresses.

Throughout the research process add information to your KWHL Chart. One trick you may want to try is to use different color marking pens each time you add information to the chart. This technique will give you a visual representation of the knowledge acquired throughout your research experience.

An example of a KWHL Chart has these headings:

■ "What we know about _____,"

■ "What we want to learn about _____,"

■ "How can I find information about _____,"

■ "What we learned about _____," and

■ "How This Relates to Us."

Other questions you can ask in a matrix format are shown in the example below.

■ What do I already know?

■ What do I want to find out?

■ How am I going to find out?

■ What did I learn?

Worksheet 7.18:
Activate a Big6™ Tool to Improve Learning (Grades 7–12)

WHAT DO I ALREADY KNOW?	
WHAT DO I WANT TO FIND OUT?	
HOW AM I GOING TO FIND OUT?	
WHAT DID I LEARN?	

The Big6™ Skills © 1987 Eisenberg & Berkowitz

7.12 Article—Know Your Information Sources (Grades 7–16)

by Susan McMullen

Related Information Literacy Skills: Big6 #2—Information Seeking Strategies

Purpose: To help students recognize various information sources and to apply appropriate criteria for selecting the best information source(s) for their particular research need.

Learning Contexts: The lesson is applicable for tasks that involve any type of information seeking, research, or report writing in secondary and higher education settings.

Discussion: When confronted with a research project, students are frequently either overwhelmed by or uninformed about their information source choices. Today's students frequently equate information seeking with the World Wide Web. They do not realize that there are a wide variety of information choices available to them, each requiring different finding methods. This exercise will help students identify different sources of information, their quality and content, and understand how they are organized. By understanding the various types of information and where information comes from, students will recognize appropriate sources for specific seeking or research topics.

Sample in Context: This lesson begins with a brainstorming activity in which the instructor asks the students to identify different information sources. If the class is small, each student may be asked to give one source. The instructor and students then review the "Know Your Information Sources" handout to get familiar with the major resources. Once familiar with these major resources, students are asked to complete the "What Source Would You Use" exercise. After this initial preparation, students are then asked to apply appropriate selection criteria to their information task.

Item: Know Your Information Sources
Using the "Know Your Information Sources" handout, determine the best information source(s) to use in the situations presented in the "What Source Would You Use" exercise. Upon completing the exercise, think about your own information task. As you prepare for research, think about the questions on the bottom half of the exercise sheet. Your answers will help you determine the most useful sources for locating information on your topic.

Worksheet 7.19:
Know Your Information Sources (Grades 7–16)

by Susan McMullen

What Source Would You Use?

N = Newspaper, PM = Popular Magazine, SJ = Scholarly Journal,
R = Reference Book, B = Book, W = Web, P = Person
Hint: You may select more than one source.

_____ to find statistics on the number of working mothers with children under the age of five

_____ to locate an in-depth article about the level of absenteeism among working mothers with children under the age of five

_____ to find out information about the day care center that XYZ corporation opened in your home town

_____ to learn about presentations offered at the National Association for Family Child Care Conference in July 2003

_____ to find current analysis of how working mothers in the 21st century are coping with child care issues

_____ to find out how much families are paying for child care

_____ to read a detailed analysis of child-care options in the workplace

_____ to learn about companies that are offering child care at the workplace

7.13 Article—Diamond Thinking by Bob Berkowitz Diamond Thinking (Grades 6–12)

by Bob Berkowitz

Related Big6™ Skills: Big6™ #4—Use of Information

Purpose: In this activity, students associate their ideas with the information they find.

Learning Contexts: Grades 6–12. Diamond Thinking is an Information Use strategy that helps students become divergent thinkers. This activity encourages students to expand their ideas as they engage and extract information from material they read, hear, or view.

Discussion: Ask students to list information from their research in the "Information" diamond (left diamond). Students then respond to that information by writing their thoughts in the "My Thoughts" diamond (right diamond). Information in the "My Thoughts" diamond may be based upon personal opinion or experience. In addition, students may fill in the "My Thoughts" with questions that were not answered by information they read, heard, or viewed.

Variation: One variation is to switch the headings and make "My Thoughts" in the left diamond, and "Information" in the right column. Using this variation, students begin by listing their ideas and opinions, and through research, complete the right diamond with information that validates or disputes their opinion.

Item: Diamond Thinking handout

Sample in Context:

Students in Mr. Lake's 12th grade health class are working on a communicable diseases unit. Mr. Lake's assignment includes accessing and locating information on the Web about communicable diseases. To help students personalize the experience, he uses the "Diamond Thinking" strategy.

As students locate and read Web-based information on their topics from the pre-selected sites, they complete the left diamond with four facts that relate to how the disease is transmitted. These facts are placed in the "Information" diamonds.

Students respond with their opinion or personal experience in the corresponding right "My Thoughts" diamond. In this way, students are able to provide their own strategies about preventing the spread of communicable diseases.

As an extension of this assignment, students may continue their research to determine the effectiveness or viability of their recommendations. Students proceed down the Diamond Thinking handout until they've completed their assignment. It is easy to see how Diamond Thinking can act as a springboard for a variety of extension activities.

Worksheet 7.20: Diamond Thinking (Grades 6–12)

by Bob Berkowitz

While you're researching your topic, use the graphic organizer below to record and think about what you've read, heard, or viewed. This exercise will help you become a divergent thinker and will help you expand your ideas as you gather (engage and extract) information from sources.

1. In the "Information" diamond below, list facts you've read, heard, or viewed about your topic.
2. In the "My Thoughts" diamond, list your thoughts, feelings, experiences, or unanswered questions that relate to your facts in the "Information" diamond.

Topic: _____

Information	My Thoughts
Information	My Thoughts
Information	My Thoughts

7.14 Article—Acing the Exam

By Rick Margolis
School Library Journal, 10/1/2002

How can librarians boost students' test scores? Bob Berkowitz shares a strategy for success.

Bob Berkowitz is tackling one of his favorite topics, high-stakes tests—those thorny competency-based exams that many students must pass before receiving their high school diplomas. As the accountability movement in American education continues to swell, an increasing number of states, including Connecticut, Texas, Michigan, and New York, have turned to formal assessments to gauge students' understanding of such disparate subjects as history, biology, language arts, physics, math, and foreign languages. In the anxiety-laden realm of big-time testing, Berkowitz is the equivalent of Mr. Goodwrench, seemingly able to fix whatever ails struggling students and perplexed instructors. In short, he's a school librarian who knows how to help kids become more sophisticated thinkers and, by extension, more savvy test takers.

The secret of Berkowitz's success is embodied in the Big6™, a generic problem-solving strategy that he and his colleague Mike Eisenberg, now dean of the University of Washington's School of Information, invented in the late 1980s. The Big6™ approach, as its name suggests, distills the decision-making process into six discrete, interrelated skills: task definition, information-seeking strategies, location and access, use of information, synthesis, and evaluation. (For more details, visit <www.big6.org>.)

The 54-year-old Berkowitz, a library media specialist at Wayne Central High School in Ontario Center, NY, is an unabashed Big6™ booster—and for good reason. Five years ago, for example, he helped transform Scott Hopsicker, a fledgling social studies teacher at Wayne Central High, into an instructional dynamo. At the time, Hopsicker's students had performed poorly on New York's American History Regents Examination: for two consecutive years, scarcely more than 50% scraped by. Yet after working with Berkowitz, an impressive 91% of his class sailed successfully through the test. More recently, Berkowitz has had similar results in the sciences, helping teacher Mike Carges prime his Wayne Central students for the advanced placement test in physics. We spoke to Berkowitz about how librarians can play a leading role in helping students excel on tough formal tests.

Describe your approach to improving students' test scores

The [most important] thing for me is this notion that instruction is a series of information problems—a very empowering idea for school librarians. What it says is that if you have an information problem-solving model as your curriculum, then you can use that model to design instruction and to teach skills so that students engage the content. Whenever you have a problem to solve or a decision to make, you can use this approach. It doesn't matter whether you're interested in finding out if whales swim on their backs, if chickens have elbows, what movie you want to go to on Friday night, or if it's the right time to refinance your mortgage.

Talk about working with teacher Scott Hopsicker

Scott is a highly motivated young teacher. We analyzed the Regents Examination and the curriculum. We also looked at his prior teaching strategy, his approach to teaching. We had to develop a collaborative relationship, things that we believed in together. For example, we brainstormed on the characteristics that were indicative of high-quality instruction. We wanted to move students from being dependent learners to being independent learners. We wanted students to be able to incorporate higher-order thinking skills, because the examinations at the end [of the year] require analysis, synthesis, and evaluation. [The exams] also require being able to move from literal to interpretive to applied levels of thinking. We wanted to incorporate [those critical thinking skills] into our instructional models.

What we found was that in the prior year when we looked over the way he taught and his instructional materials and reviewed his lesson-plan book, we discovered that he was teaching a lot of content and [neglecting] the [problem-solving] processes needed to engage that content.

Is that characteristic of most teachers?

I think that most teachers approach instruction that way. So we taught kids how to think like social scientists. Right or wrong, we decided that we were going to teach social studies as a cause-and-effect relationship between social, political, and economic [factors] and foreign affairs.

Can you give an example of what an emphasis on process, rather than content, looks like in the classroom?

One of the early assignments was a fairly traditional assignment. It was to have students make a salt map of a country that had geographic features. We had students look at the impact of rivers on social, political, economic, and foreign affairs. The impact of mountains on social, political, economic, and foreign affairs. The impact of deserts on social [events]. In other words, what's the cause-and-effect relationship of geography to this discourse. Many of these [high-stakes] exams—the Regents exam and the state competency kinds of exams—are quite willing to give students information. But what they're asking students is to use those higher-order thinking skills—analysis, interpretation, the application of information—to solve a problem or answer a question.

In the elementary school, the cue words that lead you to this notion of problem solving [are] "who," "what," "when," "where," "why," [and] "how." Those are cue words to knowing that you have a problem to solve or a decision to make. In a secondary [education] situation, those morph or change into [words] like "compare" and "contrast" and "evaluate," "analyze," "discuss." Those are all, in effect, the first words to questions on the examinations.

I encouraged him to use these kinds of questions in his teaching to move students toward a higher order of thinking. He began asking questions: "What are the relationships between?" "How does this compare to?" "What is the effect on?" "How would this change if?" He moved his questioning techniques from the literal level to this interpretative and applied thinking level. That was real hard for him.

Talk more about the nuts and bolts of making your approach work with teachers.

[Scott and I] invested a lot of time and energy into designing instruction from the perspective that I've outlined. We met formally at least twice a week for two 50-minute planning periods. Additionally, I might have spent another hour working on some aspect of a project that we were collaborating on. He might have spent two or three or [as much as] six hours during the week working on projects, designing his instruction, and then bringing that information back the next time [we met]. We were continually working on instructional activities and units, continually talking about theory and approach. As we got toward the third quarter and fourth quarter [of the school year], he became more knowledgeable, more sophisticated: one of my goals was to make him an independent Big6er. Over time, the amount of time we spent together decreased. He became more competent.

What are some of the specific ways you collaborated with him?

I did a number of things. I observed his class as a mentor. I did a little bit of co-teaching with him. I did a lot of instructional design with him. In other words, he and I would jointly design instructional units and activities. It goes back to the notion that on one side [of the learning process] there's this content and on the other side, there's Big6™. Scott knows his content. The problem wasn't that he wasn't teaching the content. The problem was that he wasn't also [initially] teaching the [problem-solving] process. So kids didn't know when to engage the content. If they couldn't, for example, analyze what the question required them to do, which is task definition, they weren't able to engage the content he had taught them. They didn't have the right cue. Or, if they didn't practice self-evaluation, they never knew when they were finished. They didn't know what it took to earn an "A," because Scott hadn't considered the notion of evaluation as being important.

How can the average library media specialist begin replicating your success with Scott?

There are some key ideas in activating this collaborative process with teachers. I think school library media specialists need to take the initiative. They need to meet with administrators. The principal is the instructional leader in the school. The administrator needs to know what your approach is, what your curriculum is, what your goals are. Administrators are interested in student performance, student success, and student achievement.

So you addressed all of those concerns?

Absolutely. And early on when I got here, there was a situation with a faculty person who was teaching advanced placement social studies. His students were doing really poorly on a document-based question that appeared on those exams back in the early '80s. I was able to go in, collaboratively design instructional strategies with this teacher, and the scores improved immensely. All of a sudden, I built a lot of value. There was a lot of credibility to what I was saying. In a period of a few months, the scores changed drastically by doing the same basic things—going over and over and over again—what we were talking about relative to Scott Hopsicker. So taking the initiative, I think, is important.

I also think it's important to identify the teachers that you can work with. You know, sometimes those are the early adopters, sometimes they're your friends. Identifying those people who you can best and most easily work with, so you can build some chits, you build some credit. I start with three questions: What do I want to have happen? How can I make it happen? What am I going to accept as evidence that it's going on? I get really focused on those ideas. Trying to find answers to those three questions is really important to me.

Is there anything else you'd like librarians to know?

It's not that I believe in teaching to the test, because there are a lot of people that talk about teaching to the test. What I'm trying to suggest is that the test is a step on the way to something else. The something else, or goal, is that we want students to become lifelong learners. We want students to be able to analyze, synthesize, and evaluate the events and information that impact their daily lives.

Librarians are in a unique position to help that happen. School library media specialists are the only ones with the unique set of training as information professionals in the schools. That's our bread and butter, that's our raison d'être as information specialists. No one else in the school has that area of expertise. They're all content experts. We have this professional obligation to act as consultants and collaborators in instructional design and development.

Author Information

Rick Margolis is SLJ's news and features editor

© 2003 Reed Business Information Reprinted with permission.

Margolis, R. (Oct. 2002). Acing the exam: How can librarians boost student's test scores? *School Library Journal* *48(10)* p. 50–52.

7.15 Article—Moving Every Child Ahead: The Big6™ Success Strategy

By Bob Berkowitz, Library Media Specialist, Wayne Central School, Ontario Center, New York, with Ferdi Serim, MultiMedia Schools Editor

MultiMedia Schools, *May/June 2002*

Leaving No Child Behind: High-Stakes Testing as Information Problem Solving

In far too many schools, the prospect of annual testing for all students in grades 3–8 has needlessly paralyzed progress toward education reform and technology integration. As schools circle the wagons to meet the challenge of high-stakes tests, fear-based responses often sacrifice the higher-order-thinking, project-based-learning approaches, upon which successful uses of technology depend, in favor of rote learning. Our cover story features a proven strategy, which instead *improves performance by improving thinking* on the part of teachers and students alike. The powerful partnership of Bob Berkowitz and Scott Hopsicker, using the Big6™ process, gives us a working model for seizing this opportunity to advance effective teaching and learning by treating the tests themselves as information-based problems.

The Big6™ is the most widely known and used approach to teaching information and technology skills in the world. Used in thousands of K–12 schools, higher-education institutions, and corporate adult training programs, the Big6™ information problem-solving model is applicable whenever people need and use information. The Big6™ integrates information search and use skills along with technology tools in a systematic process to find, use, apply, and evaluate information to specific needs and tasks. Mike Eisenberg, co-creator of the Big6™ along with Bob Berkowitz, says, "Our mission is to help all people succeed by becoming better information problem-solvers. We live in an increasingly complex information- and technology-rich world. Information and technology skills are the 'new basics.' Being able to find and use information more effectively is essential to the success of students of all ages—pre-K through adult."

As this is the most vital issue facing our profession, I encourage you to share this story with your administrators, your school board, your community, and your peers. Together, we can work our way beyond teaching to the test, to the higher ground of improved learning for all.

—Ferdi Serim

An All-Too-Common Problem

Scott Hopsicker was a social studies teacher at Wayne Central High School, near Rochester, New York, when he first came to see me in 1997–1998. Even though he'd been at Wayne Central for only two years, Scott was a very active and popular teacher. He was involved in coaching as well as teaching and was well liked by his students. But he had a problem. In his first year as a teacher, Scott's students did not perform well on the New York State Regents Exam in American History. Remembering that first year, Scott says, "Only 53% passed, and I was horrified. I looked at myself first. I didn't blame the kids. I went to Bob soon afterwards."

Concerned about his students, and wanting to do something to help them improve their scores, Scott spoke to our assistant principal, who suggested that he discuss the situation with me, in my role as the school's library media specialist. Since I'd succeeded in helping students on advanced placement tests in various subjects, perhaps I could help. Scott saw himself as a conscientious, well-prepared teacher. He obviously needed a new strategy. Enter the Big6™.

First thing, when Scott came by and dropped off a couple of binders, I said, "I can tell you right now—you probably taught every small fact, being a first-year teacher, and you didn't actually teach concepts or themes." He was more of an instructor than a teacher. Scott recalls, "I presented information and then expected the students to keep up to date on it—I was assuming things."

Eyes on the Prize

What motivates teachers? Student performance! But this involves far more than test scores, far more than "covering the content." The test is nothing more than an interim objective to a greater goal: moving students from teacher-dependent to independent and lifelong learners. People often focus on what they want kids to know and be able to do. We add to this how we want them to be: capable, confident, independent learners.

We wanted to turn the exam experience into the basis for a powerful learning experience. To do this, you have to know: Which race are you running? Which skills are you practicing? If you are in the hurdles, and all you do is practice running, never practicing jumping, on the day of the race, you're going to be in for a sad surprise! So we had to analyze all the skills required and match these up with the processes and how the content would be used to gain these skills.

The Big6™: An Umbrella Strategy

The Big6™ approach to information-based problem solving provided Scott and me with the tools we needed to reinvent his teaching. This may sound bold, but anything less would not have done the job. Working as his coach and mentor throughout the year, we treated instructional design as a series of information-based problems or decisions. This allowed Scott to change his style of teaching from a content-driven approach to a Big6™ information-process-driven approach. The payoff was huge.

After one year, his students went from a 53% passing rate to 91%. The next year the rate rose to 99%, with 75% of the students attaining mastery level. The third year (and beyond) has continued this pattern of success.

Such success required time and effort. For the entire year, I spent two hours each week with Scott, along with an additional two hours of follow-up on my own as I did my "information professional" homework. Scott spent six hours per week of his prep time—at least two of his three prep periods based on a four-day rotation—doing his homework. Then Scott had me come in and observe his teaching, so I could see his styles and strengths as well as some of his weaknesses. I also wanted to see the kids in action and how they reacted to Scott. Then we came up with activities and projects. He would tell me what content things he wanted them to know. I helped Scott decide what we wanted to base the projects on, and how often. *[Editor's note: These experiences form the basis of a new series ofBig6™ workshops and conference presentations designed to expand the reach of what's been learned. See <http://www.big6.com>.]*

Scott Hopsicker is quite direct and unapologetic. "My goal is to make my students successful on the test. Yes, we use Regents essays and questions, but we really don't water down the curriculum. We did projects in addition to the essay preparation and test-taking work. We created cause-and-effect projects so the students can see how everything is connected together, not just little pieces and fragments. History is all one piece—all one smooth flow. It's kind of like reading a book from start to finish; everything is connected somehow."

Instructional Design: A Series of Information-Based Decisions

We knew that to move from a content-driven to an information-process-driven basis of instruction, we needed to learn more about the characteristics of high-quality instruction, which include the following:

- Higher-order thinking skills
- Repetition of good practices
- Moving from teacher-dependent to independent student learning behaviors
- Levels of learning: literal, interpretive, applied

Unlike other information problem solving strategies, the Big6™ is both diagnostic and prescriptive. This is the key difference, an empowering difference, to the Big6™ approach. We look at the process, as well as student performance, all along the way. We get rid of ineffective practices that are dragging us down. We not only see what's working (and what needs to work better), but we and our students see how to change, to bring us to our goal.

For example, in a content-driven model, we focus on standards, on what is taught (teacher behavior). However, we don't focus as much on what is learned (student behavior) until the test, when it is often too late. Moving from high-stakes tests to higher-order thinking requires a different framework for instruction. Providing the tools and skills to build meaning gives them the foundation they need for understanding, not just regurgitation of short-term factoids.

Scott Hopsicker's Study Tips

© Berkowitz & Hopsicker, 1998

1. **Time Management:**
   - How much time do you spend studying?
   - How much of the time is quality time?
   - Is the time quiet, free from distractions?
   - How much time is spent searching for information?

2. **Extra Help:**
   - Do I need to get help from my teacher?
   - I can meet with Mr. Hopsicker before homeroom (starting at 6:30 a.m.), during homeroom, during his open periods, for lunch, or after school.
   - Please just make an appointment

3. **Learning Strategies:**
   - Rewrite notes/review sheets
   - Redo chapter worksheets
   - Make flash cards: person/term/or event on one side; information on other side of the card: cause/effect/impact/ contribution/ positive/negative
   - Note blanks: Cover up information in your notes, then write in missing gap
   - Use a tape recorder: Talk into a tape recorder using information, or without information
   - Read chapter and take notes on most important information
   - Review with family member, friend, or classmate
   - Use a combination of techniques listed from above
   - Use any other learning strategy that enables you to achieve your best score

Formula for Success: E1 + E2 = E3

Engage (read) +

Extract (notes, talk about it, chart) =

Ensure (result = better grades)

Discourse: Missing Links to Learning

Teachers don't think like information professionals. They don't ever ask, "How is information in this content area organized?" Scott and I approached history as "SPEFA," the interplay of social, political, economic, and foreign affairs events. We did exercises and projects that reinforced cause-and-effect relationships. So in learning geography, the impact of a river as a barrier to trade (or an aid to trade), or the different responses to various technologies in different cultures allowed students to exercise their minds, not just their memories. Now I've given them coat hangers, a place to put information, instead of just throwing it into their mental closets. If I present information as random dots and ask students to exactly recreate the pattern, there's no way that will happen. If instead I draw lines connecting the dots, creating a graphic, showing them the underlying structure of the information, they now have the tools to function at a higher level. Their learning becomes deeper and more lasting, as we know from 30 years of cognitive science.

Scott Hopsicker notes, "What I like about the Big6™ is that you assume nothing and that it's really common sense. You just apply the common sense you use in everyday life to school things."

We were surprised to learn that vocabulary needs went beyond the content we wanted to teach. Vocabulary within the instructions was a significant barrier for many students, particularly at-risk kids without a history of success and confidence. Students can be thrown off and perform at levels far below their capabilities and preparation simply by not grasping what they're being asked to do. Scott says, "We focus on difficult vocabulary words in the essay instructions. Instructions such as 'identify and discuss' are different than 'compare and contrast.' Even in high school, students still won't know what those words mean. We quiz them on the words and continually reinforce their correct use."

We used the information we gathered on a daily basis, both in terms of what was being taught, and the feedback we got from student performance. One key strategy we used was having daily quizzes . . . success breeds success and "points are cheap." Another key strategy was involving parents as part of the solution. (See the sidebars "Scott Hopsicker's Study Tips" and "Helping With Homework: A Big6™ Assignment Organizer")

Scott notes another key student need. "One of the problems students in high school have is writing essays. So we created a new essay strategy for them—how to find, organize, and present information for essays. We used something called the "perfect chart" (see the sidebar "Perfect Chart: Cases and Issues"), which helps the students outline the essay first. The students develop charts, and I develop one, too. My chart is the "perfect" one—it includes all the information needed to get a perfect 100 score on the essay. So, there is no guessing game. The students know exactly what it takes to get a 100."

Helping with Homework: A Big6™ Assignment Organizer

Assignment _____ **Due Date** _____

Complete Big6™ Skills #1-5 BEFORE you BEGIN your assignment. Complete Big6™ Skill #6 BEFORE you TURN IN your assignment.

Big6™ Skill #1: Task Definition

What does this assignment require me to do? What information do I need in order to do this assignment?

Big6™ Skill #2: Information Seeking Strategies

What sources can I use to do the assignment? Circle the best sources.

Big6™ Skill #3: Location & Access

Where can I find my sources?
Do I need help? If so, who can help me?

Big6™ Skill #4: Use of Information

What do I have to do with the information?

_____ read/view/listen _____ chart and/or write an essay

_____ take notes _____ copy and highlight

_____ answer questions _____ properly cite

_____ other: _____

Big6™ Skill #5: Synthesis

what product does this assignment require?

Big6™ Skill #6: Evaluation

Student self-evaluation checklist:

_____ I did what I was supposed to do (see Big6™ #1, Task Definition)

_____ The assignment is complete.

The Big6™ Eisenberg & Berkowitz, 1990. Assignment Organizer © Berkowitz & Hopsicker, 1997.

Another surprise was the balance of content and process. Scott remembers, "I had someone from another school take a look at our essays strategy. She thought we were watering down the curriculum because we gave them the answers in the perfect chart. She didn't understand. It doesn't matter that we're giving them the content—it's the process that counts. We want them to actually spend more time concentrating on how to put [information] in their own words, and spend less time finding it. And, along the way, they are learning the content."

There were two kinds of evaluation: formative and summative. Formative involves diagnosing student performance during learning so that adjustments can be made before students turn in their work (or take a high-stakes exam!). Adjustments may include the following:

- Redirecting planned instruction to focus on areas in which students are having trouble

- Providing special learning activities not previously planned

- Helping students apply relevant technology tools

- Redefining the problem or returning to a previous Big6™ stage

- Offering one-on-one tutoring

- Brainstorming alternative approaches

Of course, the summative evaluation for this project was the Regents exam. It is vital to keep in mind the power of the affective side. All year long, we'd done this through confidence-building activities, daily quizzes, exposing students to high-quality work, and a number of other strategies. Perhaps the most amazing was the 'Academic Pep Rally."

Picture the scene: 130 kids in the cafeteria, as Scott Hopsicker gives the Knute Rockne speech. "You've worked hard, and I believe in you. You will do well. If you get nervous, raise your hand. I won't be able to tell you the answer, but I'll stand beside you and give you my confidence."

Even now that Scott was lured away from Wayne Central and teaches in the Brockport (New York) Central School District, his results have followed him, as he puts the Big6™ process to the test, and his students continue to move ahead, pointing the way for the rest of us. You are the most crucial link for making these results happen in your school. We can improve scores by improving thinking!

Big6™ Skill 1: Task Definition

- To move from a 53% passing rate to the maximum possible

- To understand the tasks required of students by the Regents exam and prepare all students to succeed at every task

- To turn the exam into a learning experience

Big6™ Skill 2: Information-Seeking Strategies

To review and analyze all aspects of the teaching and learning process, Hopsicker and Berkowitz relied on multiple sources: review of lesson plans, curriculum, textbooks, classroom observations, and student journals. These were then compared to the performance tasks embedded in the Regents exam.

Big6™ Skill 3: Location and Access

How many kids truly engage with the information from the textbook? We created guided reading sections, with the 10–15 key sentences found in each section. Students would find key vocabulary, definitions, and explanations. They had to have those sheets with them to walk in the door. It was an easy way to get an A. Highlighting sections, underlining keywords on all multiple-choice worksheets, and tape-recording notes and then transcribing them—all contributed to strengthening these skills.

Big6™ Skill 4: Use of Information

Students must know what to do with information. Simply knowing the content is not enough. For example, students needed help with vocabulary contained within the questions, not just with the content. Knowing the difference between "identify and discuss" and "compare and contrast" involved learning the processes required for success. This skill had to be mastered first.

Big6™ Skill 5: Synthesis

Essay writing was the most difficult task for students. We provided tools, templates, and models to build their skills and confidence throughout the year.

Big6™ Skill 6: Evaluation

Evaluation was a continual process, leading up to the "main event" of the Regents exam itself. Students measured their own work against examples of quality work and learned to assess their efforts. More importantly, they came to understand their strengths and gaps and developed strategies that improved their performances.

Communications to the author may be addressed to Bob Berkowitz, Library Media Specialist, Wayne Central School, Route 350, Ontario Center, NY 14520; e-mail: Bberkowitz@wayne.kl2.ny.us. For more information, visit <http://www. big6.com>.

Perfect Chart: Cases and Issues

McCulloch v. Maryland (1819)—federalism
Dred Scott v. Sanford (1857)—property rights
Plessy v. Ferguson (1896)—civil rights

Korematsu v. U.S. (1944)—Presidential power
Engel v. Vitale (1962)—freedom of religion
Miranda v. Arizona (1966)—due process

Choose all cases from the list. For each one chosen:

1. show how the constitutional issue listed was involved in the case,
2. state the Supreme Court's decision in the case, and
3. discuss an impact of the decision on United States history.

Case	How Constitutional Issue Was Involved	Supreme Court Decision	Impact of the Decision
McCulloch v. Maryland	Federalism = The division of power between state and national government Issue: Whether the state of Maryland could tax the National Bank.	Maryland could not tax the bank because it was created by the federal government.	Federal agencies are immune from control by the states.
Dred Scott v. Sanford	Issue: Whether Dred Scott could sue for his freedom because he was a slave.	Slaves are property, not citizens. Therefore slaves can't sue for their freedom.	Greater distrust between abolitionists and pro-slavery citizens, making compromises to avoid the Civil War worthless.
Plessy v. Ferguson	Issue: Whether separate facilities for blacks and whites were constitutional.	Separate, but equal is constitutional and it does not violate the 13th and 14th Amendments.	Separate facilities were not equal for blacks and the decision was later reversed by Brown v. Board of Education. Separate was not equal; segregation ended.
Korematsu v. U.S.	Issue: Whether the war powers of President FDR justified placing Japanese-Americans in internment camps.	Internment camps were justified because presidential powers expand during war or national crisis.	Rights of citizens can be suspended during war or national crisis.
Engel v. Vitale	Issue: Can schools force students to say a school prayer to start each day?	School prayer was contrary to the 1st Amendment because the Amendment provides for religious freedom but prevents government from establishing a religion.	A couple of Presidents since have called for a constitutional amendment allowing school prayer.
Miranda v. Arizona	Issue: Can the police deny you your right to an attorney during questioning?	The 5th Amendment protecting from self-incrimination and the 6th Amendment providing a right to an attorney were violated by the police when questioning Miranda.	All suspects must be read their rights when questioned and have the right to an attorney.

This *MultiMedia Schools* article emphasizes the importance of teaching information literacy skills and encourages educators to share their success stories with others in their communities.

7.16 Article—Plagiarism by Mike Eisenberg

Plagiarism is an increasing problem in K-12, higher education, and beyond. We believe in "fighting" plagiarism with a positive, not punitive, approach. It's not just okay to cite sources, it's expected and appreciated! Students should cite their sources of information all the time. So should classroom teachers, teacher-librarians, and administrators.

We need to turn the emphasis from focusing on citation format or citation policing to making citing part of the school's culture. Schools can create a "culture of citing" by introducing citing at a very early age (e.g., through Super3 Citation Stickers or by using rubber stamps), by modeling (e.g., citing by teachers), by expecting citations in all work (e.g., even homework), by not accepting or by deducting points from assignments that do not include citation, and by generally making citing so common that students would find it strange not to cite sources of information.

The slides presented here offer practical, positive actions and approaches to address plagiarism.

Fighting Plagiarism

Help!

"What can we do to stop students from just copying and pasting and presenting the work as their own?"

Create a culture that promotes "citing in context."

▸ Have students learn to cite at an early age.

▸ Model citing in teachers' work.

▸ Show "bad" examples – exaggerate plagiarism.

▸ Have students cite all sources all the time.

▸ Do not accept work without citing.

▸ Expect citing in class discussions as well.

Citing Sources

✓ **It is important for students to tell where they found their information.**

✓ **Citing makes their work more trustworthy and credible.**

✓ **Citing helps teachers to troubleshoot difficulties in information problem-solving (i.e., Big6 stages)**

Super3 Lesson
Creating a "Culture of Citing"

	Rubber stamps	Super3 Sam Citing stickers
▸ Book		
▸ Computer		
▸ Person		
▸ Self		

Big6 Lesson

• **Work separately on <u>Use of Information</u> and <u>Synthesis</u> before requiring both be done together.**

  ▸ Have students provide "direct quote" answers before requiring them to do so in their own words.

  ▸ Give students the "direct quote" answers and then have them put them in their own words.

  ▸ Do not advance until they can do each of these skills successful on their own.

Citing

- **Focus on citations in context more than bibliographies.**

- **Require "annotated" bibliographies – with annotations of "why" students selected a particular source as well as their "credibility" analysis of the source.**

© Eisenberg & Berkowitz

Fighting Plagiarism

Ask good questions.

- Give assignments that are simply "descriptive" are easily copied.
- Give assignments that ask students to make judgments or defend a position require thinking and are not easily copied.

DESCRIPTIVE	INFERENTIAL
Do a report on a region of the U.S. (or world).	Your business is considering moving to another region. Based on research about this region, decide whether you think it's a good idea.
Write a paper on humpback whales.	Write a paper on whether humpback whales are still endangered and should or should not be protected.

© Eisenberg & Berkowitz

There are many more micro planning lessons, units, activities, worksheets, and readings available on the Big6 Web site (http://www.big6.com), and in the *Big6 eNewsletter* (http://www.big6.com/category/enewsletter/), as well as in books and teaching materials published by Linworth and Big6 Associates.

If you have prepared lessons, teaching ideas or materials to share, please contact us via e-mail at info@big6.com.

Part 8:
Assessment

▶ **8.0 Introduction** **231**

▶ **8.1 Assess the Process** **231**

▶ **8.2 Self-Assessment** **232**

▶ **8.3 Assessment Exercise** **233**

▶ **8.4 Article—Assessment: Big6™
Scoring Guides for Diagnosis
and Prescription** **233**

The BIG6 Assessment

8.0 Introduction

- Have students learned what was intended?
- Are students proficient in the overall Big6 process?
- Are students able to solve information problems across a range of situations, subjects, and settings?
- Are students skilled in each Big6 stage and sub-stage?

Answering these four questions is what assessment is all about. Assessment is often dreaded because it comes across as negative and difficult to accomplish. This need not be the case. Assessment can be used to recognize strengths and highlight skills that need improvement, and assessment can be handled in a straight forward manner. We emphasize that teachers need to communicate expectations as well as the techniques they will use to evaluate student performance in relation to expectations. The evidence required to assess Big6 proficiency may be gathered within the context of existing assignments, tests, products, and other forms of assessment.

8.1 Assess the Process

Assessment from a Big6 perspective means going beyond simply whether the students learned the content that was taught. Teachers must also determine students' abilities in terms of the processes involved. For example, it is important to know whether students were able to clearly articulate their assignment and the information needed (Task Definition) or whether they were able to acquire the information they were supposed to get (Information Seeking Strategies and Location & Access). And, could they pull out the valuable information and apply it to the task (Use Information and Synthesis)? Last of all, were the students able to recognize and correct deficiencies in their own work (Evaluation)? In other words, classroom teachers and teacher-librarians must be able to assess performance within the information problem-solving process itself and then develop ways for students to address deficiencies and problems.

8.2 Self-Assessment

We also believe that assessment is the responsibility of students as well as teachers. Students must be able to assess the results of their efforts by analyzing the effectiveness of their products and their efficient use of the information problem-solving strategy. It is crucial to help students learn to:

- Value and recognize quality work

- Reflect on the ways they undertake assignments and tasks

- Determine how they can improve

- Recognize the relationship between self-discipline and achievement

- Gain self-confidence in solving information problems

Students often have no idea why they scored as they did on an assignment. At best, they might speculate on what they did wrong. It's more likely that they won't even think about it. Students must be encouraged to assume ownership of their own work through self-assessment. Students can and must also learn this assessment process. They need to know how to identify the factors that define a job well done, determine whether or not they found all of these factors, and compare their final products with an exemplar.

But that is not enough. Students must then judge whether they were properly engaged in the process. They should be able to determine whether they managed time efficiently, developed a product, or even handled assessment. In addition, students must develop skills to judge their own effectiveness. They need to know that they can recognize exemplary work when they see it.

It's important to take the guesswork out of assessment. If a student judges his or her work to be "good or excellent," but the teacher rates it as just "fair or adequate," there's a gap between teacher and student understanding and that's clearly a communication problem. By learning and using the Big6, we hope that students and teachers can eliminate that gap. Improved self-assessment can take place when students learn to assess their own products and skills according to the same criteria that teachers use. We talk about having students think like their teachers or "getting inside their teachers' heads." Students can also learn to assume ownership for their own learning, to diagnose problems, and to select solutions.

8.3 Assessment Exercise

This exercise is designed to help educators develop competence in assessing students' Big6 abilities. The aids—particularly the Big6 Scoring Guides—are useful mechanisms for documenting and planning assessment criteria and evidence.

For example, Bob's in-service workshop on assessment is built around the "Postcard" Assessment Exercise. Bob asks the teachers to analyze the assignment from a Big6 perspective. What is required of the students? What are the key Big6 Skills? What criteria will be used to assess student performance? Bob and the teachers (sometimes working in groups) then start to fill in the Big6 Scoring Guide matrix:

1. First, members need to agree upon a grading scale (e.g., "Highly Competent to Not Yet Acceptable").

2. Next, members discuss which stages of the Big6 are represented or emphasized in the assignment in some way. They determine the "degree of focus" for each Big6 Skill to be assessed and assign a relative percentage in the rightmost column.

3. Then teachers define the criteria within each Big6 Skill and level; for example, whatever the "best case" would be for Task Definition becomes the expectation for Highly Competent. Bob and the teachers work through each level down to "Not Yet Acceptable."

4. The matrix is completed by determining what evidence will be used to assess student performance. They go through each Big6 stage to determine the qualities and quantities of work expected and the evidence required to measure the work. Last, they apply the weight or percent of focus for each skill.

After the Scoring Guide is defined, the teachers divide into small groups to assess the sample postcards. Teachers gain scoring experience by applying their new assessment tool to actual student work. Debriefing includes discussing the value and approaches to assessing both the Big6 process and the final products of student work.

8.4 Article—Assessment: Big6™ Scoring Guides for Diagnosis and Prescription

The article on Big6 Scoring Guides, from *The Big6 Newsletter*, provides further explanation about the various scoring forms and how to use them.

Worksheet 8.1:
Data Collection Sheet

Worksheet 8.2:
Postcard Assessment Exercise

Review the following instructional activity. Determine the Big6™ skills attributes, focus, and the criteria to assess student performance.

You have just won the grand prize in the Spanish 2 Cultural Sweepstakes. The prize is an all expenses paid trip to South America, Central America, or Spain. Because Mrs. Hoffman is a terrific teacher, you have decided to write her two postcards to describe your trip.

Your task is to write two picture postcards, either from a Spanish speaking country in South America or Central America, or from Spain. One card's content should focus on topics from the "social" list below and the second card should focus on topics from the "political" list below.

The front of each postcard must have a graphic (picture or drawing) that illustrates the content of the written message.

Social:

_____ recreation
_____ clothing
_____ celebrations
_____ customs and traditions
_____ sports/games
_____ food
_____ communication
_____ religion
_____ family life
_____ school
_____ art
_____ shopping
_____ housing
_____ music
_____ entertainment

Political:

_____ government structure
_____ history
_____ currency
_____ employment
_____ climate
_____ regions (beaches, mountains, etc.)
_____ historical personalities
_____ population statistics
_____ exports/imports
_____ sites of interests/places to visit
_____ current events
_____ historical landmarks

Dear Mrs. Hoffman,
Madrid is great! Shopping here is excellent. The malls here are gigantic and beautiful (see front) Most malls have more than 150 stores. Madrid is called the "capitol of joy and contentment." Our tour guide told us that the UN had to invent the word 'la movida' to describe Madrid's bustling night life! Madrid's restaurants offer a variety of food from around the world. The city's most popular dish is Madrid Stew. Some of ingredients are potatoes, chickpeas, black pudding, and meat. There are more than 140 art galleries in Madrid. Every year, there is a contemporary Art Fair. It is one of the most important art fairs in the world. Well, I have to go. We're going to an open-air cafe for lunch. See you soon!

Katie

Mrs Hoffman
6200 Ontario Ctr. R
Ontario, NY
14520

Dear Mrs Hoffman,
Hi! I'm in Madrid. Yesterday, I visited the Plaza Mayor. It is the sight for many things such as: bullfights, dances, concerts, and fairs. Every Sunday, there is a stamp and coin show. There is a place in Madrid called 'zero kilometre'. It has been there ever since the 19th century. It is the distance marker for all the roads leading out of the city. My tour guide told me that the population of Madrid is about 3,124,000. That's almost three times the population of Barcelona! I was also told about Spain's exports. They are citrus fruits, olive oil, wine, footwear, and vegetables. I have to go now. We're going to the park for a picnic See you later!

Katie

Mrs. Hoffman
6300 Ontario Ctr. Rc
Ontario, NY
14520

Assessment Exercise (cont.)

Dear Mrs. Hoffman,

    Brazil is very hot and humid. I was very tired when I got in my hotel room. And that was only one minute after I got out of my "El Taxi!" It is so boring here, I miss Panama! The only thing I liked about this country is the weather at night...........

        Hasta Luego

        Sarah

Mrs. Hoffman

6200 ont. centr. Rd

ont. centr. N.Y

14568

Dear Mrs. Hoffmann,

Ohhh man...I just love those malls. They are humongous. They have 76 stores. One of them is all souvenirs and party gifts, another is a history store with ancient jewels and other old stuff. Of course I'm talking about Brazil. I started to like it when I got used to the weather. Now I love this place................
    C-Ya Later,
    SARAH

Mrs. Hoffman
6200 ont. centr. rd
Ont. centr. N.Y 14568

Assessment: Big6™ Scoring Guides for Diagnosis and Prescription

by Bob Berkowitz

Big6™ Scoring Guides are designed to communicate expectations for students' work and achievement in ways that students can understand and use. Big6™ Scoring Guides focus on the process of solving information problems as well as the final result. Therefore, guides are useful both during and after working on assignments—for both formative and summative assessment.

Formative assessment, as explained in previous articles, involves diagnosing students' performances during learning so that adjustments can be made before students turn in their work. Adjustments may include:

■ redirecting planned instruction to focus on areas where students are having trouble

■ providing special learning activities not previously planned

■ helping students to apply relevant technology tools

■ redefining the problem or returning to a previous Big6™ stage

■ offering one-on-one tutoring

■ brainstorming alternative approaches

These types of adjustments are prescriptions for improving learning. Of course, Big6™ Scoring Guides can also be used to assess final products—summative assessment. In working with teachers, we find that post-assignment debriefings—built around Big6™ Scoring Guides—are effective ways of involving students in the assessment process.

To create Big6™ Scoring Guides

1. Define the curriculum objectives within a Big6™ context.

2. Determine which Big6™ Skills are important (the focus) for this particular assignment.

3. Develop criteria across a scale (from "highly competent" to "not yet acceptable"). There may be more than one aspect to each criteria.

Consider which aspects are essential.

4. Determine what evidence will be examined to determine student performance for each Big6™ skill.

5. Conduct the assessment.

6. Share the assessment with students.

7. Revise as necessary.

Figure A: Muscular Action Worksheet

Your task is to design a controlled experiment to test the hypothesis below. Your experiment should be designed so that it can be conducted in a 15 to 20 minute period.

Hypothesis:
When there is an increase in muscular activity, there is a corresponding increase in the energy used by muscles. This energy increase causes heat as well as a corresponding increase in oxygen consumption.

Material:

Procedure:

Result: (tabulate data and represent in an appropriate graph)

Conclusion:

Questions:
● What variable(s) did you test?
● What are the constants?
● What is the experimental control?
● Evaluation/Scoring Guide

For example, assume that completing Figure A is the task for students in ninth-grade biology studying "muscular activity." Figure B is the Big6™ Scoring Guide designed to assess students' performance. This guide is designed to include multiple assessments by student (S), teacher (T), and library media specialist (L). This allows students and teachers to quickly identify gaps in their views of perceived performance. Focusing on gaps can lead to clarification of misunderstandings and highlighting the need for further instruction.

The column labeled "Evidence" indicates the products or techniques used to assess specific skills. Examples of evidence include written, visual, or oral products, assignments, homework, projects, tests, observation, or even self-reflection. This is an essential piece of the Scoring Guide since it identifies the specific context for assessing student performance.

The last column, "Focus," relates to the relative importance of each skill being evaluated. It is not necessary or desirable to assess all Big6™ skills equally in every learning situation. The assigned focus should be based on the goals and objectives of the unit in terms of Big6™ skill development and content learning. For example, in the muscle example, a percentage of emphasis is assigned to each of the Big6™ skills. Location & Access is not a skill emphasized in this situation while Task Definition, Information Seeking Strategy, and Synthesis are.

Figure C is an elementary curriculum example that uses a Big6™ Scoring Guide in context. The curriculum context is a science lab experiment on the effects of light on seed growth. The Scoring Guide is an easy way to compare student and teacher assessment on key Big6™ Skills: Location & Access, Use of Information, and Synthesis.

Figure B: Big6 Scoring Guide for Muscular Action

Big6™ Assessment Scoring Guide — Muscular Exercise

Big6™ Skills Eisenberg/Berkowitz © 1988		Highly Competent 10 points		Competent 8 points		Adequate 7 points		Not Yet Acceptable 5 points	Evidence	Focus
1. Task Definition 1.1 Define the problem. 1.2 Identify the information needed.	S T L	Experiment meets 15–20 minute requirement. Procedure tested: oxygen consumption and levels of heat.	S T L	Experiment limited to15–20 min. requirement. Procedure tested: oxygen consumption or levels of heat.	S T L	Experiment did not meet time requirement. Procedure tested: oxygen consumption or levels of heat, but not both.	S T L	Experiment did not meet time requirement. Procedure did not test for either: oxygen consumption or levels of heat.	Experiment	20%
2. Information Seeking Strategies 2.1 Determine all possible sources. 2.2 Select the best source.	S T L	Procedure can be repeated exactly and produce the same results. Procedure tests the hypothesis.	S T L	Procedure tested the hypothesis but is not easily followed.	S T L	Procedure tests the hypothesis but is not easily followed and does not give the same results.	S T L	Procedure does not test the hypothesis. Procedure cannot be repeated at all.	Procedure	40%
3. Location & Access 3.1 Locate sources. 3.2 Find information within sources.	S T L		S T L		S T L		S T L			
4. Use of Information 4.1 Engage (e.g., read, hear, view). 4.2 Extract relevant information.	S T L	Complete and accurate data tables. Complete and accurate graphs.	S T L	Accurate data tables. Appropriate but incomplete graphs.	S T L	Incomplete data tables. Incomplete and inaccurate graphs.	S T L	No data tables. No graphs.	Results	10%
5. Synthesis 5.1 Organize information from multiple sources. 5.2 Present the result.	S T L	Appropriate conclusion. Answers all questions completely.	S T L	Appropriate conclusion. Answers all questions poorly.	S T L	Conclusion attempted but is inappropriate. Questions poorly answered and/or only some questions answered.	S T L	No conclusion. No questions answered.	Conclusion Question	20%
6. Evaluation 6.1 Judge the result (effectiveness). 6.2 Judge the process (efficiency).	S T L	Scoring Guide thoughtfully completed.	S T L		S T L		S T L	Scoring Guide was not completed.	Scoring Guide	10%

(S) Student, (T) Teacher, (L) Library Media Specialist

Big6™ Skills Eisenberg/Berkowitz © 1988

The hardest part of creating Big6™ Scoring Guides is writing the specific statements of performance under each criteria and Big6™ skill. We find that people get much better at this over time. Figure D is provided as a template to help you practice.

We also find that collaboration helps. Try working with library media specialists, other teachers, and even students. In fact, having students participate in creating their own Big6™ Scoring Guides is an excellent technique for teaching the Big6™ Skills of Task Definition and Evaluation.

Figure C: Elementary Science Experiment: Light and Seed Growth

Objectives:

1. To study the impact of light on seed growth.
2. To gather necessary materials and conduct an experiment.
3. To keep a daily journal of observations.
4. To write up a lab and draw logical conclusions.

Procedures:

Working in pairs, students are to:
1. Line two glasses with paper towels and stuff the inside of the glasses with more paper towels to hold the paper towel liner against the glass.
2. Place four bean seeds, evenly spaced and half-way down, between the glass and the paper towels.
3. Dampen the paper towels with water.
4. Put one glass in a dark cupboard or cabinet and place the other glass on a windowsill.
5. Each day, moisten the paper towels in each glass.
6. Make observations in a journal each day for seven days. Note date, time, actions taken, observations.
7. Write up the experiment in scientific lab format. Include a written summary of results and a conclusion based on observations.

Assessment: Big6™ Scoring Guide for Light and Seed Growth Experiment

Big6™ Skills	Expert Scientist	Scientist	Lab Assistant	Novice
3. Location & Access 3.1 Locate sources. 3.2 Find information within sources.	Gathers lab materials: independently; appropriately.	Gathers lab materials: with some assistance; appropriately.	Needs assistance: missing some materials.	Needs assistance: missing most materials.
4. Use of Information 4.1 Engage (e.g., read, hear, view). 4.2 Extract relevant information.	Journal includes daily entries; is appropriate to task; is accurate.	Journal includes almost daily entries; is appropriate to task; is accurate.	Journal includes some entries; is inappropriate to task; is accurate or inaccurate.	Journal includes few or no entries.
5. Synthesis 5.1 Organize information from multiple sources. 5.2 Present the result.	Lab write-up complete and has proper format. Logical conclusion based on results.	Lab write-up not complete or problems with format. Logical conclusion based on results.	Lab write-up okay. Conclusion needs work.	Problems with lab write-up and/or format. Conclusion needs work.

Worksheet 8.3: Big6™ Assessment Scoring Guide

Big6™ Skills Eisenberg/Berkowitz © 1988		Highly Competent 10 points	Competent 8 points		Adequate 7 points		Not Yet Acceptable 5 points		Evidence	Focus
1. Task Definition 1.1 Define the problem. 1.2 Identify the information needed.	S T L		S T L		S T L		S T L			
2. Information Seeking Strategies 2.1 Determine all possible sources. 2.2 Select the best source.	S T L		S T L		S T L		S T L			
3. Location & Access 3.1 Locate sources. 3.2 Find information within sources.	S T L		S T L		S T L		S T L			
4. Use of Information 4.1 Engage (e.g., read, hear, view). 4.2 Extract relevant information.	S T L		S T L		S T L		S T L			
5. Synthesis 5.1 Organize informa- tion from multiple sources. 5.2 Present the result.	S T L		S T L		S T L		S T L			
6. Evaluation 6.1 Judge the result (effectiveness). 6.2 Judge the process (efficiency).	S T L		S T L		S T L		S T L			

(S) Student, (T) Teacher, (L) Library Media Specialist

The Big6™ Skills © 1987 Eisenberg & Berkowitz.

Worksheet 8.3: Big6™ Assessment Scoring Guide (Cont.)

Big6™ Skills Eisenberg/Berkowitz © 1988		Highly Competent 10 points	Competent 8 points	Adequate 7 points	Not Yet Acceptable 5 points	Evidence	Focus
1. Task Definition 1.1 Define the problem. 1.2 Identify the information needed.	S T L						
2. Information Seeking Strategies 2.1 Determine all possible sources. 2.2 Select the best source.	S T L						
3. Location & Access 3.1 Locate sources. 3.2 Find information within sources.	S T L						
4. Use of Information 4.1 Engage (e.g., read, hear, view). 4.2 Extract relevant information.	S T L						
5. Synthesis 5.1 Organize information from multiple sources. 5.2 Present the result.	S T L						
6. Evaluation 6.1 Judge the result (effectiveness). 6.2 Judge the process (efficiency).	S T L						

(S) Student, (T) Teacher, (L) Library Media Specialist

The Big6™ Skills © 1987 Eisenberg & Berkowitz.

Part 9:

Macro Planning: How to Develop School and District Information Literacy Programs

▶ **9.0 Introduction** **247**

▶ **9.1 Curriculum Information
Seeking Strategies** **253**

▶ **9.2 Data Collection** **254**

▶ **9.3 Integrating Big6™ Skills into the
Program: Curriculum Mapping** **259**

▶ **9.4 Planning an Integrated
Program** **266**

The BIG6 Macro Planning

9.0 Introduction

In Part 7, we noted two levels of instructional design planning: micro and macro. Part 7 focused on the micro level for lesson and unit design. Here, however, we discuss ways to implement the Big6 on the macro level. The goal of the macro level is to integrate information skills instruction on graduated levels, including the classroom, school, district, region, and even the state level.

Often we hear educators say, "We don't have time to plan; we already have too much to do." Planning provides a process for educators, administrators, and parents to engage in an action-oriented framework. A definite plan helps establish a common mission, goals and priorities, and practical approaches for implementation.

We provide figures and worksheets in this chapter to help guide the discussion and facilitate the planning process on the macro level.

A set of simple, yet effective questions guide the strategies presented in this part of the *Workshop Handbook.*

What do we want the learners to know, to do, and to be like, really?

- How can instruction motivate learners?

- Is the value and relevance of the instruction apparent to students?

- Are learners required to use their knowledge and skills to solve problems and make decisions in authentic performance tasks?

- Is the learning environment rich in information, guidance, and support?

Yes, planning goals, objectives, and benchmarks does take time, but there are benefits as well. The most successful projects begin with a strategic plan designed to fulfill a vision. And planning is an excellent way to get people involved and invested in a new program. In the ending stage, effective planning is critical to overall success.

Our approach to systematic macro planning is straightforward:

1. Gather information about classroom and subject area curriculum.
2. Analyze that curriculum information to determine the units and assignments that are well suited for integration with Big6 instruction.
3. Determine which Big6 Skills to emphasize in instruction.
4. Create planning charts (**Unit x Big6 Matrix**) to link classroom curriculum and assignments to the Big6, technology, and standards (if appropriate).

To begin, create a matrix; we call it a **Unit by Big6 Matrix (or Unit x Big6 Matrix),** for an upcoming marking period or for an entire school year. The matrix is a formal plan to merge Big6 information and technology skills instruction with curriculum assignments. Furthermore, after the instruction is complete, the **Unit x Big6 Matrix** documents what was taught in an integrated Big6 instructional program.

We continually stress that Big6 instruction is fully compatible with existing subject area and classroom curriculum. The Big6 provides students with the ability to have control of information and harness thinking skills necessary to carry out the various learning tasks determined by curriculum standards and frameworks. However, to successfully integrate Big6 instruction requires accurate, up-to-date, and specific information about the classroom, school, or district level curriculum. Access to curriculum information is a key component of macro planning.

In essence, we have an information problem of our own to solve—what is the "real" curriculum taught to students? We use Worksheet 9.1, "Curriculum Information Seeking Strategies Worksheet," provided in this section to brainstorm and analyze information-seeking alternatives for curriculum information.

For example, school, district, or state curriculum guides are widely available sources of curriculum information. These guides provide some degree of detail on the curriculum as intended, but they do not provide specifics of the actual curriculum as experienced by students and teachers. Useful curriculum information may also be available in textbooks or on Web sites.

Since the mid-1970s, Mike has used a technique called "curriculum mapping" to gather, organize, and present reliable curriculum information. Curriculum mapping is now widely known and used in K-12 education. There are even software programs (e.g., Atlas Curriculum Mapping, http://www.rubicon.com/) to assist with curriculum mapping.

If your school or district currently engages in some form of curriculum mapping, you can easily use that for the kind of curriculum analysis described in this part of the *Workshop Handbook*. But if your school does not, we offer a tried and tested "Eisenberg-style" method that does not require an overwhelming effort or time commitment.

Curriculum mapping provides a mechanism for gathering specific and accurate information on the various attributes of classroom curriculum. The primary building block of curriculum in K-12 schools is the curriculum ***unit***. Therefore, curriculum mapping is based on gathering data—generally from teachers, but sometimes from students—about actual curriculum units or units intended for teaching.

Curriculum mapping Eisenberg-style involves two steps:

1. Systematically collect information about what's actually going on in the classroom, and

2. Combine classroom activity information into charts and tables that describe the curriculum in a particular setting.

The "Curriculum Mapping Data Collection Worksheet"[1] is the primary tool to use when gathering data on curriculum units. We provide multiple copies of the data collection worksheet (Worksheet 9.2) so that audiences can experience the ease of filling out one or two and still have some blank sheets left over. It only takes 5 to 10 minutes to complete a Curriculum Mapping Data Collection Worksheet. We have revised the Curriculum Mapping Data Collection Worksheet dozens of times over the years, and users should individualize the worksheet to local school settings. To save time and effort, do not ask for data that is already available. List the school name on the form, and use local vocabulary terms to describe various teaching methods and assignments.

The Curriculum Mapping Data Collection Worksheet itself is not a curriculum map. A curriculum map is developed from the information compiled from multiple Worksheets. We provide a blank form to create your own curriculum map (Worksheet 9.3), but you can also use a computer database or electronic spreadsheet program. We also provide several sample curriculum maps (Figures 9.2–9.7) to show how useful and flexible the technique is for classroom, school, subject area, and district levels as well as across grade levels in elementary, middle, and high school situations.

Once maps are created, the task is to use the information in curriculum maps to plan Big6 instruction that is integrated with classroom and subject area curriculum. Planning integrated instruction involves systematically reviewing the curriculum maps and selecting units that are best suited to integrated information and technology skills instruction. This step involves creative analysis of the various aspects of units in relation to the Big6 and technology. Assignments are a key, and Worksheet 9.4 is an Integration Planning Worksheet to help with the analysis of assignments in relation to the Big6 and technology.

We try to identify the "big juicy" units, those information-rich curriculum units that are filled with information needs, resources, and processing. These are the units that offer strong opportunities to teach specific Big6 Skills within the overall Big6 process.

For example, units that are good candidates for Big6 Skills instruction generally have these characteristics. Units will:

■ Have a longer duration

■ Reach many students

---

1. Electronic versions of the worksheets and figures in this section are available on the Big6 Web site: http://tinyurl.com/big6templates. Scroll down to the bottom of the screen.

- Involve a report, project, or cumulative product
- Use multiple resources
- Involve a range of teaching methods.

Once desirable units are selected, enter them into the Unit x Big6 Matrix (Worksheets 9.5–9.6).

If the Unit x Big6 Matrix is developed before the beginning of the school year or before an upcoming marking period, the Matrix becomes a blueprint for integrated information skills instruction. Update the Matrix after instruction is completed during the year to reflect what actually took place. Then, at the end of the marking period or school year, the Matrix provides detailed documentation of what was actually accomplished. The Unit x Big6 Matrix also serves as the basis for follow-up planning by teachers for the next year and for other teachers who will have the same students the next year in the next grade.

Create Unit x Big6 Matrices for individual teachers, teams, subject areas, schools, or even districts. We provide examples of various matrices. Another way to represent the integrated curriculum-Big6 plan is on a timeline. Figure 9.12 presents a K-12 example while Worksheet 9.7 is a blank timeline that you can use.[2]

We cannot over-emphasize the importance of teaching all Big6 Skills in context. The process of systematically reviewing curriculum, identifying valuable units for integrated instruction, and developing and documenting plans is important to a successful Big6 program. The tools provided here give educators practical means for accomplishing meaningful, integrated Big6–classroom curriculum instruction.

---

2. Note: Templates of the figures in this part are available on the Big6™ Web site: www.big6.com.

Context

#1 - the process
- information problem solving = the Big6
- information literacy = the Big6

#2 - technology in context
- technology in the process
- technology standards in the process

#3 - curriculum
- real needs in real situations
- assignments: papers, reports, projects
- units and lessons
- curriculum standards

© Eisenberg & Berkowitz

Context #1: Process

1. Task Definition
2. Info Seeking Strategies
3. Location & Access
4. Use of Information
5. Synthesis
6. Evaluation

The BIG6

© Eisenberg & Berkowitz

Context #2: Technology in Context

TASK DEFINITION	Students use e-mail, chat, audio-, video-, and web-conferencing, txt messaging, group e-mail; Twitter, and other online communication methods to clarify assignments and brainstorm problems. Students also use software to generate timelines, charts, mind maps, etc. to plan and organize complex problems.
INFO SEEKING STRATEGIES	Students identify and assess electronic resources (e.g., article databases, online encyclopedias, websites, blogs) as they develop information seeking strategies toward their problem.
LOCATION & ACCESS	Students use article search engines, Web search engines, online catalogs, and other electronic searching tools find sources and information within sources.
USE OF INFORMATION	Students process information in online or locally stored electronic information sources, view, download, and decompress files, and use copy-and-paste features to extract relevant information. Students also use presentation or world processing software for note-taking and documentation.
SYNTHESIS	Students organize and communicate their results using all forms of media production and presentation software (e.g., word processing, database management, spreadsheet, presentation, graphics, multimedia editing and production) and distribute their projects via e-mail, Web publishing or hosting, or other media.
EVALUATION	Students evaluate their technology-based products as well as the impact, effectiveness, and efficiency of the types and specific technology systems used. Students use a range of communications technologies to share their assessments with teachers, parents, and each other.

© Eisenberg & Berkowitz

Context #3

- Real needs in real situations
  - school, life, work
  - assignments: papers, reports, projects
  - integrated units and lessons
  - curriculum standards or frameworks

© Eisenberg & Berkowitz

Curriculum – Big6 Integration

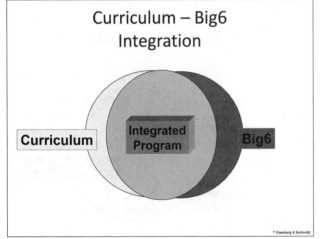

© Eisenberg & Berkowitz

"Big Juicies"

Are important units in the curriculum:
- have a longer duration
- reach many students
- involve a report, project, or product
- use multiple resources
- involve a range of teaching methods

© Eisenberg & Berkowitz

Figure 9.1

Curriculum Contexts

Math class working on graphing equations
Political Science discussion of current issues
Microbiology lab
English writing
Health reports

Any assignment, particularly a
project, report, or paper!!

Any personal decision that calls for
information, e.g., selecting a TV show,
buying a product...

© Eisenberg & Berkowitz

The Big6
Examples

- **1st grade – language arts – ABC book**
- **7th grade – Leon - recycling project**
- **10th grade – probability**

© Eisenberg & Berkowitz

The Big6 Example:
7th Grade Social Studies

- Leon -
- Recycling project
- Short paper and oral presentation on the problems and solutions regarding recycling of one type of waste.

© Eisenberg & Berkowitz

The Big6 Example:
Assignment—Whales

GRADE 2	Create a picture book on whales.
GRADE 5	Make a presentation (with multimedia aids) on types of whales and their habits.
GRADE 8	Project: Are whales still endangered?
GRADE 12	Argumentative essay: Should Native Americans be allowed to hunt whales?

© Eisenberg & Berkowitz

The Big6 Example:
Freshman English Class

Information technology project -
- **Paper and oral presentation on the opportunities and challenges of living in the information age.**
- **"Is freed today and in the future enhanced or threatened by information and technology?**

© Eisenberg & Berkowitz

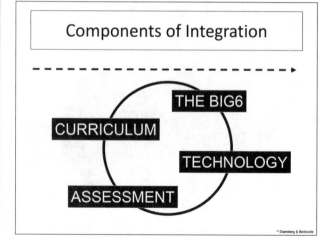

© Eisenberg & Berkowitz

Figure 9.1 (*continued*)

Worksheet 9.1:
Curriculum Information Seeking Strategies

Exercise:
- **Brainstorm all possible sources**
- **Note strengths and weaknesses**
- **Circle top 2 sources**

Possible Sources	Strengths	Weaknesses

Big6™ Skills Eisenberg/Berkowitz © 1988

Worksheet 9.2:
Data Collection

School:	

Date:	

Grade:	
Teacher:	
Subject:	
Unit:	

Number of Sections:	
Number of Students:	
Total Teaching Time:	
Marking Period:	

Level of Instruction:
- ☐ introduced
- ☐ reinforced
- ☐ expanded

Notes:

Resources:
- ☐ text
- ☐ one source
- ☐ multiple sources
    - ☐ articles (online, print)
    - ☐ websites
    - ☐ reference (online, print)
    - ☐ book (nonfiction)
    - ☐ book (fiction)
    - ☐ person(s)
    - ☐ organization
    - ☐ other:

Organization of Instruction
- ☐ large group
- ☐ small group
- ☐ individual

Notes:

Primary Teaching Method
- ☐ desk work
- ☐ lecture
- ☐ demonstration
- ☐ video, film, multimedia
- ☐ lab, hands-on
- ☐ discussion
- ☐ independent study
- ☐ multimedia project
- ☐ report
- ☐ other:

Assignment(s):
- ☐ test
- ☐ short written assignment
- ☐ report
- ☐ project/product
- ☐ observation
- ☐ other:

Notes:

Technologies:
- ☐ **tool** (word processing, database, presentation, spreadsheet)
- ☐ **communication** (e-mail, chat, txt audio/video conferencing, social network)
- ☐ **information** (web, articles, ebooks, blogs, vido, picture, graphic)
- ☐ other:

Notes:

Standards (State/District):
- ☐
- ☐
- ☐
- ☐
- ☐
- ☐
- ☐

Notes:

Comments/Notes:

Big6™ Skills Eisenberg/Berkowitz © 1988

Worksheet 9.2: (*continued*)

School: _____

Date: _____

Grade: _____
Teacher: _____
Subject: _____
Unit: _____

Number of Sections: _____
Number of Students: _____
Total Teaching Time: _____
Marking Period: _____

Level of Instruction:
- ☐ introduced
- ☐ reinforced
- ☐ expanded

Notes:

Resources:
- ☐ text
- ☐ one source
- ☐ multiple sources
  - ☐ articles (online, print)
  - ☐ websites
  - ☐ reference (online, print)
  - ☐ book (nonfiction)
  - ☐ book (fiction)
  - ☐ person(s)
  - ☐ organization
  - ☐ other:

Organization of Instruction
- ☐ large group
- ☐ small group
- ☐ individual

Notes:

Primary Teaching Method
- ☐ desk work
- ☐ lecture
- ☐ demonstration
- ☐ video, film, multimedia
- ☐ lab, hands-on
- ☐ discussion
- ☐ independent study
- ☐ multimedia project
- ☐ report
- ☐ other:

Assignment(s):
- ☐ test
- ☐ short written assignment
- ☐ report
- ☐ project/product
- ☐ observation
- ☐ other:

Notes:

Technologies:
- ☐ **tool** (word processing, database, presentation, spreadsheet)
- ☐ **communication** (e-mail, chat, txt audio/video conferencing, social network)
- ☐ **information** (web, articles, ebooks, blogs, vido, picture, graphic)
- ☐ other:

Notes:

Standards (State/District):
- ☐
- ☐
- ☐
- ☐
- ☐
- ☐
- ☐

Notes:

Comments/Notes:

Big6™ Skills Eisenberg/Berkowitz © 1988

Worksheet 9.2: (*continued*)

School:	

Grade:	
Teacher:	
Subject:	
Unit:	

Date:	

Number of Sections:	
Number of Students:	
Total Teaching Time:	
Marking Period:	

Level of Instruction:
- ☐ introduced
- ☐ reinforced
- ☐ expanded

Notes:

Resources:
- ☐ text
- ☐ one source
- ☐ multiple sources
  - ☐ articles (online, print)
  - ☐ websites
  - ☐ reference (online, print)
  - ☐ book (nonfiction)
  - ☐ book (fiction)
  - ☐ person(s)
  - ☐ organization
  - ☐ other:

Organization of Instruction
- ☐ large group
- ☐ small group
- ☐ individual

Notes:

Primary Teaching Method
- ☐ desk work
- ☐ lecture
- ☐ demonstration
- ☐ video, film, multimedia
- ☐ lab, hands-on
- ☐ discussion
- ☐ independent study
- ☐ multimedia project
- ☐ report
- ☐ other:

Assignment(s):
- ☐ test
- ☐ short written assignment
- ☐ report
- ☐ project/product
- ☐ observation
- ☐ other:

Notes:

Technologies:
- ☐ **tool** (word processing, database, presentation, spreadsheet)
- ☐ **communication** (e-mail, chat, txt audio/video conferencing, social network)
- ☐ **information** (web, articles, ebooks, blogs, vido, picture, graphic)
- ☐ other:

Notes:

Standards (State/District):
- ☐
- ☐
- ☐
- ☐
- ☐
- ☐
- ☐

Notes:

Comments/Notes:

Big6™ Skills Eisenberg/Berkowitz © 1988

Worksheet 9.2: (*continued*)

School:

Grade:

Teacher:

Subject:

Unit:

Date:

Number of Sections:

Number of Students:

Total Teaching Time:

Marking Period:

Level of Instruction:
- ☐ introduced
- ☐ reinforced
- ☐ expanded

Notes:

Resources:
- ☐ text
- ☐ one source
- ☐ multiple sources
  - ☐ articles (online, print)
  - ☐ websites
  - ☐ reference (online, print)
  - ☐ book (nonfiction)
  - ☐ book (fiction)
  - ☐ person(s)
  - ☐ organization
  - ☐ other:

Organization of Instruction
- ☐ large group
- ☐ small group
- ☐ individual

Notes:

Primary Teaching Method
- ☐ desk work
- ☐ lecture
- ☐ demonstration
- ☐ video, film, multimedia
- ☐ lab, hands-on
- ☐ discussion
- ☐ independent study
- ☐ multimedia project
- ☐ report
- ☐ other:

Assignment(s):
- ☐ test
- ☐ short written assignment
- ☐ report
- ☐ project/product
- ☐ observation
- ☐ other:

Notes:

Technologies:
- ☐ **tool** (word processing, database, presentation, spreadsheet)
- ☐ **communication** (e-mail, chat, txt audio/video conferencing, social network)
- ☐ **information** (web, articles, ebooks, blogs, vido, picture, graphic)
- ☐ other:

Notes:

Standards (State/District):
- ☐
- ☐
- ☐
- ☐
- ☐
- ☐
- ☐

Notes:

Comments/Notes:

Big6™ Skills Eisenberg/Berkowitz © 1988

Worksheet 9.2: (*continued*)

| School: | | Date: | |

Grade:	
Teacher:	
Subject:	
Unit:	

Number of Sections:	
Number of Students:	
Total Teaching Time:	
Marking Period:	

Level of Instruction:
- ☐ introduced
- ☐ reinforced
- ☐ expanded

Notes:

Resources:
- ☐ text
- ☐ one source
- ☐ multiple sources
    - ☐ articles (online, print)
    - ☐ websites
    - ☐ reference (online, print)
    - ☐ book (nonfiction)
    - ☐ book (fiction)
    - ☐ person(s)
    - ☐ organization
    - ☐ other:

Organization of Instruction
- ☐ large group
- ☐ small group
- ☐ individual

Notes:

Primary Teaching Method
- ☐ desk work
- ☐ lecture
- ☐ demonstration
- ☐ video, film, multimedia
- ☐ lab, hands-on
- ☐ discussion
- ☐ independent study
- ☐ multimedia project
- ☐ report
- ☐ other:

Assignment(s):
- ☐ test
- ☐ short written assignment
- ☐ report
- ☐ project/product
- ☐ observation
- ☐ other:

Notes:

Technologies:
- ☐ **tool** (word processing, database, presentation, spreadsheet)
- ☐ **communication** (e-mail, chat, txt audio/video conferencing, social network)
- ☐ **information** (web, articles, ebooks, blogs, vido, picture, graphic)
- ☐ other:

Notes:

Standards (State/District):
- ☐
- ☐
- ☐
- ☐
- ☐
- ☐
- ☐

Notes:

Comments/Notes:

Big6™ Skills Eisenberg/Berkowitz © 1988

Worksheet 9.3:
Curriculum Mapping

GR	TCHR	SUBJ	UNIT	#SEC	#STUD	TIME	MAR_PER	LEV	RESOURCES	ORG	METHODS	ASSIGN	TECH	Standards	DATE

The Big6™ Skills © 1987 Eisenberg & Berkowitz

Curriculum Mapping Sample

GR	TCHR	SUBJ	UNIT	#SEC	#STUD	TIME	MAR_PER	LEV	RES	ORG	METHODS	ASSIGN	TECH	STANDARDS	DATE
00-00	LIE	LA	Colors	1	24	40	1234	I	mult	lg	disc/hands-on	worksheet	none		01/03/10
01-01	REB	LA	ABC book	1	25	15	x2xx	R/E	mult	lg/ind	demo/ind study	product	none	WA Comm 3: Selects a topic to inform or tell a story, with teacher guidance.	01/03/10
01-01	MAB	Math	Whole/Parts	1	32	10	x2xx	I	text/mult	lg	lect/desk work	worksheet	none	WA Math 4.2: Organize and interpret information.	01/03/10
03-03	RDY	Sci	Planets	1	33	15	xx3x	I	mult	sg/lg	lect/group	project	Web, Graphics		01/03/10
03-03	RDY	Sci	Endangered Animals	1	33	15	xxx4	I	mult	lg/ind	lect/disc/ind	project	Web, PowerPoint, Graphics		01/03/10
03-03	RDY	SS	Community	1	33	20	x2xx	R/E	mult	sg/lg	lect/disc/trip	project	PowerPoint, e-mail	WA Comm. 3: The student who is information literate uses information accurately and creatively.	01/03/10
03-04	CAL	LA	Letter Writing	1	27	8	x2xx	I	mult	ind	lect/desk work	product	Word Processing	WA Writing 1: writes clearly and effectively.	09/27/09
03-04	CAL	Math	Graphs	1	27	15	xxx4	I	text	lg/ind	lect/desk work	product	none	WA Math 3.1 analyze information from a variety of sources;	09/27/09
03-04	CAL	Sci	Simple Machines	1	27	40	1xxx	I/R	text/mult	sg	lab/ind study	products	none		09/27/09
03-04	CAL	Sci	Work & Energy	1	27	8	xxx4	I	text	lg	lect	test	none		09/27/09
05-05	MBE	Library	Biography	5	120	2	xx3x	R/E	mult	lg	lect/disc	none	online catalog, Web	WA Reading 3.1: Read to learn new information.	01/03/10
06-06	SEW	LA	Folktales and Legends	1	29	20	x23x	R/E	mult	lg	lect/disc/desk work	homework/test	none	WA Reading 3.2: Expand comprehension by analyzing; interpreting, and synthesizing…in literary and informational text.	01/03/10
06-06	SEW	Sci	Vocabulary	1	29	3	1xxx	R/E	text	lg/ind	lect/desk work	homework	none	WA Reading 2.2: Understand and apply knowledge of text components to comprehend text.	01/03/10
06-06	SEW	SS	Current Events	1	29	40	1234	I/R/E	mult	lg/ind	disc/ind study	report	Web, online articles		01/03/10
06-06	SEW	SS	Native Cultures	1	29	10	x2xx	I	single	lg	lect/desk work, group	test, product	Web	Arts 2.1: Reflects for the purpose of elaboration and self evaluation.	01/03/10

Figure 9.2 Curriculum Mapping Sample (K–6)

Curriculum Mapping Sample

GR	TCHR	SUBJ	UNIT	#SEC	#STUD	TIME	MAR_PER	LEV	RES	ORG	METHODS	ASSIGN	TECH	STANDARDS	DATE
07-07	MBE	Info Lit	Dictionary Skill	6	150	2	1xxx	R/E	one	lg	lect/desk work	short written assignment	none		01/03/10
07-07	TMJ	Sci	Weather	3	87	15	xx3x	R/E	text	lg	lect/disc	test	Web	WA Sci GLE 1.3.6. Analyze the relationship between weather and climate and how ocean currents and global atmospheric circulation affect weather and climate.	01/03/10
07-07	TCH	SS	Recycling	3	87	15	x23x	R/E	mult	lg/ind	lect/ind	report	Web/ Word Proc/ PowerPoint/Online Articles/ e-mail		01/03/10
9-Sep	TMJ	Sci	Classification	2	45	40	x2xx	R-E	mult	sg/lg/ind	demo/disc	product (classification website)	Web/articles/ PowerPoint/Graphics	WA Sci 1.1.6: Understand how to classify organisms by their external and internal structures.	09/27/09
9-Sep	MBE	Info Lit	Web authoring	9	20	10	x2xx	I	mult	ind	demo/prod/ind study	product (web page)	Web Authoring// Graphics	WA Ed Tech 2.3 Select and Use Applications: Use productivity tools and common applications effectively and constructively.	09/27/09
9-Sep	HJW	SS	Map Skills	4	111	10	1xxx	R/E	mult	lg	worksheet	worksheet	Web	WA SS 3.1: Understands the physical characteristics, cultural characteristics, and location of places, regions, and spatial patterns on the Earth's surface.	01/03/10
9-Sep	CER	Health	Diet & Nutrition	10	250	20	1x3x	R/E	mult	lg/sg	lect/disc/prod	posters	Web/ PowerPoint	WA Health 1.5: Understands relationship of nutrition and food nutrients to body composition and physical performance.	01/03/10
12-Oct	CER	Health	Tobacco & Smoking	10	250	10	1x3x	R/E	mult	lg/sg	lect/disc	test	none	WA Health 4.1: Analyzes personal health and fitness information.	01/03/10
12-Oct	CER	Health	Drugs	10	250	10	x2x4	R/E	mult	lg/sg	lect/disc/prod	product	Web/ Word Processing/ PowerPoint/Graphics	WA Health 4.1: Analyzes personal health and fitness information.	01/03/10
10-10	BAB	Math	Probability	4	104	20	xx3x	R/E	text	lg/ind	lect/desk work	homework	none	WA Math 2.4: Core ontent: Probability	01/03/10
10-12	RBW	Physics	Light Lab	1	17	4	xx3x	I/R/E	laser, lab apparatus, text	lg - pairs	lect/lab	lab report	Word Processing/ Spreadsheet	WA Sci 2.1.2. Understand how to plan and conduct systematic and complex scientific investigations.	09/27/09
10-12	RBW	Physics	Light	1	17	15	xx3x	I/R/E	text	lg	lect/disc	test	Word Processing/ Spreadsheet	WA Ed Tech 2.3 Select and Use Applications: Use productivity tools and common applications effectively and constructively.	09/27/09
11-12	CJC	LA	Catcher in the Rye	3	86	10	xx3x	I	mult	lg	lect/disc	report	Word Processing/ Online Articles/Web		09/27/09
11-12	MAB	Spanish 4	Spanish Cooking	1	14	10	xxx4	E	mult	ind	ind	product	Web/Graphics		01/03/10
11-12	BDE	SS	Supply & Demand	3	68	20	xx3x	I/R	mult	sg/lg	lect/disc	obs/swa	Word Processing	WA SS Economics 2.2 Understands how economic systems function.	09/27/09

Figure 9.3 Curriculum Mapping Sample (7–12)

Curriculum Mapping Sample

GR	TCHR	SUBJ	UNIT	#SEC	#STUD	TIME	MAR_PER	LEV	RES	ORG	METHODS	ASSIGN	TECH	STANDARDS	DATE
01-01	REB	LA	ABC book	1	25	15	x2xx	R/E	mult	lg/ind	demo/ind study	product	none	WA Comm 3: Selects a topic to inform or tell a story, with teacher guidance.	01/03/10
03-03	RDY	Sci	Planets	1	33	15	xx3x	I	mult	sg/lg	lect/group	project	Web, Graphics		01/03/10
03-03	RDY	Sci	Endangered Animals	1	33	15	xxx4	I	mult	lg/ind	lect/disc/ind	project	Web, PowerPoint, Graphics		01/03/10
03-03	RDY	SS	Community	1	33	20	x2xx	R/E	mult	sg/lg	lect/disc/trip	project	PowerPoint, e-mail	WA Comm. 3: The student who is information literate uses information accurately and creatively.	01/03/10
03-04	CAL	LA	Letter Writing	1	27	8	x2xx	I	mult	ind	lect/desk work	product	Word Processing	WA Writing 1: Writes clearly and effectively.	09/27/09
03-04	CAL	Math	Graphs	1	27	15	xxx4	I	text	lg/ind	lect/desk work	product	none	WA Math 3.1 Analyze information from a variety of sources;	09/27/09
03-04	CAL	Sci	Simple Machines	1	27	40	1xxx	I/R	text/ mult	sg	lab/ind study	products	none		09/27/09
06-06	SEW	SS	Current Events	1	29	40	1234	I/R/E	mult	lg/ind	disc/ind study	report	Web, online articles		01/03/10
06-06	SEW	SS	Native Americans - NW Tribes	1	29	10	x2xx	I	single	lg	lect/desk work, group	test, product	Web	Arts 2.1: Reflects for the purpose of elaboration and self evaluation.	01/03/10

Figure 9.4 Curriculum Mapping Sample (K–6)

Curriculum Mapping Sample

GR	TCHR	SUBJ	UNIT	#SEC	#STUD	TIME	MAR_PER	LEV	RES	ORG	METHODS	ASSIGN	TECH	STANDARDS	DATE
07-07	TCH	SS	Recycling	3	87	15	x23x	R/E	mult	lg/ind	lect/ind	report	Web/ Word Proc/ PowerPoint/Online Articles/ e-mail		01/03/10
9-Sep	TMJ	Sci	Classification	2	45	40	x2xx	R-E	mult	sg/lg/ind	demo/disc	product (classification website)	Web/articles/ PowerPoint/ Graphics	WA Sci 1.1.6: Understand how to classify organisms by their external and internal structures.	09/27/09
9-Sep	MBE	Info Lit	Web authoring	9	20	10	x2xx	I	mult	ind	demo/prod/ ind study	product (web page)	Web Authoring// Graphics	WA Ed Tech 2.3 Select and Use Applications: Use productivity tools and common applications effectively and constructively.	09/27/09
12-Oct	CER	Health	Diet & Nutrition	10	250	20	1x3x	R/E	mult	lg/sg	lect/disc/ prod	posters	Web/ PowerPoint	WA Health 1.5: Understands relationship of nutrition and food nutrients to body composition and physical performance.	01/03/10
12-Oct	CER	Health	Drugs	10	250	10	x2x4	R/E	mult	lg/sg	lect/disc/ prod	product	Web/ Word Processing/ PowerPoint/ Graphics	WA Health 4.1: Analyzes personal health and fitness information.	01/03/10
10-12	RBW	Physics	Light Lab	1	17	4	xx3x	I/R/E	laser, lab apparatus, text	lg - pairs	lect/lab	lab report	Word Processing/ Spreadsheet	WA Ed Tech 2.3 Select and Use Applications: Use productivity tools and common applications effectively and constructively.	09/27/09
11-12	CJC	LA	Catcher in the Rye	3	86	10	xx3x	I	mult	lg	lect/disc	report	Word Processing/ Online Articles/Web		09/27/09
11-12	MAB	Spanish 4	Spanish Cooking	1	14	10	xxx4	E	mult	ind	ind	product	Web/Graphics		01/03/10

Figure 9.5 Curriculum Mapping Sample (7–12)

Curriculum Mapping Sample

GR	TCHR	SUBJ	UNIT	#SEC	#STUD	TIME	MAR_PER	LEV	RES	ORG	METHODS	ASSIGN	TECH	STANDARDS	DATE
05-05	MBE	Library	Biography	5	120	2	xx3x	R/E	mult	lg	lect/disc	none	online catalog, Web	WA Reading 3.1: Read to learn new information.	01/03/10
03-03	RDY	SS	Community	1	33	20	x2xx	R/E	mult	sg/lg	lect/disc/trip	project	PowerPoint, e-mail	WA Comm. 3: The student who is information literate uses information accurately and creatively.	01/03/10
03-03	RDY	Sci	Planets	1	33	15	xx3x	I	mult	sg/lg	lect/group	project	Web, Graphics		01/03/10
03-03	RDY	Sci	Endangered Animals	1	33	15	xxx4	I	mult	lg/ind	lect/disc/ind	project	Web, PowerPoint, Graphics		01/03/10
01-01	MAB	Math	Whole/Parts	1	32	10	x2xx	I	text/mult	lg	lect/desk work	worksheet	none	WA Math 4.2: Organize and interpret information.	01/03/10
06-06	SEW	SS	Current Events	1	29	40	1234	I/R/E	mult	lg/ind	disc/ind study	report	Web, online articles		01/03/10
06-06	SEW	LA	Folktales and Legends	1	29	20	x23x	R/E	mult	lg	lect/disc/ desk work	homework/ test	none	WA Reading 3.2: Expand comprehension by analyzing, interpreting, and synthesizing…in literary and informational text.	01/03/10
06-06	SEW	SS	Native Cultures	1	29	10	x2xx	I	single	lg	lect/desk work, group	test, product	Web	Arts 2.1: Reflects for the purpose of elaboration and self evaluation.	01/03/10
06-06	SEW	Sci	Vocabulary	1	29	3	1xxx	R/E	text	lg/ind	lect/desk work	homework	none	WA Reading 2.2: Understand and apply knowledge of text components to comprehend text.	01/03/10
03-04	CAL	Sci	Simple Machines	1	27	40	1xxx	I/R	text/mult	sg	lab/ind study	products	none		09/27/09
03-04	CAL	Math	Graphs	1	27	15	xxx4	I	text	lg/ind	lect/desk work	product	none	WA Math 3.1 Analyze information from a variety of sources;	09/27/09
03-04	CAL	LA	Letter Writing	1	27	8	x2xx	I	mult	ind	lect/desk work	product	Word Processing	WA Writing 1: Writes clearly and effectively.	09/27/09
03-04	CAL	Sci	Work & Energy	1	27	8	xxx4	I	text	lg	lect	test	none		09/27/09
01-01	REB	LA	ABC book	1	25	15	x2xx	R/E	mult	lg/ind	demo/ind study	product	none	WA Comm 3: Selects a topic to inform or tell a story, with teacher guidance.	01/03/10
00-00	LIE	LA	Colors	1	24	40	1234	I	mult	lg	disc/hands-on	worksheet	none		01/03/10

Figure 9.6 Curriculum Mapping Sample (K–6)

Curriculum Mapping Sample

GR	TCHR	SUBJ	UNIT	#SEC	#STUD	TIME	MAR_PER	LEV	RES	ORG	METHODS	ASSIGN	TECH	STANDARDS	DATE
10-12	CER	Health	Diet & Nutrition	10	250	20	1x3x	R/E	mult	lg/sg	lect/disc/ prod	posters	Web/ PowerPoint	WA Health 1.5: Understands relationship of nutrition and food nutrients to body composition and physical performance.	01/03/10
10-12	CER	Health	Tobacco & Smoking	10	250	10	1x3x	R/E	mult	lg/sg	lect/disc	test	none	WA Health 4.1: Analyzes personal health and fitness information.	01/03/10
10-12	CER	Health	Drugs	10	250	10	x2x4	R/E	mult	lg/sg	lect/disc/ prod	product	Web/ Word Processing/ PowerPoint/Graphics	WA Health 4.1: Analyzes personal health and fitness information.	01/03/10
07-07	MBE	Info Lit	Dictionary Skill	6	150	2	1xxx	R/E	one	lg	lect/desk work	short written assignment	none		01/03/10
09-12	HJW	SS	Map Skills	4	111	10	1xxx	R/E	mult	lg	worksheet	worksheet	Web	WA SS 3.1: Understands the physical characteristics, cultural characteristics, and location of places, regions, and spatial patterns on the Earth's surface.	01/03/10
10-10	BAB	Math	Probability	4	104	20	xx3x	R/E	text	lg/ind	lect/desk work	homework	none	WA Math 2.4: Core ontent: Probability	01/03/10
07-07	TMJ	Sci	Weather	3	87	15	xx3x	R/E	text	lg	lect/disc	test	Web	WA Sci GLE 1.3.6. Analyze the relationship between weather and climate and how ocean currents and global atmospheric circulation affect weather and climate.	01/03/10
07-07	TCH	SS	Recycling	3	87	15	x23x	R/E	mult	lg/ind	lect/ind	report	Web/ Word Proc/ PowerPoint/Online Articles/ e-mail		01/03/10
11-12	CJC	LA	Catcher in the Rye	3	86	10	xx3x	I	mult	lg	lect/disc	report	Word Processing/ Online Articles/Web		09/27/09
11-12	BDE	SS	Supply & Demand	3	68	20	xx3x	I/R	mult	sg/lg	lect/disc	obs/swa	Word Processing	WA SS Economics 2.2 Understands how economic systems function.	09/27/09
09-09	TMJ	Sci	Classification	2	45	40	x2xx	R-E	mult	sg/lg/ ind	demo/disc	product (classification website)	Web/articles/ PowerPoint/Graphics	WA Sci 1.1.6: Understand how to classify organisms by their external and internal structures.	09/27/09
09-09	MBE	Info Lit	Web authoring	9	20	10	x2xx	I	mult	ind	demo/prod/ ind study	product (web page)	Web Authoring// Graphics	WA Ed Tech 2.3 Select and Use Applications: Use productivity tools and common applications effectively and constructively.	09/27/09
10-12	RBW	Physics	Light	1	17	15	xx3x	I/R/E	text	lg	lect/disc	test	Word Processing/ Spreadsheet	WA Ed Tech 2.3 Select and Use Applications: Use productivity tools and common applications effectively and constructively.	09/27/09
10-12	RBW	Physics	Light Lab	1	17	4	xx3x	I/R/E	laser, lab apparatus, text	lg - pairs	lect/lab	lab report	Word Processing/ Spreadsheet	WA Sci 2.1.2. Understand how to plan and conduct systematic and complex scientific investigations.	09/27/09
11-12	MAB	Spanish 4	Spanish Cooking	1	14	10	xxx4	E	mult	ind	ind	product	Web/Graphics		01/03/10

Figure 9.7 Curriculum Mapping Sample (7–12)

Worksheet 9.4:
Integration Planning Worksheet

Assignment	Big6	Technologies

The Big6™ Skills © 1987 Eisenberg & Berkowitz

Unit x Big6™ Matrix

Worksheet 9.11: Unit x Big6 Skills Matrix: ELEMENTARY SCHOOL

GR	TCHR	SUBJ	UNIT	M_PER	ASSIGN	TECH	The Big6						COMMENTS
							1	2	3	4	5	6	
00-00	LIE	LA	Colors	1234	worksheet	none	X	-	-	X	X	X	intro to Super3 and overall process
01-01	REB	LA	ABC book	x2xx	product	none	X	-	-		X		emphasize TD and Synthesis
01-01	MAB	Math	Whole/Parts	x2xx	worksheet	none							use of worksheets
03-03	RDY	Sci	Planets	xx3x	project	Web, Graphics		X	X	-	X	X	fun project; could use more time
03-03	RDY	Sci	Endangered Animals	xxx4	project	Web, PowerPoint, Graphics		X	X				
03-03	RDY	SS	Community	x2xx	project	PowerPoint, e-mail	X	X	-	-	X	X	brainstorm and narrow - hit hard
03-04	CAL	LA	Letter Writing	x2xx	product	Word Processing							
03-04	CAL	Math	Graphs	xxx4	product	none				X	X		introduce spreadsheet and graphing? Presentation in different formats
03-04	CAL	Sci	Simple Machines	1xxx	products	none	X				X		
03-04	CAL	Sci	Work & Energy	xxx4	test	none							
05-05	MBE	Library	Biography	xx3x	none	online catalog, Web	X	X	X				look to integrate into subject area
06-06	SEW	LA	Folktales and Legends	x23x	homework/test	none							
06-06	SEW	Sci	Vocabulary	1xxx	homework	none							
06-06	SEW	SS	Current Events	1234	report	Web, online articles	X	X	X	X	X	X	all year long - can teach all Big6 stages.
06-06	SEW	SS	Native Cultures	x2xx	test, product	Web				X	X	X	emphasize the output side of the Big6 process

The Big6™ Skills © 1987 Eisenberg & Berkowitz

Figure 9.8 Unit x Big6™ Matrix—Elementary

Unit x Big6™ Matrix

Worksheet 9.12: Unit x Big6 Skills Matrix: SECONDARY SCHOOL

GR	TCHR	SUBJ	UNIT	M_PER	ASSIGN	TECH	The Big6						COMMENTS
							1	2	3	4	5	6	
07-07	MBE	Info Lit	Dictionary Skill	1xxx	short written assignment	Web	-			X	X		Web and print sources
07-07	TMJ	Sci	Weather	xx3x	test	Web				X	X		organizing notes for studying for a test
07-07	TCH	SS	Recycling	x23x	report	Web/ Word Proc/PowerPoint/ Online Articles/ e-mail		X	X	-	X	-	lots of technology
08-08	TMJ	Sci	Classification	x2xx	product (classification website)	Web/articles/ PowerPoint/ Graphics	X						complex assignment; ways of organizing
08-08	MBE	Info Lit	Web authoring	x2xx	product (web page)	Web Authoring//Graphics					X		good design techniques
08-08	HJW	SS	Map Skills	1xxx	worksheet	Web		X		X			Web and print sources
09-12	CER	Health	Diet & Nutrition	1x3x	posters	Web/ PowerPoint	X	X	-	-	X	-	health reaches all students; repeats 2x year
09-12	CER	Health	Tobacco & Smoking	1x3x	test	none	X			X	X	-	cooperative teacher, test-taking strategies & the Big6
09-12	CER	Health	Drugs	x2x4	product	Web/ Word Processing/ PowerPoint/Graphics		X			X		presentation skills and design techniques
10-10	BAB	Math	Probability	xx3x	homework	none							
10-12	RBW	Physics	Light Lab	xx3x	lab report	Word Processing/ Spreadsheet					X		lab report format and style
10-12	RBW	Physics	Light	xx3x	test	Word Processing/ Spreadsheet							
11-12	CJC	LA	Catcher in the Rye	xx3x	report	Word Processing/Online Articles/Web		X	X				look for extensive analysis sources
11-12	MAB	Spanish 4	Spanish Cooking	xxx4	product	Web/Graphics		X			X		
11-12	BDE	SS	Supply & Demand	xx3x	obs/swa	Word Processing				X	X		recognizing credible information

The Big6™ Skills © 1987 Eisenberg & Berkowitz

Figure 9.9 Unit x Big6™ Matrix—Secondary

Unit x Big6™ Matrix

Figure 9.13: Sample Skills x Unit Matrix: MS. HALL - 4TH GRADE TEACHER

TCHR	SUBJ	UNIT	M_PER	PERS	TECH	1	2	3	4	5	6	COMMENTS
Spelling	Language Arts	Test	1234	40					X	-		strategies for learning/remembering spelling
State History	Social Studies	Written Report	12xx	30		X	X	X	X	X	X	major unit - lessons on all Big6
Geography	Social Studies	Maps, Product	1x3x	20	Paint, Draw, Picture Editor	X				X		computer graphics to produce maps
Listening Skills	Language Arts	Test	1xxx	10	digital recorder, audio books	X			X			note-taking, use digital recorder, audio books
Personal Hygiene	Health	Ads, Product	1xxx	15	PowerPoint	X	-			-	X	evaluating ads, creating posters
Letter Writing	Language Arts	Product	1xxx	15		X				X	X	what makes a good letter? Using word processing.
Food Groups	Health	Product (chart, posters, ads)	x2xx	15	PowerPoint, Web, Articles databases	X	X	X	X			articles in databases and on the Web.
Multiplication Tables-10s	Math	Test	x2xx	20					-			just mention ways to memorize
Structure of Plants	Science	Experiment, Test	xx34	20	Excel, Word					X		lab reports - use spreadsheet and word processor template
Rocks and Minerals	Science	Worksheet, Test	xx3x	20	Web		X	X				use sources for worksheet - focus on brainstorm, narrow, and keywords
Metric Measurements	Math	Test	xx3x	20			X	X				test will include examples of the metric system in action. Will need sources.
Deserts/Life, Weather	Social Studies/ Science	Written and Oral Report	xx3x	30	Articles databases	X	X	X				2 subjects, lots of electronic information seeking strategies, location & access
Mixed Numbers	Math	Worksheet	xx3x	20							X	self-evaluation

The Big6™ Skills © 1987 Eisenberg & Berkowitz

Figure 9.10 Unit x Big6™ Matrix—Ms. Hall—4th Grade Teacher

Unit x Big6™ Matrix

Worksheet 9.14: Unit x Big6 Skills Matrix: SOCIAL STUDIES DEPARTMENT

GR	TCHR	UNIT	M_PER	ASSIGN	TECH	The Big6						COMMENTS
						1	2	3	4	5	6	
7	Hussain	Recycling	1xxx	product	Web, electronic resources, PowerPoint	X	X	X	-	X	-	*major unit, Big6 overview*
7	Hussain	Global Communities	x23x	product	Web, electronic resources, PowerPoint	X	X	X	-	X	-	*emphasize information technology sources*
8	Sprague	Rainforest	1xxx	test, swa, project	Web, PowerPoint	X				X		*focus on problem definition*
8	Sprague	Climate Change	xx3x	project	spreadsheet, Web		X		X			*make charts, credibility of sources*
9	Sullivan	Latin America	1xxx	Test		X	-	-	-	X	X	*test taking strategies - task definition, synthesis*
9	Sullivan	Northern Africa	x2xx	Test, Report	Web		X	X	X		-	*sources - web searching, note-taking*
9	Sullivan	India	xx3x	Maps, Product	Web, Graphic					X		*computer software to create various kinds of maps*
10	Ryan	Between the Wars	12xx	Test, Short Written Assignment	Word Processing					X		*essay writing strategies*
10	Ryan	WW I	1xxx	Test		X				X		
10	Ryan	WW II	x2xx	Project, Test	Electronic resources		X	X	-	-		
10	Ryan	Cold War	xx3x	Test							X	
10	Ryan	Vietnam	xxx4	Oral Report	Web, electronic resources, PowerPoint	-	-	-	X	X	-	*presentation and graphics software*
11	Jackson	Constitution	x2xx	Written and Oral Report	PowerPoint					X	X	
11	Jackson	Civil War	xx3x	Test		X						*nature of test*
11	Rossini	Colonization of Western Hem.	1xxx	Test		X			X			*extracting relevant information from the textbook and notes*
11	Rossini	Civil War	xx3x	Report, Project	Web for archival materials	X	X	X	X			*using primary and secondary sources*
12	Alarby	The New Information Economy	x2x4	industry analysis and profile	Web, electronic resources, e-mail	-	X	X	X	-	-	*uses community mentors*
12	Petruso	Street Law	xxx4	Project	Electronic resources, web		X			X		*community resources and law libraries*
12	Valesky	Stock Market	1234	Project	Web, electronic resources	X	X	X	-	-	X	*full-year, competitive intelligence*

Figure 9.11 Unit x Big6™ Matrix—Social Studies Department

The Big6™ Skills © 1987 Eisenberg & Berkowitz

Worksheet 9.5:
Unit x Big6™ Matrix

Worksheet 9.15: Unit x Big6 Skills Matrix

GR	TCHR	SUBJ	UNIT	M_PER	ASSIGN	TECH	The Big6						COMMENTS
							1	2	3	4	5	6	

The Big6™ Skills © 1987 Eisenberg & Berkowitz

Worksheet 9.5: (continued)

Worksheet 9.15: Unit x Big6 Skills Matrix

GR	TCHR	SUBJ	UNIT	M_PER	ASSIGN	TECH	The Big6						COMMENTS
							1	2	3	4	5	6	

The Big6™ Skills © 1987 Eisenberg & Berkowitz

Worksheet 9.6:
K–12 Integrated Big6™ / Curriculum Timeline

GR	Tchr	Subject	Assignment	1	3	5	7	9	11	13	15	17	19	21	23	25	27	29	31	33	35	37	39	1	2	3	4	5	6

The Big6™ Skills © 1987 Eisenberg & Berkowitz

Sample Integrated Big6™ / Curriculum Timeline

GR	Tchr	Subject	Assignment	Curriculum (Timeline)	Big6: 1	2	3	4	5	6
00-00	LIE	LA	worksheet	COLORS************	X	-	-	X	X	X
01-01	REB	LA	product		X	-	-		X	
01-01	MAB	Math	worksheet	ABC Book				X		X
03-03	RDY	SS	project	COMMUNITY***	X	X	-	-	-	-
03-03	RDY	Sci	project	**PLANETS**	X	X	X	-	X	
03-04	CAL	Sci	products	SIMPLE MACHINES*****	X				X	X
03-04	CAL	Math	product	GRAPHS				X	X	X
06-06	SEW	SS	report	Current Events************	X	X	X	X	X	X
06-06	SEW	SS	test	Native Cultures****				X	X	X
07-07	TCH	SS	product	RECYCLING	X	X	-	-	X	-
08-08	HJW	SS	worksheet	Map Skills / NOISE**********	X	-	X	X	X	
08-08	TMJ	Sci	wr report		-	X	X	-	X	-
09-12	CER	Health	posters	Diet/Nuitrition	X	X	X	-	X	-
09-12	CER	Health	test	Smoking	X	X	X	X	X	X
09-12	CER	Health	product	DRUGS**	X	-	-	-	-	X
11-12	CJC	LA	report	Catcher/Rye	X	X	X	-	X	
11-12	BDE	SS	obs/swa	Supply & Demand**	X	X	X	-	X	

Figure 9.12 Sample Integrated Big6™/Curriculum Timetable

The Big6™ Skills © 1987 Eisenberg & Berkowitz

Part 10:
The Parent Connection

▶ **10.0 Introduction** **279**

▶ **10.1 Overview Slides** **281**

▶ **10.2 Parent Exercises**. **283**

▶ **10.3 Hopsicker Letter** **285**

▶ **10.4 Article—Helping With
Homework**. **287**

The BIG 6™ The Parent Connection

10.0 Introduction

This Part of the *Big6 Workshop Handbook* focuses on the parent or caregiver connection to information literacy. Educators, parents and caregivers are important partners in helping students to gain information skills and to succeed in school. We often hold parent and community workshops to encourage parents to get involved in their child's education in constructive and meaningful ways. We find that parents are eager audiences and we encourage you to use the materials in this section (as well as our *Helping with Homework* book) to conduct your own parent community sessions.

Parent sessions do not need to be long—one hour maximum or even as short as 15 to 20 minutes. The point is to help parents understand the Big6 and then learn to guide their children through assignments and tasks using the Big6 approach. Our sessions usually undertake the following outline:

- The information age: Implications for learning & teaching
- Information literacy: The Big6 Skills process & approach
- The parent role
- The technology connection
- Q&A.

The "Overview" slides explain the parent role. We emphasize that parents can help and use the Super3 and Big6 at three different times:

- Before children actually start their homework: talk through the process (i.e., to outline the assignment and develop an action plan in order to complete the work.

- During the work: help children find and use appropriate resources, troubleshoot with their children if they get stuck, monitor progress and check work.

- After their children are finished: review their work.

The detailed chart, "Helping with Homework," (Figure 10.2) provides three different examples of guiding and coaching. We find that this chart helps adult audiences understand how to use the Big6 to guide students.

Two exercises (Worksheets 10.1–10.2) help parents develop guiding and coaching skills. The first exercise deals with a single assignment (the astronomy paper) while the second present scenarios from a variety of situations. We sometimes divide parent/community audiences into groups, work through the sample exercises, and then discuss findings with the full audience.

The "Hopsicker Letter" (Figure 10.3) is an example of communication from a teacher to parents to explain the information skills-to-classroom connection. The "Helping With Homework: A Big6 Assignment Organizer" is a tool to help students manage their assignments.

Last of all, the article, "Helping With Homework: A Parent's Guide to Information Problem-Solving," brings parent-guide concepts all together. This article is based on our book, *Helping with Homework: A Parent's Guide to Information Problem-Solving.* You have permission to photocopy and widely distribute the article.

Parents and caregivers can and should have an important role to help their children succeed. However, while parents are well-intentioned and wish to provide assistance, they often lack the necessary understanding and an effective approach to truly help. In fact, many times, parent-child help sessions end abruptly in conflict and confrontation.

We encourage parents to avoid confrontation by using the Big6 and Super3 to help guide or coach. With the Super3 and Big6 approach, parents are not asked to teach—because that usually leads to their child exclaiming "that's not the way my teacher does it!" Rather, the parent needs to guide their child on teacher-determined, established goals and curriculum.

10.1 Overview Slides

Helping With Homework
The Big6 Approach

The Parent Connection:
Helping with Homework

"Parents can make a difference by helping, not by teaching or doing."

"Parents can assist children to learn how to approach information problems (both in and out of school) and to choose the tools to solve those problems."

from *Helping with Homework*, 1997

Approach for Parents

- **Parent as helper-guide**
  - ‣ before homework: talk through
  - ‣ during homework: troubleshoot
  - ‣ after homework: check
- **Using the Big6™ process**
  - ‣ a tool for solving information problems
  - ‣ context for use of technology

Figure 10.1 Overview

Helping with Homework Chart

Information Problem Solving Process	1st Grade Language Arts—Maria's homework is to make an ABC book.	7th Grade Social Studies—Leon has to do a social studies report on recycling (three minute oral report with visual aids).	10th Grade Math—Joanne is working on probability homework problems. She missed two days of school this week.
Task Definition	■ After the teacher explains the assignment, Maria decides that she will make an ABC book based on the topic of food. While talking with her mother, Maria realizes she will need to gather lots of foods (and spellings).	■ Leon decides to narrow the topic of recycling to investigate ways to recycle tires.	■ Joanne realizes that because she missed school, she doesn't really know how to do the problems assigned.
Information Seeking Strategies	■ Maria decides to ask her mother for help to get information about foods. Together they realize that a cookbook might help and that maybe she can find one for kids in the school library.	■ Leon talks to the school teacher-librarian about his idea. She suggests newspaper and magazine articles in the online databases and government Web sites as two good sources.	■ Joanne asks her older brother what she should do. He asks what the teacher relies on most—the textbook or class notes. Joanne says that the class notes are most important.
Location & Access	■ The school teacher-librarian helps Maria find a children's cookbook.	■ Leon searches in the online databases and also uses Google to search the WWW.	■ Joanne calls her friend Tonya and arranges to go over to her house to look over her notes.
Use of Information	■ Maria reads through the book to find the names of fruits, vegetables, and other foods. She writes each name on a card.	■ Leon reads the articles on the screen and is able to copy and paste text directly into his word processor document.	■ Tonya explains how the notes are organized and shows Joanne the pages that specifically relate to the homework. Joanne copies Tonya's notes.
Synthesis	■ Maria uses pictures from magazines, construction paper, and crayons to illustrate her book. She puts all the pages in alphabetical order and staples them together. Maria practices reading her ABC book to her mother.	■ He practices his oral presentation. He makes a few changes in order to be more specific about the benefits of recycling tires.	■ Joanne is able to do three of the problems, but gets stuck on the other three. She writes a note on her homework that she needs additional help.
Evaluation	■ Maria decides that she likes her book, but that maybe next time she can create her book using a computer.	■ Leon reviews his draft and realizes he has plenty of specific information about recycling tires but needs to add more general information about recycling in the introduction.	■ Joanne realizes that she still needs direct information from her teacher and arranges to come in for extra help.

The Big6™ Skills © 1987 Eisenberg & Berkowitz

Figure 10.2 Helping with Homework Chart

282   *The Big6™ Workshop Handbook, Implementation and Impact, Fourth Edition*

10.2 Parent Exercises

Worksheet 10.1: Parent Exercise: Developing an Understanding in Context

Parent Exercise: The Astronomy Paper. Your child is studying astronomy. The assignment is to write a paper about a trip to a planet or other body in the solar system. Please try to identify the relevant Big6™ stage and note possible actions that you might take. Note: There are six situations, one for each Big6™.

Situation	Big6™	Your Possible Actions
Your child says, "I can't find anything about Mars. How am I supposed to do this project anyway?"		
Your child is confused about exactly what to do and asks, "Isn't this just a typical astronomy report?" What could you do?		
Your child has trouble creating a picture using a computer paint program. What can you do?		
Your child has trouble reading from your neighbor's college astronomy textbook. How can you help?		
Your child asks you to check if all the necessary parts are included. What can you do?		
Your child has trouble finding information on Callisto in the encyclopedia. How can you help?		

The Big6™ Skills © 1987 Eisenberg & Berkowitz

Worksheet 10.2:
Big6™ Situations: Possible Actions

General Exercise: Parent-Student Interactions. Below are examples of problems that students might have in a variety of situations. Please try to identify the relevant Big6 skill and note possible actions that you might take. Note: More than one Big6 may apply to a given situation and not all Big6™ are necessarily used.

Situations	Big6	Your Possible Actions
Your 11th grade daughter is flipping through a thick guide to colleges. She's frustrated and anxious and says, "Maybe I just won't go to college."		
Your son is working on a 4th grade science experiment. He asks for help because he doesn't know how he should take notes on his observations.		
Your daughter and her friend complain that they don't know what's on tomorrow's test.		
Your son just finished his literary criticism paper. You ask, "How did you do?" He responds, "I haven't a clue."		
You rush in the room after your daughter screams, "I just can't do this!" You see her staring at the shoebox full of notecards for her geography report.		
Calvin says, "If I had a computer, I'm sure I'd get better grades on my book reports."		

The Big6™ Skills © 1987 Eisenberg & Berkowitz

10.3 Hopsicker Letter

Sample Parent Letter

SAMPLE • SAMPLE • SAMPLE • SAMPLE • SAMPLE • SAMPLE • SAMPLE

Mr. Scott Hopsicker
Wayne Central High School
Social Studies Department

October 8, 2009

Dear Parent or Guardian,

As a teacher, and more importantly your student's Social Studies teacher, I know that parents/guardians can be key partners in helping their children be successful in school. I am asking for your help because parents/guardians can provide an atmosphere that fosters achievement and success. However, the question is, "What can parents/guardians do to help their students that will have the biggest impact?" Answer: Assignments—especially homework.

U.S. History and Government is designed to be a conceptual course aimed at giving students an understanding of events and issues that impact social, political, economic, and foreign policy concerns. The course covers such topics as: the Constitution, impact of the presidents, and Supreme Court cases throughout America's history. Homework is assigned on a regular basis. Assignments are ways for my students to show me what they know. They are also ways for students to learn, review, remediate, or extend what is taught in my classroom. To be successful on quizzes and tests in this course, the homework must be done.

You can help your student be successful with their homework assignments by guiding, assisting, and generally making it easier for them to succeed. The attached "Homework Planner" offers a framework that you can use to guide students through assignments and homework. I think that this simple tool can make a big difference. I will make copies available for all students and encourage that they be used to help organize homework assignments. I hope you will help me by using this organizer with your student whenever he/she has homework in U.S. History and Government.

Please feel free to contact me at the high school whenever you have any concerns. If you leave a message at the main office, I will return your call as soon as possible.

Thank you in advance for your support and cooperation.

Sincerely,

Scott Hopsicker

Reprinted with author's permission.

SAMPLE • SAMPLE • SAMPLE • SAMPLE • SAMPLE • SAMPLE • SAMPLE

Figure 10.3 Sample Parent Letter

Worksheet 10.3: Assignment Organizer

Assignment:_____ Date Due:_____

Complete Big6 Skills #1–5 BEFORE you BEGIN your assignment.
Complete Big6 Skill #6 BEFORE you TURN IN your assignment.

Big6 Skill #1: Task Definition

What does this assignment require me to do?

What information do I need in order to do this assignment?

Big6 Skill #2: Information Seeking Strategies

What sources can I use to do the assignment?
Make a list, then circle the best sources.

Big6 Skill #3: Location & Access

Where can I find my sources? Do I need help?
If so, who can help me?

Big6 Skill #4: Use of Information

What do I need to do with the information?

_____ read/view/listen

_____ take notes

_____ answer questions

_____ other: _____

_____ chart and/or write an essay

_____ copy and highlight

_____ properly cite

Big6 Skill #5: Synthesis

What product does this assignment require?

Big6 Skill #6: Evaluation

Student self-evaluation checklist:

_____ I did what I was supposed to do (see Big6 #1, Task Definition)
_____ The assignment is complete.

The Big6 Eisenberg & Berkowitz, 1987. Assignment Organizer © Berkowitz & Hopsicker, 1997.

10.4 Article—Helping with Homework

A Parent's Guide to Information Problem-Solving

by Robert E. Berkowitz

Introduction:

Parents and caregivers can help their children succeed in school, but they need an effective approach to do this well. The approach taken in the book, *Helping with Homework: A Parent's Guide to Information Problem-Solving,* is based upon the Big6 Skills problem-solving approach. The Big6 Skills apply to any problem or decision-making activity that requires a solution or result based upon information. An abundant amount of information is available, and the Big6 can help parents deal effectively with that information to guide their youngsters through school assignments.

- The Big6 Approach: The Big6 approach has six main components: task definition, information seeking strategies, location and access, use of information, synthesis, and evaluation.

- Task Definition: In the task definition stage, students need to determine what is expected from the assignment. They will also need to determine the information requirements.

- Information Seeking Strategies: Once students know what's expected of them, they need to identify the range resources they will need to solve the task as defined, then select the most useful sources.

- Location & Access: Next the students must find potentially useful resources and the information within each source. Location and access is the stage of implementation of the information seeking strategy.

- Use of Information: Use of information requires the students to engage the information (e.g., read, view, and listen) and decide how to use the information to meet their task.

- Synthesis: Synthesis requires the students to construct, communicate, and repackage the information to meet the requirements of the task as defined.

- Evaluation: Finally, students need to evaluate the quality of their work on two levels before it is turned in to the teacher. Students need to know if their work will meet their teacher's and their own expectations for (1) quality and (2) efficiency.

Students may apply the Big6 stages in any order, but must complete all stages.

Parents' Role and Students' Role:

The Big6 approach requires parents and students to adopt a working role. The parent assumes the role of a "coach" and the child assumes the role of "thinker and doer." As a coach, the parent will use the Big6 Skills to guide the student through all the stages required to complete the assignment. The parent will first ask their child to explain an assignment in his or her own words. This is "task definition"—a logical first step. Parents can also help by discussing possible sources of information. This is "information seeking strategies." Parents can then help their children implement information seeking strategies by helping their children find useful resources. This is the Big6 stage called "location and access." Location and access may have to be repeated during an assignment because some children may not identify everything they need at the beginning. Parents can facilitate by brainstorming with their children alternate places where information might be available. In the "use of information" stage, parents can discuss whether the information the child located is relevant, and if so, help the child decide how to use it. In the "synthesis" stage, parents can ask for a summary of the information in the child's own words, and ask whether the information fits the requirements identified in the "task definition" stage. The end of any assignment is the final check, an evaluation of all the work that has been done. Parents can help their children with the "evaluation" stage by discussing whether the product answers the original question, whether it meets the teacher's expectations, and whether the project could have been done more efficiently. This is all part of a self-evaluation process.

As children work through each Big6 stage, they need to think about what to do, and then find appropriate ways to do it. This is their role—"thinker and doer." Parents should encourage children to be as independent as possible, but children often have difficulty beginning an assignment because they are confused about what is expected of them. Whatever the reason is for their inability to get started, students are ultimately responsible for doing their work. When parents act as coaches, they can help their children assume responsibility for school work; engage them in conversation about what is expected of them; and guide them throughout the assignment using the Big6 Skills.

Why Assignments?

In addition to contributing to school achievement, many teachers believe that homework teaches students to take responsibility for tasks, and homework teaches students how to work independently. Homework helps children learn and develop transferable skills that will help them not only throughout their school career, but also through life. Specifically, homework helps students learn how to plan, organize tasks, manage time, make informed decisions, and solve problems. These are among the essential skills that contribute to functioning effectively in the world of work, families, and school.

Schools with a strong homework policy believe they produce students who achieve more, when compared to classes and schools that assign less homework. Teachers believe that homework has a positive effect on student achievement. Homework's impact on achievement is a result of well-placed effort more than time. When students focus on their homework—because it is intrinsically motivating or because they have good homework habits—achievement increases. Assignments provide students with an opportunity to review and practice new material, to correct errors in

understanding and production, and to assess personal levels of mastery.

Nearly every assignment is an information problem that can be solved using the Big6. For example, the goal of many homework assignments is to have students practice a skill taught in class. If a child has a problem understanding an assignment, the parent may encourage the child to explain what he or she does not understand. The parent can use information seeking strategies to help the child identify information sources by asking questions such as: "Is there another student in your class who can help you understand how to do this?" or, "Did the teacher give any other examples?" The parent can help the child identify information sources and suggest ways to get them. For instance, the public television network may have a homework hotline, the public library may have study guides, or a neighborhood child may be in the same class.

Technology and The Big6:

Technology is widely accepted as a teaching tool in classrooms; therefore, extending the use of technology to the home by assigning meaningful homework provides an opportunity for students to practice valuable technology skills that will serve them well beyond the completion of the homework itself.

Technology for student learning activities outside the classroom has changed rapidly in recent years. From the Big6 approach perspective, wikis, webcasts, podcasts, threaded discussions, blogs, e-mail lists, and social networking sites all provide homework opportunities for students and extend student learning.

The Big6 approach encompasses the benefits associated with the use of technology in education. Information technology can help students learn, practice, and extend both content and information literacy skills. Information technology tools and software can connect students to information and help students organize information. Technology tools can also help students to edit written work, check grammar and spelling, chart and graph quantities, and construct outlines. Technology and its accompanying software can help with time management, setting priorities, and evaluating efficiency.

Conclusion:

It is an axiom of American education that parents are partners in their children's education. Parents have traditionally participated in the education process by helping their children with homework. The Big6 approach can help parents effectively guide their children through assignments and at the same time help their children become independent learners and users of information.

Bibliography and Recommended Reading:

American Psychological Association. 1998, March 4. "Research Shows Homework Does Boost Academic Achievement; but Overemphasizing Grades and Performance May Lead to Cheating." *ScienceDaily,* http://www.sciencedaily.com/releases/1998/03/980304073520.htm#.

Bailey, L. 2006. "Interactive Homework: A Tool for Fostering Parent-Child Interactions and Improving Learning Outcomes for at-Risk Young Children." *Early Childhood Education Journal,* 34 (2): 155–67.

Clark, C. 2006. "The Heavy Burden of Homework Is Heaping Stress on Parents and Kids." *The Province* (Vancouver, BC), (December 10): A.24.

Cooper, H. 2006. "Homework Helps Students Succeed in School, as Long as There Isn't Too Much." Study. Duke University, Durham, NC.

Eisenberg, M. B., and R. E. Berkowitz. 1990. *Information Problem Solving: The Big6 Skills Approach to Library and Information Skills Instruction.* Norwood, NJ: Ablex. Ablex Publishing Corporation, 355 Chestnut St. Norwood, NJ 07648 ($22.95). Document not available from EDRS. (ED 330 364)

Eisenberg, M. B., and R. E. Berkowitz. 1992. "Information Problem-Solving: The Big Six Skills Approach." *School Library Media Activities Monthly,* 8 (5): 27–29, 37, 42. (EJ 438 023)

Eisenberg, M. B., and R. E. Berkowitz. 1995, August. "The Six Study Habits of Highly Effective Students: Using the Big Six to Link Parents, Students, and Homework." *School Library Journal,* 41 (8): 22–25. (EJ 510 346)

Eisenberg, M. B., and R. E. Berkowitz. 1996. "Helping with Homework: A Parent's Guide to Information Problem-Solving." Syracuse, NY: ERIC Clearinghouse on Information and Technology. Available from Big6 Associates, LLC.

Eisenberg, M. B., and L. L. Spitzer. 1991, October. "Skills and Strategies for Helping Students Become More Effective Information Users." *Catholic Library World,* 63 (2): 115–20. (EJ 465 828)

Eren, Ozkan, and Daniel J. Henderson. 2006, May. "The Impact of Homework on Student Achievement." *Social Sciences Research Network,* http://ssrn.com/abstract=917447.

Granowsky, A. 1991. "What Parents Can Do to Help Children Succeed in School." *PTA Today,* 17 (1): 5–6. (EJ 436 757)

Indiana State Department of Education. 1990. "Get Ready, Get Set, Parent's Role: Parent Booklet." [Booklet]. Indianapolis, IN: Author. (ED 337 264)

Konecki, L. R. 1992. "Parent Talk: Helping Families Relate to Schools and Facilitate Children's Learning." Paper presented at the Annual Meeting of the Association of Teacher Educators (Orlando, FL, February 17, 1992). (ED 342 745)

Lankes, R. D. 1996. "The Bread & Butter of the Internet: A Primer and Presentation Packet for Educators." (IR-101). Syracuse, NY: ERIC Clearinghouse on Information & Technology. (ED 402 924)

Scarnati, J. T., and R. B. Platt. 1991, October. "Lines and Pies and Bars, Oh My! Making Math Fun." *PTA Today,* 17 (1): 9–11. (EJ 436 759)

Trautwein, U. 2007. "The Homework/Achievement Relation Reconsidered: Differentiating Homework Time, Homework

Frequency, and Homework Effort." *Learning & Instruction*, 17 (3): 372–88.

U.S. Department of Education, National Center for Education Statistics. 2007. *The Condition of Education 2007. Indicator 21: Time Spent on Homework.* Washington, DC: U.S. Government Printing Office. [NCES 2007064].

Van, J. A. 1991, October. "Parents Are Part of the Team at Hearst Award Winner's School." *PTA Today*, 17 (1): 7–8. (EJ 436 758)

vanVoorhis, F. L. 2003. "Interactive Homework in Middle School: Effects on Family Involvement and Science Achievement." *Journal of Educational Research*, 96 (6): 323–38.

Think Sheet

Part 11:
Big6™ and Super3™ Program Planning

▶ **11.0 Introduction** **295**

▶ **11.1 Personal Planning** **297**

▶ **11.2 School or District Planning** **298**

▶ **11.3 Program Assessment** **299**

▶ **11.4 Next Steps Planning** **300**

▶ **11.5 Putting it all Together** **302**

Big6™ and Super3™ Program Planning

11.0 Introduction

After working through the content, worksheets, exercises, and readings in this *Big6™ Workshop Handbook*, you should be well-informed about the Big6 processes and approach. You should also have some conceptual frameworks and practical methods for planning and implementing Big6 and Super3 Skills instruction on the classroom, school, and district levels.

The Big6 is an approach to information and technology skills instruction that puts students in a position to be successful information problem-solvers—from young elementary students through the college years. In this *Handbook*, we emphasize:

■ The nature and scope of the Super3 and Big6 processes and skills.

■ How information and communications technology skills are fully integrated into the Big6 approach.

■ Needs and mechanisms for instructional design and planning on the macro and micro levels.

■ The role of assessment in terms of efficiency and effectiveness.

■ Planning and implementing a comprehensive Big6 information literacy program on the classroom, library, building, or district level.

■ Collaborative roles for all educators as well as parents, community members, and even students in implementing meaningful Big6 instruction.

Now what remains is the formal plan for the future; to take all of these parts and shape them into a cohesive whole. This action plan will require you to do the following:

Assess the current status of your own level of expertise as well as the status of integrated skills instruction at the school or district level:

- Determine what Big6 Skills the students needs to attain
- Determine what curriculum, technology, and planning will help meet students needs
- Establish a timeframe to accomplish these goals.

In this Part, we provide content and worksheets (11.1–11.5) to begin long-term planning for effective Big6 Skills instruction. These worksheets will consider students' needs as well as the status of personal, school, and district situations. The worksheets provide a mechanism to gauge the needs of students, the extent of your own expertise, and the current degree of the school community's engagement. You can then use this base to plan for further personal and systemic development.

We urge you to "think big!" Information and technology skills instruction is not optional; it's not an add-on. Big6 Skills instruction is part of a basic skills education in the 21st century. Being information literate is as essential as reading, writing, and arithmetic.

To borrow from the mission statement of the American Association of School Librarians and the Association for Educational Communications and Technology (with an edit suggested by Joyce Valenza), our goal is "to ensure that students are effective users [and producers] of ideas and information" (*Information Power*, 1988, 1998; Joyce Valenza, personal communications 2009).

We are confident that you will use the ideas, strategies, and tools offered in this *Handbook* to make a difference in your schools and communities. We encourage you to customize and personalize the various forms and activities in order to envision, analyze, plan, implement, and evaluate on your own.

Again—think Big(6)!

11.1 Personal Planning

Worksheet 11.1: Personal Planning

	Current Status	Needs	Time Frame
Big6™ Information and Technology Skills			
Technology: Personal Skills			
Technology: Context			
Curriculum: Instructional Design			
Planning: Micro			
Planning: Macro			

The Big6™ Skills © 1987 Eisenberg & Berkowitz

11.2 School or District Planning

Worksheet 11.2:
School or District Planning

	Current Status	Needs	Time Frame
Student Skills and Needs			
Curriculum			
Big6™ Information and Technology Skills Instruction			
Technology			
Planning: Macro			

The Big6™ Skills © 1987 Eisenberg & Berkowitz

11.3 Program Assessment

Worksheet 11.3: Program Assessment

1. Determine key indicators for a quality Big6™ program.
2. Review the current status for each indicator.
3. Comment to help guide action planning.

Indicator	Current Status	Comment
Example: ■ Big6 Skills are integrated throughout the curriculum.	Example: ■ There is a Long Range Curriculum Planning Team that includes classroom teachers, library media specialist, and technology teacher. ■ An analysis of the Curriculum Map shows Big6 "Bonanza" units in science, social studies, and language arts—grades 6 and 8. Also, strong Big6 units in science and health—grade 7.	Example: ■ Need to develop or redesign units in art, music, and math—grades 6 through 8.

The Big6™ Skills © 1987 Eisenberg & Berkowitz

11.4 Next Steps Planning

Worksheet 11.4: Benefits

Answer these questions being as specific as possible. Be prepared to share your answers with others in the workshop.

1. The integration of the Big6 approach into the instructional program at my school and district can benefit students by:

2. The integration of the Big6 approach into the instructional program at my school and district can benefit classroom teachers, technology teachers, teacher-librarians, and other educators by:

3. The integration of the Big6 approach into the instruction program at my school can benefit subject area programs, library information & technology programs, and school or district initiatives and priorities by:

4. I can help my school or district implement Big6 approach by:

Worksheet 11.5:
Next Steps Planning

Next Steps Planning Worksheet

	Immediate	Short Term	Long Term
What do I want to have happen?			
How can I make it happen?			
Who can help me and how can they help?			
What will I accept as evidence that I am achieving my goals?			
What will I do tomorrow?			

The Big6™ Skills © 1987 Eisenberg & Berkowitz

Worksheet 11.6: Putting it all Together

Summary—Problems

- Information overload
- Information quality
- Student lack of information & technology skills
- Technology out of context

© Eisenberg & Berkowitz

Summary—Solutions

- Focus on process, not just content
- Information & technology literacy – the Super3 and Big6
- In context—not an add-on!
  - Within the process
  - Tied to existing curriculum, instruction, assignments

© Eisenberg & Berkowitz

Final Suggestions

- Recognize the challenges of the information age
- Remember context #1—the information problem-solving process (the Big6).
- Remember context #2—technology in a Big6 context.
- Remember context #3—the curriculum and real needs.
- To make it happen: a partnership: classroom teachers, library/info professionals, technology teachers, administrators, staff, students, community.

© Eisenberg & Berkowitz

1 + 1 + 1 + 1

**Classroom Curriculum
+
Big6
+
Technology
=
STUDENT LEARNING**

© Eisenberg & Berkowitz

Think Sheet

Index

A

Achieving Educational Standards Using the Big6 (Murray), 127
Acing the Exam (Margolis), 214–217
Administrators, 31, 161, 171, 217
American Association of School Librarians (AASL), 125, 176
American Library Association, 125
Anderson, Cyndee, xvi
Applied level application, 49
ARCS Model of Motivational Design, 182, 205–207
Assessment, 231–244
  Big6™ scoring guides, 233
  Exercise, 233
  Introduction to, 231
  Process of, 231–232
  Self, 232
  Worksheets, 234–244
Association for Educational Communications and Technology (AECT), 162
Association of College and Research Libraries (ACRL), 6
Association of Supervision and Curriculum Development (ASCD), 160
Attention, in ARCS Model, 182, 205–206

B

Bartow, Colet, 125, 127
Baseline technology, defined, 96
Beginning stage, Super3, 27, 29
Benchmarks, 124
Berkowitz, R. E. (Bob), xvi, 97, 110, 112, 162, 167, 168, 173, 183, 208–209, 212–213, 218, 222, 223–224, 287–290
Big6™
  Content standards, 153–155
  Introduction to, 3–22
  Learning, 45–77
  Macro planning, 245–275
  Micro planning, 179–228
  Program planning, 295–303
  Standards, 123–128
  Technology and, 95–119

  Tests, 156–177
  Themes of, 81–91
Big6™, learning, 47–77
  Answer key, 76–77
  Curriculum connection worksheet, 74
  Information literacy, 48–49
  Introduction to, 47–48
  Worksheet, applied level, 69–73
  Worksheet, information literacy, 48–49
  Worksheet, interpretive level, 58–68
  Worksheet, literal level, 58–65
Big6™, technology and, 95–119
  Information, communication, and technology (ICT) skills, 112–115
  Introduction to, 95–97
  Web resources for, 107–109
  Worksheets, 98–106
Big6™, themes of, 81–91
  Introduction to, 95–97
  Worksheets, 98–106
Big6™ standards, 123–128
  Educational standards and, 124
  Information literacy and ICT, 125
  Subject area content, 125–128, 153–155
Big6™ tests, 156–177, 123–129
  PowerPoint slides on, 156–158
  State tests and, 128–129
  Web information sources, 126–127
Bruett, Karen, 175
Bynum, Marjorie, 176

C

Carges, Mike, 214
CCOT, 4
Change
  Elements that effect, 4
  Key points about, 4–5
  Planning for, 13
Charts, Big6, 48
Compatibility, as element of change, 4
Complexity, as element of change, 4
Confidence, in ARCS Model, 182, 205, 206
Curriculum mapping, 248–250

Curriculum Mapping Data Collection
    Worksheet, 254
Curriculum unit, 249–250, 251–252

D

Darrow, Rob, 107
Diamond Thinking, 212–213
Do, as Super3 stage, 29

E

Educational standards, 124
Educational Testing Service (ETS), 174
Effort, expectancy-value theory and, 205
Eisenberg, M. B. (Mike), xvi, 97, 110, 112, 129,
    159, 162, 164, 168, 182, 218, 226, 248
End stage, Super3, 28, 30
English Language Learners (ELL), 30
Essential learnings, 124
Ewing, Tom, 175
Expectancy-value theory, 205

F

Frameworks, 124

G

Grade level expectations, 124

H

Homework, helping with, 287–290
Hopsicker, Scott, 214, 215, 217–220, 221, 223,
    285

I

Information, communication, and technology
    skills (ICT), 95, 110–119
    Big6 Skills approach, 111, 112–115
    Information problem-solving, 110–119
    Standards, 125
Information literacy, xi, xiii, 5–6, 14, 18–22, 48–49
    Parents and, 279–290
Information literacy standards, 125
Information Literacy Standards for Student
    Learning, 176
Information problem-solving, ICT skills for,
    110–119

Evaluation, 115
    Information seeking strategies, 112–113
    Locate/access information, 113–114
    Relevant information, extracting, 114
    Synthesis, 114–115
    Task definition, 112
Information seeking strategies, 112–113
    Information sources and, 210
Information sources, 210
Information Technology Association of
    America, 176
Instructional change, understanding, 5
Instructional Materials Motivation Survey
    (IMMS), 206
International Society for Technology in
    Education (ISTE), 111, 125, 176
    National Educational Technology
        Standards for Students, 111, 162, 176
Interpretive level application, 49
It's All About Learning (Eisenberg article),
    159–173
    Content area standards, 163–165
    Information skills instruction, 162–163
    Library media programs, 160–161
    Standardized testing, 159–160, 166–171

J

Johnson, Doug, 97, 110, 112

K

Keller, John M., 205, 206
Kuhlthau, Carol, 161, 162
KWHL Chart, 208–209

L

Lance, Keith Curry, 160
Landgraf, Kurt M., 174
Library Media Connection, 125
    Eisenberg article in, 159–173
Library media programs, 160–161
Literal level application, 49

M

Macro planning, Big6™, 245–275
    Context, 255–257
    Curriculum mapping, 252–253

Introduction, 247–252
Worksheets, 253–274
Mankato Schools Information Literacy Curriculum Guideline, 111
Margolis, Rick, 214
McMullen, Susan, 83, 210–211
Micro planning, Big6™, 181–228
Big6™ skills, 182
Diamond Thinking, 212
Improving student test scores, 1214–215
Information sources, 210–211
Introduction to, 181–183
KWHL Chart, 208–209
Margolis, Rick article, 214–217
Plagiarism, 108, 226–228
Small, Ruth article, 205–207
Success strategy, 218–225
Super3™ sample lessons, 194–204
Worksheets, 184–193
Middle stage, Super3, 29
Motivational Delivery Checklist, 206
Motivational quality assessment instruments, 206–207
Motivation in Instructional Design (Small), 205–207
Murray, Janet, 125, 127, 133, 162, 174

N

National Assessment of Educational Progress (NAEP), 128
National Educational Technology Standards for Students (NETS-S), 176
No Child Left Behind act, 159
Number connecting exercise, 7–12

O

Observability, as element of change, 4
Occupational Outlook Handbook, 176

P

Parents, Super3™ and, 30–31
Parents and information literacy, 279–290
Helping with homework chart, 282
Introduction to, 279–280
Overview slides, 281
Worksheets, 283–286

Partnership for 21st Century Skills, 110, 175
Plagiarism, 108, 226
Plan, as Super3 stage, 27, 29
Process, Super3, 28
Program planning, Big6™ and Super3™, 295–302
Introduction to, 295–296
Worksheets, 297–301

R

Redefining Literacy for the 21st Century (Warlick), 176
Reich, Robert B., 176
Relevance, in ARCS Model, 182, 206, 207
Research, as 4th "r," xiv
Review, as Super3 stage, 30, 32
Robinson, Laura, xvi, 182

S

Satisfaction, in ARCS Model, 182, 206, 207
Self-assessment, 232
Serim, Ferdi, 218
Small, Ruth, 182, 205
Special needs children, Super3™ and, 30
Standardized testing, 159–160, 171
Standards, Big6™, 123–128
Educational standards and, 124
Information literacy and ICT, 125
Subject area content, 125–128
Subject area content standards, 125–128
Compilations of, 125–128
Organizational Web sites for, 126
PowerPoint slides on, 130
State Web sites for, 126
Super3™
Information literacy and, 5–6
Introduction to, 3–4
Learning, 27–31
Process, 28
Program planning, 295–302
Stages, 27–30
Worksheet, information literacy, 20–21
Super3™, learning, 27–31
Answer key, 43
Beginning plan stage, 29
End stage or review, 30

Exercises, 34
Introduction to, 27
Middle stage, 29
Older students, 30
Parents and, 30–31
Special needs children, 30
Think process, 28
Worksheets, 34–42
The Super3: Information Skills for Young Learners (Eisenberg/Robinson), 182

T

Technology literacy, 110–111
Testing Information Literacy Skills (Murray article), 174–177
Tests, Big6™, 128–129, 166–177
PowerPoint slides on, 156–158
State tests and, 128–129
Web information sources, 125–127
Texas Assessment of Academic Skills (TAAS), 161
3 R's, xiii
Todd, Ross, 160
Try-ability, as element of change, 4

U

UNESCO (United Nations Educational, Scientific and Cultural Organization), xiii
U.S. Department of Education, 160
National Center for Educational Statistics (NCES), 128

W

Warlick, David, 176
Web resources, Big6™ and technology, 107–109
Website Motivational Analysis Checklist (WebMAC), 206–207

Web sites
Compilations, 126–127
Organizations, 126
Standardized state/national test information, 126–127
State, 126
Woo-Lun, Marlene, xiv
Work of Nations: Preparing Ourselves for 21st Century Capitalism (Reich), 176
Worksheets
Assessment, 234, 235, 243–244
Big6™ technology, 98–106
Information age, learning/teaching implications, 15–16
Information literacy, 14, 20–24
Learning Big6™, 54–74
Macro planning, Big6™, 253–274
Micro planning, Big6™, 184–196, 209, 211, 213
Parents and information literacy, 283–286
Planning for change, opening questions, 13
Program planning, Big6™ and Super3™, 297–301
Themes of Big6, 83, 84, 88, 90
Understanding Super3™, 34–42
Workshop Handbook activities
Assessment exercise, 233–239
Information and technology literacy, 99–103, 105–106
Macro planning, 253–274
Number connecting exercise, 7–12
Standards and tests, 131–132, 135–137, 144, 145
Themes of the Big6, 80, 84, 88, 90
World Wide Web, standards documents on, 126–127
Wurster, Sue, xiv, 164